THE ADMINISTRATIVE STATE IN CANADA

PUBLIC ADMINISTRATION
VALUES, POLICY, AND CHANGE

Edited by O.P. Dwivedi
with a foreword by John Meisel

The Administrative State in Canada

Essays in Honour of J.E. Hodgetts

University of Toronto Press
Toronto Buffalo London

Toronto Buffalo London
Printed in Canada

Canadian Cataloguing in Publication Data

Main entry under title:
The Administrative state in Canada
Festschrift published in honour of J.E. Hodgetts.
'Bibliography of the main works by J.E. Hodgetts': p.
ISBN 0-8020-5603-2 (bound). – ISBN 0-8020-6480-9 (pbk.)
1. Hodgetts, J.E., 1917- – Addresses, essays, lectures. 2. Canada – Politics and government – 1867- – Addresses, essays, lectures. I. Hodgetts, J.E., 1917- II. Dwivedi, O.P., 1937-
JL65 1982 A45 320.971 C82-094363-0

Contents

JOHN MEISEL

Foreword

The festschrift is a curious literary form. It is a tribute from contemporary scholars to a colleague whose work is so important and inspiring as to call for a special intellectual celebration. But, in truly austere academic style, what these scholars write does not as a rule address the achievements and characteristics of the person to be honoured. The various essays for the most part deal with some intellectual problem. Since the contributors are colleagues and often students of the scholar being recognized, the articles tend naturally to represent one field.

Although the origin of this genre of writing is, as the name suggests, in central Europe, the form has a somewhat puritanical aura about it: it seems to spring from the premise that work is prayer, that the best way of expressing one's appreciation of someone's accomplishments is not by talking about them but by doing one's own work (or 'thing' as we say nowadays) as best one can. The authors, like so many *jongleurs de Notre Dame*, contribute their own scholarship to the volume which then constitutes an offering in praise of the one who inspired it.

Still, there is often one item designed to focus on the person to whose homage the whole enterprise is dedicated. This piece, however, invariably runs into difficulties which, perhaps, explain why biographical essays and critiques are usually eschewed: the scholar whose writings have stimulated the preparation of the festschrift is very much alive and kicking, busily adding further laurels to an already high reputation. It is exceedingly dangerous to try to pinpoint and evaluate work still continuing to evolve.

The present volume is a case in point. It pays its respects to a man who, while retiring from one of his long-standing careers – teaching –

is at the height of his creative powers, who is, in fact, just embarking on a new major project – a study of the public service in Ontario. His *œuvre* is thus still in the process of unfolding, and the volume wisely does not attempt to review its scope and significance. But this short foreword provides an opportunity for expressing a few personal observations about the man whose existing intellectual contribution is being fêted.

One of the striking characteristics of J.E. Hodgetts' writing is the consistency of its central concern – the effectiveness of government. 'Effectiveness,' here, embraces not merely the efficiency of the operations – although this aspect is by no means excluded – but effectiveness in a fundamental, humane sense: the contribution of government to the well-being of citizens in the liberal democratic context. More than most of his contemporaries, Ted Hodgetts has throughout his scholarly life stuck to the intensive exploration of this one major theme. Starting with a pioneer study of royal commissions and more recently tackling the thorny issues arising from the need for accountability in the public service, he has only rarely strayed far from this motif.

His disciplined concentration on one of the central preoccupations of public administration, of course, reflects more than just his professional style. It is wholly consistent with the personal values and priorities of a citizen who is socially responsible and active, whether the sphere of concern relates to his university, his profession, the world of his community, or family.

As a teacher, Ted Hodgetts has always been warm and approachable, showing a personal concern for his students. His interest has occasionally gone to quite extraordinary lengths – I believe that he still now and then exchanges philatelic goodies with a one-time student who will soon be contemplating his own retirement. A course he designed dealing with political ideas is still being offered, modified only a little some twenty-five years after its inception.

The success of his teaching resulted from a sure mastery of his material; lively, wide-ranging interests; and unusual skill in communicating ideas. The latter talent is reflected in the freshness of his written style and has found ready application in numerous editorial feats, from the editing of various books, through the reshaping of the *Queen's Quarterly* and the subduing of royal commission reports, to the general editorship of the Canadian Public Administration Series.

Although his books and articles have on occasion tackled subjects which appear at first blush to defy lively or exciting treatment, he has never written a dull page. An erudition going well beyond his academic preoccupations, a vivid sense of humour, and an eye for the striking phrase have combined to make every one of his publications an enjoyable 'read' as well as a useful contribution to knowledge.

More profoundly, the intellectual appeal of his writing is probably so great because of the ever-present philosophical concern which infuses all of his works. Even the aspects of public administration which appear the most prosaic and nitty-gritty are sooner or later related to some of the fundamental issues of liberal democracy, notably the best realization of public interests. It is not surprising that J.A. Corry invited him to update and revise his classic *Democratic Government and Politics*, a quintessential expression of the ideas of liberal democracy.

Although the influences of Toronto and Chicago were probably more profound than that of Queen's, J.E. Hodgetts nevertheless fitted extremely well into the atmosphere of Queen's university. In one respect in particular, his work so far is completely congruent with that of such famous Queensmen as O.D. Skelton, Adam Shortt, W.A. Macintosh, J.A. Corry, and J.J. Deutsch. Like them, he has combined a vital scholarly interest with a practical concern for the quality of our government.

Canada, unlike the United States, has not seen large-scale, direct cross-fertilization between the universities and government. It has been uncommon for academics to serve occasional stints in Ottawa or in the provincial capitals. J.E. Hodgetts is outstanding in the degree to which he has complemented his academic work and university preoccupations with sorties into the governmental orbit, usually in connection with special inquiries touching on his basic academic interests. Thus keeping a foothold in both camps, his work in each has shown a marvellous balance between the academic and the applied, the bookish and the practical. Eschewing the fads and untested novelties of his discipline and of avant-garde administrators, he has allowed his impressive scholarship to improve the management of public business, at the same time that his intimate knowledge of the latter informs his scholarship: a rare and happy combination which continues to make for rare and happy results!

Ottawa
December 1981

Preface

In honouring Ted Hodgetts, who has affectionately been called 'the academic's academic' as well as the 'father' of the discipline of public administration in Canada, the editor and the contributors – friends, colleagues, and former students – have attempted no assessment of his achievements, but rather each has written on a topic that seemed to him a significant aspect of the central theme of the 'administrative state,' a theme which has been an enduring concern of Professor Hodgetts.

For their assistance in the editorial part of this undertaking I am grateful to Meyer Brownstone, Jack Grove, Kenneth Kernaghan, and, especially, Richard Phidd and Vince Wilson. To all the contributors who gave their time and talent to prepare these essays, I express my gratitude. And I owe a debt to R.I.K. Davidson of the University of Toronto Press for his invaluable help in the publication of this festschrift.

The book has been published with the help of a grant from the Social Science Federation of Canada, using funds provided by the Social Sciences and Humanities Research Council of Canada.

O.P.D.
University of Guelph
December 1981

THE ADMINISTRATIVE STATE IN CANADA

V. SEYMOUR WILSON AND O.P. DWIVEDI

Introduction

The steady growth of government, both at the federal and provincial levels, has been one of the most distinctive and important developments in Canadian history during the twentieth century.[1] As the role of government in Canadian society expanded, the centre of gravity of its powers has shifted from Parliament and the legislatures to the executives and bureaucracies.[2] The characteristic patterns that underlie this shift can be detected both in the spectacular growth of expenditure patterns and bureaucratic expansion by the provincial governments and in the proliferation of regulatory activity by the federal government.[3] Recently the Economic Council of Canada documented that the federal government passed as many statutes designed to regulate economic activity between 1970 and 1978 as it had done in the previous thirty years.[4]

Students of public administration, more in the United States than elsewhere, have written extensively about the implications of this growth, particularly as it affects the relationship between bureaucracy and democracy.[5] This is not the place to chronicle the profound debate among American writers, but it should be noted that the writings of such scholars as Fritz Morstein Marx, Charles Hyneman, Dwight Waldo, John Gaus, Marshall Dimock, Norton Long, Frederick Mosher, Emmette Redford – the list seems almost endless – have explored some of the most fundamental theoretical questions in democratic governance: the role of senior public servants in the process; the interaction of the governmental bureaucracy with interest groups; the increasing complexity and growth of regulation; the proliferating growth of public corporations and the consequent fuzziness between the private and public sectors; and the democratic imperative to maintain political control of delegated legislation.

As a next step some scholars attempt to explain why this complexity has occurred, giving a list of reasons such as greater demands on government by the deprived and the rich leading to more and more government agencies; the perceived threats of multinational enterprises; the growth of imitative organizations by voluntary groups and labour unions to ensure their own survival in an organizational world; the explosion of technology and mass production. In addition, others such as John Kenneth Galbraith are well known for their hypothesis that such big and technologically advanced organizations can be explained in terms of long-term forward planning.

Canadian scholars too have been concerned with both the *extent* and *cause* of the growth of government, but, when compared to that of our American neighbours, our debate has had some rather marked differences. On the whole, American thought on this subject is dominated by a highly critical or suspicious attitude to any form of (much less an increase in) bureaucratic powers. As this volume demonstrates, J.E. Hodgetts, along with some of his contemporaries and former students, has thought long and hard about some of the patterns of relationships enumerated above. However, these ideas have been generally characterized by a much more sympathetic attitude towards governmental intrusions in society. The reasons for these differences are no doubt many and complex, but the most obvious reason is a rather philosophical one: Americans possess a trait of debating contemporary issues in terms of fundamental principles. We are constantly struck by this American predisposition to return continuously to the writings of Jefferson, Madison, Hamilton, Paine, and other founding fathers to reaffirm the basic nature of the American polity. Public administration in America has never been exempt from this searching fundamental examination of the nature of democratic governance.[6] In contrast we in Canada are much more pragmatic. In the recent constitutional debates the institutions and processes of public administration were barely mentioned or even seriously considered as important aspects of constitutionalism in Canada. This dismissal of our bureaucratic institutions is joined with a pervasive pragmatism about government. No Delphic phrases and fundamental philosophies about government preoccupy our thoughts on the nature of governmental institutions. 'Canadians [are] more prone to identify liberty and democracy with legal traditions and procedures than with populism, the right of the people to rule or with the freedom of business and enterprise.'[7] Thus while Americans have extensively debated the advent and nature of their administrative state, in contrast Canadians have been less concerned about their ubiquitous government.

For purposes of this volume, the administrative state denotes the phenomenon by which state institutions influence many aspects of the lives of citizens, especially those aspects which relate to the economic and social dimensions. It describes a system of governance through which public policies and programs, affecting almost all aspects of public life, are influenced by the decisions of public officials.[8] Consequently, the administrative process becomes a principal instrument in the formulation and implementation of a highly expanded public agenda.

The bureaucratic sector in such a state is accorded a schizophrenic position in its relations with other sectors of society. On the one hand, it can be construed as an instrument fashioned to implement or give expression to the public will as enunciated by the people's representatives, the politicians. On the other hand, this 'instrument' can project an image of strong autonomous powers, more important than the powers of political and participatory sectors in determining the course of public affairs and in influencing the behaviour of the state. It should be stressed that these conceptions are ideal types or logical constructions rather than descriptions of any real state. But scholars do contend that, increasingly, Western industrialized societies exhibit various tendencies characteristic of the logical construction of bureaucratic power. As French sociologist Michel Crozier puts it, 'there is always [this] double belief in the superiority of bureaucratic rationality in the domain of efficiency and in its threatening implications in the domain of human values.'[9] Why is this Janus-like image associated with the administrative state?

The first image construes the administrative state as some sort of societal instrument for the achievement of higher social purposes in society, all of which is done efficiently and effectively. This usage is associated with the turbulence of world events over the last four or five decades. Beginning in the 1930s, the economic crisis which the industrialized world experienced made it abundantly clear to political leaders everywhere that governments must assume a more active role in attempting to ameliorate the severe social and economic problems of their societies.

Before the Great Depression most liberal democratic governments were suspicious of their own powers. Most of these governments, to be sure, did believe that there was some limited scope for governmental intervention in the economy. What is even less frequently remarked is that these governments believed most firmly in the propriety of governmental intervention and regulation in the areas of public taste and public morality. But beyond this, the economic arrangements of the state were largely construed, in Adam Smith's memorable phrase, as a 'system of natural liberty': the less we saw and heard from government the better it was for democratic governance. Government must visualize its role as a routine, restricted servant, an instrument providing certain minimal services to the public.[10]

This image of a restricted servant soon changed to one of an omnipotent servant as governments were forced to move to help in various ways in filling the void left by the collapse of the economic order. Governments quickly became initiators of programs aimed at inducing major social changes in society. To North Americans, the administrative state meant that the servants of the state were increasingly engaged in managing the affairs of their societies and providing leadership, financial support, and technical know-how in activities which required imagination, initiative, and energy in the pursuit of public purposes. Thus, in the US, the administrative state implied the strengthening of the President's *executive powers* to include *management capabilities* as well.[11] In Great Britain the term 'welfare state' was preferred, the emphasis being on the ability of the state to meet the clearly identified needs of its citizenry. In Canada, the term generally used was the 'positive state.' The discernible political ideology behind this usage of these terms was a Fabian socialist concern to enhance the performance of the state institutions as instruments for the furtherance of social equity.[12] Whether one dubbed the phenomenon the administrative state, the welfare state, or the positive state, the implications were clearly the same: namely, the instrumental nature of the state's institutions as rationally conceived means to the realization of expressly announced group goals.[13] Its structures are understood as tools deliberately established for the efficient and effective realization of these group purposes.[14]

The second image closely associated with the administrative state is one which admittedly predated its advent – an image of an overpowering leviathan. Originally associated with the seventeenth-century states of Prussia and France, the image increasingly emphasized the lack of human compassion which came to characterize state officials engulfed by fixed rules, established routines, and delays in public functions. Franz Kafka's novel, *The Castle*, is perhaps the most celebrated example of this 'anomie' or alienation from humanity and human values. Other more contemporary writers have emphasized the same theme, for example Orwell in *Animal Farm* or Solzhenitsyn in *The First Circle*.

The feeling of utter perplexity and helpless passivity thus created among the public is closely associated with a perception of power purportedly in the all-embracing grip of the bureaucrats. Thus Harold Laski defined the growing bureaucracy of the late 1930s as 'a system of government the control of which is so completely in the hand of officials that their power jeopardizes the liberty of ordinary citizens.'[15] Similarly in North America various commentators viewed with increasing alarm the growth of large-scale organizations,[16] the impending bureaucratization of the world,[17] and the rise of the 'organization man.'[18]

These two powerful images – social servant and state juggernaut – have merged in our present-day conception of the administrative state in Canada. J.E. Hodgetts demonstrates this fact quite well by his argument that the 'shift from laissez-faire to collectivism has been accompanied by an unprecedented shift in the balance of real power, discretion and initiative – away from courts, legislatures and even cabinets to public servants.' The public, he further notes, fears the administrative state (power in the hands of 'faceless' people and mandarins) and suspects 'that their rights are being invaded even as they are ostensibly being served by [these] public employees.'[19] But exactly how have these tendencies been demonstrated in Canada? Earlier we suggested that there are some marked differences in the Canadian experience with the administrative state compared to that of other Western countries and particularly to that of the United States. Some further elaboration of this theme is needed.

In any serious discussion of Canadian economic development the contention is always made that such development could only have been accomplished by a national government which acted aggressively to establish and maintain economic unity.[20] Alexander Brady's comment is unequivocal: 'the role of the state in the economic life of Canada is really the modern history of Canada.' Furthermore, he contends, the positive, pragmatic state was an absolute necessity because of 'the pioneer nature of the country, the physical structure of the half continent, the imperial sweep of settlement after 1867, the influence of the interacting ideas and institutions of Britain and the United States, and the quick response of the whole society to the advance of western industrialism.'[21] Other social commentators have concurred with this analysis: this 'positive state' in the age of laissez-faire was a deliberate national policy to transform Canada into a modern nation.

Writing in 1952 Vernon Fowke argued that 'the term "national policy" includes collectively the group of policies which were designed to transform the British North American territories of the mid-nineteenth century into a political and economic unit. As thus defined, the national policy was fully formulated in its main outlines prior to Confederation which was its main constitutional instrument.'[22] Pointing to a lack of 'doctrinal limitations' on the part of the Canadian government, W.A. Mackintosh contended that 'in a period where laissez-faire policies were at their peak of respectability, the Canadian attitude to the question of public versus private enterprise was purely pragmatic. In the vital field of railway transportation there was not generally any clear view on the merits of public versus private action so long as the railways were actually built.'[23] What is indeed most interesting is that this state activism was conducted by a relatively small bureaucracy. In 1867, with a population of approximately four million people, the size of the federal bureaucracy has been estimated at around 3,000, that is, approximately one public servant to every 1,300 or so members of the population.[24] Of the 3,000 only 263 were then located in Ottawa, the rest situated in other parts of the country and collectively called members of the Outside Service.[25] By the beginning of the First World War, some fifty years later, the total civil service had grown to 25,000.[26]

There seem to be several reasons for this growth, but the most important factors were the consequences which flowed from the *political perception* that the bureaucracy was strictly *instrumental* in character. Put in another way, the growth of the federal bureaucracy, from 3,000 to 25,000 in five decades, can be explained not in terms of some imperialistic designs of the mandarins but in terms of the nation-building tasks assigned by the politicians to the bureaucracy. In the nineteenth century Canadian politicians heavily financed their nation-building ventures through financial subventions to private enterprise and assigned the instrumental technical tasks (surveying, road, canal and bridge building) and the performance of essentially routine repetitive jobs of a clerical nature, for which the public demand was great (the postal service), to the public service. Hodgetts noted that at Confederation the Department of Public Works was regarded as 'one of the giant planets' of the civil service, impressively combining 'the labours of a Department of Transport with those of a central housekeeping agency.'[27]

Whatever trends towards self-aggrandizement that existed in the federal bureaucracy then seem to be largely attributable to political interference after each election. As the *Canadian Monthly* of November 1876 so graphically put it: 'Serve the party day and night, secure us an electoral triumph by fair means or foul, and you shall be quartered for life on the public treasury.' But perhaps the greatest reason for growth was the political mandate handed the federal Department of the Interior in the 1870s – managing and preparing western land resources for the eventual influx of immigrants and an anticipated export boom. For close to fifty years the department served admirably the hinterland development policies of successive national governments. By the 1930s, however, this mandate had been fulfilled, and the Liberal government of the day simply abolished this large department whose service had been crucial in formulating and executing the policies of 'defensive expansionism' in this country.[28]

Another glimpse at this instrumental nature of our bureaucracy can be gleaned from the role it has had to play in the regulatory functions of government. Commentators have identified the regulatory functions of democratic government, particularly since the Second World War, as one of the most crucial determinants of bureaucratic influence and growth.[29] Much of the literature about the nature of regulation and regulatory activity originates in the United States. For Americans, regulatory activity is essentially a policing role by government, that is, ensuring that economic activity approximates competitive market conditions. Thus, the criterion for the utility of regulation in America lay essentially in an assessment of it as a tool of economic efficiency. This is emphatically not the case in Canada. The growth of regulation and the regulatory activity of governments in Canada can be largely explained in terms of political objectives crucial to nation-building (or what Richard Schultz calls 'the three p's': policing, promoting, and planning).[30] For example, in Canada national unity and regional income redistribution have been explicitly a part of freight-rate and air-fare setting, and the establishment of agricultural marketing boards has been a deliberate political attempt to transfer income from consumers to producers.[31] That we have today public servants wielding substantial discretionary powers of regulation is due to the political decisions made by our elected representatives to create these delegated powers. Moreover, informed commentators point to the extensive political controls exercised over the regulatory process. These commentators have noted that, unlike the American regulatory process, Canadian agencies are not 'independent' but are much more controlled by executive action and decrees.[32]

In summary then, Canadian historical experience shows bureaucracy as an instrument of overriding political purpose. The particularistic and localistic nature of Canadian democracy required a bureaucracy, which has expanded under explicit political directions and which has been subject to democratic political direction. The instrumental and indeed beneficent role of bureaucracy as the core of modern government is a theme which is well developed in the literature of public policy and administration.[33]

At the same time, however, the generally held view these days of the bureaucracy as leviathan cannot be easily dismissed. In Canada, as elsewhere, there has been a gnawing concern about 'the bureaucracy problem.' Since the Second World War there has been a tremendous growth in government personnel. For example, between 1946 and 1971, while federal public service employment increased from 120,577 to 216,488 (almost double), the provincial public services combined witnessed over a five-fold increase, from 38,370 to 209,760 employees.[34] During that same period Canada's population increased by only 71 per cent (12.5 million to 21.5 million). However, if one includes all those who work in hospitals, educational institutions, government enterprises, and municipal governments, total employment in the public sector by 1975 had reached the level of 2,243,100.[35] This meant that about 24 per cent of the labour force in Canada worked directly in the service of a government.[36] But even these statistics do not tell the whole story: if one includes those who are 'indirectly' employed in contractual work as well as in casual employment for governments, one arrives at an estimate of approximately 3.1 million people in governmental service.[37] This figure represented about one-third of the employed labour force in Canada. Despite the most rational and erudite reasons given for this expansion, it does worry and alarm those who fear a creeping leviathan.[38]

Bigness is, however, only one dimension of this problem. The very existence of bureaucracy is a constant reminder that human society is dependent upon the regulation, control, production, and manipulation characteristic of such complex organizations. The very conventional practices devised to ensure that society controls its bureaucracies – anonymity, secrecy, neutrality, hierarchy – are now construed as manipulative tools through which bureaucracy controls its nominal master, the public.[39] Furthermore, the problem is made even more complex in that the voices which complain about the overpowering anonymity, control, and impenetrability of bureaucracy are often the same as those demanding the regulations, the controls, and the productivity which are the daily concerns of bureaucracy.[40]

It is not only that the administrative state can be seen to wield too much discretionary power; other critics have been increasingly pointing to another dimension of this problem. The present difficulties with public bureaucracies, they contend, stem not so much from too much zeal in the exercise of power but an 'inadequate enthusiasm' in the pursuit of public objectives. One result of this is that goals or ends can be either intentionally or unintentionally thwarted in a quagmire of means.

An excellent study of the management of Canadian national security by French and Belliveau emphasizes this theme. As the authors put it, the recent history of security 'is the product not primarily of the odd irresponsible soul, nor of an organized and nefarious conspiracy. It is the product of a systematic breakdown in the nexus of responsibilities and obligations which legitimizes the exercise of exceptional powers in the general interest of a democratic state.' Pointing to the indifference in cabinet, the lack of vision and interest among senior officials, and a host of other managerial problems at the top and middle levels of management, French and Belliveau persuasively argue that 'the jerry-built network of half-hearted programs, rigid traditionalism, fragments of law, pious hopes, and a lot of whistling in the dark ... collapsed into a bitter aftermath of civil liberties violated, public confidence shaken, and the effectiveness of the Security Service eroded.'[41]

Such perspectives suffice to demonstrate the paradoxical reality of the administrative state. Administrative power is part of political power and part of our continuing collective ambivalence about power. The essays in this volume can touch on only some aspects of this reality, but each attempts to grapple with the dilemma. The first five contributions examine administrative power bequeathed to the bureaucratic élite at the federal level, aspects of the bureaucratic revolution both in Quebec and British Columbia, the complex issues of regulatory activity, and the changes in communications patterns which have fostered an elaborate network of interest groups and the decline of political parties as communication agents.

The next three essays shift the focus somewhat by concentrating on one of Hodgetts' most passionate and enduring concerns, namely, our efforts to hold the officials of the administrative state to account. Obvious themes are examined here: the nature and extent of delegated legislation and the effectiveness of parliamentary control; an examination of the contemporary debate on ministerial responsibility and the accountability and answerability of federal public servants; and a searching look at the issue of administrative secrecy, including a clarion call for effective improvement of the law to combat secrecy's baneful influence.

The last three essays begin with reflections on whether atomic scientists and engineers have presented us with a problem that administration cannot control, continue with a study of the similarities and differences between Canada and Australia and of Professor Hodgetts' place in the ideologies that attempt to shape public administration, and conclude with a summary of the issues forged in the conflict between administrative efficiency and the egalitarianism of democracy.

All the essays are implicitly concerned with the need to build a democratic theory which grapples seriously with the realities of the administrative state – one which explains how 'adequate public control' ought to be redefined in the light of modern conditions. Thus, as J.E. Hodgetts, writing with J.A. Corry, emphasized:

> If the government is going to perform many positive services for the community, there must be greater concentration and less dispersion of power than that which marked the age of laissez faire. But wherever power is lodged, devices are needed to ensure that it can be called to account. The more power is concentrated, the more nicely calculated the means of controlling it must be. The elaboration of new and more effective controls has not kept pace with the growing concentration of power. More thought must be given to such controls in the immediate future.[42]

1 Richard M. Bird, *The Growth of Government Spending in Canada* (Toronto: Canadian Tax Foundation, 1970), esp. chaps. 2 and 3

2 This shift occurred both at the federal and provincial levels of government. For example, see G. Bruce Doern and Peter Aucoin, eds., *The Structures of Policy-Making in Canada* (Toronto: Macmillan, 1971); Fred Schindeler, 'The Prime Minister and Cabinet: History and Development,' in Thomas A. Hockin, ed., *Apex of Power: The Prime Minister and Political Leadership in Canada*, sec. ed. (Scarborough: Prentice-Hall, 1977, pp. 22-47; F.F. Schindeler, *Responsible Government in Ontario* (Toronto: University of Toronto Press, 1969), esp. chap. 8.

3 W.T. Stanbury, 'Restraining the State: The Role of Deregulation,' in Peter Aucoin, ed., *The Politics and Management of Restraint in Government*, pp. 145-66.

4 *Responsible Regulation* (Ottawa, November 1979), p. 16

5 An exploration of this extensive debate is found in V. Seymour Wilson, *Canadian Public Policy and Administration: Theory and Environment* (Toronto: McGraw-Hill, 1981) in chap. 4.

6 Two recent publications, for example, are Vincent Ostrom, *The Intellectual Crisis in American Public Administration* (Alabama: University of Alabama Press, 1973), and James O. Freedman, *Crises and Legitimacy: The Administrative Process and American Government* (New York: Cambridge University Press, 1980).

7 Seymour Martin Lipset, 'Revolution and Counterrevolutiojn: The United States and Canada,' in O.M. Kruhlak *et al.* eds., *The Canadian Political Process: A Reader*, rev. ed. (Toronto: Holt, Rinehart and Winston, 1973), p. 24

8 For more on this theme, see Wilson, *Canadian Public Policy*, esp. chaps. 2 and 3.

9 *The Bureaucratic Phenomenon* (Chicago: University of Chicago Press, 1964), p. 176

10 Norton E. Long, 'Federalism and Perverse Incentives,' *Publius: The Journal of Federalism*, vol. 8, no. 2 (spring 1978), pp. 77-97

11 Frederick C. Mosher, *Democracy and the Public Service* (New York: Oxford University Press, 1968), pp. 79-84

12 R.M. Titmuss, *Essays on the Welfare State* (London: Allen and Unwin, 1958)

13 Fritz Morstein Marx demonstrates this interconnection of the various usages by the following remark: 'the new liberal's faith in "positive government" is a far cry from the earlier liberal ideal of government restricted to the role of "night watchman". But if the new liberal cannot be expected to take kindly to a loaded phrase such as "welfare state", he has come to make his peace with the more neutral concept of the "administrative state", especially with its practical realities.' *The Administrative State: An Introduction to Bureaucracy* (Chicago: University of Chicago Press, 1957), p. 2

14 A clear exposition of this viewpoint is found in Victor A. Thompson, *Without Sympathy or Enthusiasm: The Problem of Administrative Compassion* (Alabama: University of Alabama Press, 1975).

15 'Bureaucracy,' *Encyclopedia of the Social Sciences*, vol. 3 (New York: Macmillan, 1930), p. 70
16 E. Strauss, *The Ruling Servants* (London: Allen and Unwin, 1967)
17 Henry Jacoby, *The Bureaucratization of the World*, trans. Eveline Kanes (Berkeley and Los Angeles: University of California Press, 1973)
18 William H. Whyte, Jr, *The Organization Man* (New York: Simon and Schuster, 1956). These overpowering images of an inexorable juggernaut have in turn spurred the sociologist Alvin Gouldner to write a resounding critique of what he calls a 'metaphysical pathos' in bureaucratic theory. See his 'Metaphysical Pathos and the Theory of Bureaucracy,' *American Political Science Review*, vol. 49 (1955), pp. 496-507, essentially reproduced in Amitai Etzioni, ed., *Complex Organizations: A Sociological Reader* (New York: Holt, Rinehart and Winston, 1961), pp. 71-82.
19 'Challenge and Response: A Retrospective View of the Public Service of Canada,' *Canadian Public Administration*, vol. VII, no. 4 (December 1964), p. 421
20 Herschel Hardin, *A Nation Unaware: The Canadian Economic Culture* (Vancouver, 1974), esp. Part II, The Canadian Enterprise Culture, pp. 54-140
21 'The State and Economic Life,' in George W. Brown ed., *Canada* (Berkeley: University of California Press, 1950), p. 353
22 'The National Policy – Old and New,' *Canadian Journal of Economics and Political Science*, vol. 18 (1952), 271-86
23 'Canadian Economic Policy: Scope and Principles,' ibid., vol. 16 (August 1950), p. 317
24 J.E. Hodgetts and O.P. Dwivedi, *Provincial Governments as Employers* (Montreal: McGill-Queeen's University Press, 1974), p. 1
25 J.E. Hodgetts, *Pioneer Public Service: An Administrative History of the United Canadas 1841-1867* (Toronto: University of Toronto Press, 1955), p. 274
26 Privy Council Office, *Submissions to the Royal Commission on Financial Management and Accountability* (Ottawa, 1979), pp. 3-19
27 *Pioneer Public Service*, pp. 183-4
28 Hugh G. Aitken, 'Defensive Expansionism: The State and Economic Growth in Canada,' in H.G. Aitken, ed., *The State and Economic Growth* (New York: Social Science Research Council, 1959), pp. 79-114
29 Barry M. Mitnick, *The Political Economy of Regulation: Creating, Designing and Removing Regulatory Forms* (New York: Columbia University Press, 1980)
30 'Comments for Panel Discussion on Regulation,' *Canadian Public Policy*, vol. 4 (autumn 1979), pp. 486-90
31 G.B. Reschenthaler, 'Direct Regulation in Canada: Some Policies and Problems,' in W.T. Stanbury, ed., *Studies on Regulation in Canada* (Montreal: Institute for Research on Public Policy, 1978), pp. 37-112

32 As an example, see the arguments in Robert E. Babe, 'Public and Private Regulations of Cable Television: A Case Study of Technological Change and Relative Power,' *Canadian Public Administration*, vol. 17, no. 2 (summer 1974), pp. 187-225.

33 To develop this theme here from the comparative evidence would distract us from our main argument. For an insightful piece which develops this relationship between bureaucracy and democracy, see Norton Long, 'Bureaucracy and Constitutionalism,' *American Political Science Review*, vol. 46 (September 1958), pp. 808-18.

34 Hodgetts and Dwivedi, *Provincial Governments as Employers*, pp. 10, 13

35 Richard Bird, *Growth of Public Employment in Canada* (Toronto: Butterworth, 1979), p. 40

36 Ibid., p. 34

37 Ibid.

38 Elliott Jaques, *A General Theory of Bureaucracy* (New York: John Wiley 1976), Alan C. Cairns, 'The Governments and Societies of Canadian Federalism,' p. 700

39 See Wilson, *Canadian Public Policy*, chaps. 7 and 8.

40 Jacoby, *The Bureaucratization of the World*, pp. 9-35, 61-112

41 Richard French and André Beliveau, *The R.C.M.P. and the Management of National Security* (Toronto: Butterworth, 1979), p. 76

42 J.A. Corry and J.E. Hodgetts, *Democratic Government and Politics* (Toronto: University of Toronto Press, 1946). This quotation is from the third edition, p. 649.

KENNETH KERNAGHAN AND T.H. McLEOD

Mandarins and Ministers in the Canadian Administrative State

The line between politics and administration is difficult to maintain under normal party circumstances, but it is likely to disappear altogether when one party holds office for a long time. J.E. HODGETTS

There are few areas in the field of Canadian public administration that have not been illuminated by the inquiry and intellect of J.E. Hodgetts. While others have lamented the darkness in many parts of the field, he has at the very least lit a candle and on numerous occasions he has provided a beacon for others to follow. His distinguished contributions to the study of administrative history in Canada have been combined with an abiding interest in the interaction of politicians and bureaucrats. This essay builds upon Professor Hodgetts' work by examining the evolution of relations between ministers and senior officials during 'the mandarin generation' which extended from the late 1930s to the late 1960s.

The central feature of the evolution of the administrative state in Canada, as elsewhere among modern urban-industrial communities, has been the increasing interpenetration of the policy and administrative functions of public servants.[1] The influence of public servants both on the policy-making processes and on policy itself increased steadily during the early decades of this century. It accelerated even more rapidly during the 1930s and the Second World War. The advisory and discretionary powers of public servants were greatly enhanced as governments intervened more actively in society generally and in the economy in particular.

J.W. Pickersgill, on the basis of long experience both as a politician and a bureaucrat, asserted in 1972 that 'there is nothing very new about the participation of bureaucrats in policy-making; it was at least as prevalent in 1937 as it is in 1972.'[2] However, the nature of bureaucratic participation in the policy process has changed significantly since 1937. Much has been written on the evolution of the policy role of public servants during the period from the mid 1960s to the present. Comparatively little scholarly attention has been devoted to the earlier and historically significant 'mandarin generation.'

The term 'mandarin' is used much less frequently today, but it occasionally appears in the popular press as a convenient (and often pejorative) label for an influential senior public servant. In this essay the term is defined more narrowly to refer to a member of a relatively small group of public servants who, as individuals, though often acting collectively, have exercised enormous influence on government decision-making over an extended period of time. There is no doubt that even today certain senior officials play a central role in policy-making, but the exercise of power seems now to be more dispersed both among the public servants themselves and among other actors in the political system.

This essay focuses on two key aspects of the mandarin period, namely the growth in the policy influence of the mandarins and the change in government in 1957.

The growing influence of senior officials on the shape of Canadian public policy during the mandarin years constituted a patent denial of the traditional mythology about the neutrality and anonymity of public servants. Probably the most repeated but the least satisfactory explanation for this increased influence is that it resulted simply from natural human tendencies to seek and exercise power. It is more accurate to explain the evolving role of the public service generally and its mandarins in particular in the context of unique environmental conditions which both demanded and facilitated the intermingling of policy and administration. This intermingling may best be seen as an appropriate response both to the needs and the possibilities of the times.

It is likely that Pickersgill's assessment is correct. The influence of the senior echelons of the bureaucracy has always been pronounced, if not profound. But in the pre-1930 days of low-profile government in a low-technology society, bureaucratic influence did not affect any broad range of public affairs. Though this influence might have been noticeable, it was not a matter of great consequence. Most of the problems faced by governments were amenable to political, non-professional (non-technocratic) solutions. In that technologically unsophisticated society, not much was expected of government. However, the sequence of events affecting the human condition through the 1930s and onward has altered substantially the political-administrative equilibria of government, as well as our expectations of it.

It may not be wholly fortuitous that, except for the Diefenbaker interlude from 1957 to 1962, it was a series of Liberal governments that was required to respond to the changed environment in which politicians and bureaucrats interacted. It is noteworthy of the King–St Laurent–Pearson continuum (to which the name of Trudeau may now be added) that none established his position of primacy through the line of political progression. Three of the four served their governmental apprenticeships as bureaucrats. The fourth (St Laurent) 'grew up' in the world of the private corporation. Of this lineage, King, as the progenitor of a professional public service with its mandarin class, is probably the key figure.

King surrounded himself and his cabinet ministers with a group of extremely competent advisers. The central bureaucratic actors of this period were O.D. Skelton, Undersecretary of State for External Affairs (from 1925 to his death in 1941) and W.C. Clark, Deputy Minister of Finance (from 1932 to his death in 1952). Both Skelton and Clark attracted men of great ability to their own and to other departments. To External Affairs came Norman Robertson (who succeeded Skelton), Hume Wrong, Arnold Heeney, Lester (Mike) Pearson, and Gordon Robertson. To Finance came Clark's protégés, among whom were Robert Bryce, Kenneth Taylor, Ross Tolmie, Harvey Perry, Kenneth Eaton, and John Deutsch. To other departments and agencies came Graham Towers, Donald Gordon, Louis Rasminsky, W.A. Mackintosh, and Mitchell Sharp. Some members of this third group were brought into government during the Second World War by C.D. Howe, the Minister of Reconstruction and Supply. Finally, Jack Pickersgill exercised continuing influence through his service in the Prime Minister's Office from 1937 to 1952.

This coterie of able and energetic men, together with a few others, constituted on educational and intellectual grounds a bureaucratic elite. They exercised great influence on policy-making, but they also had an excellent appreciation of the appropriate role of a public servant. For example, King said that Skelton 'believed that men in the public service could best carry on their work by remaining in the background of anonymity ... and that reflection and silence become a trusted servant of the people far more than speech and the glitter of the limelight.'[3] And Mitchell Sharp, one of those persons attracted to Ottawa during the war, said that Clark's contribution to Canada 'will never be fully appreciated, because the story can never be told of his influence upon the course of events.' Moreover, Clark 'worked anonymously ... his views and his actions finding their expression in official utterances of Ministers and in the statutes approved by Parliament ... He inculcated into all of us his ideal of the good civil servant.'[4] On the other hand, it is significant that King worried that Skelton participated 'to the extent of *unduly* influencing government policy.'[5] And St Laurent said that Clark had had 'a *decisive* part in shaping the wartime financial and economic policies' of Canada.[6] Several features of our present-day administrative state, including the scale of the public bureaucracy and the extensive publicity attending its work, make it difficult for senior officials to exert such influence or to retain such anonymity.[7]

Obviously the growth in the size and influence of the mandarinate reflected more than the orientation of prime ministers or the wishes of their advisers. The ways in which the various players, mandarins and politicians alike, developed and played out their roles during the mandarin years can be explained largely by a series of other events.

First in time was the Great Depression which brought with it acceptance of certain principles of economic management, particularly as these crystallized eventually in the propositions of John Maynard Keynes. Beyond the depression itself, but certainly of no less importance to Canadian public policy, was the 'post-Depression psychosis.' This was a state of mind that prompted active propagation over the succeeding years of the view that economic and social management ('social engineering' to some) was the most appropriate, if not the only appropriate, recipe for avoiding a repetition of the disastrous experience of the 1930s.

Then came the Second World War which provided opportunities for a vast exercise in economic and social management – the vastest the free world had known – and produced the archetype of the social engineer at work in C.D. Howe and his management apparatus. With the encouragement of Canada's mandarins, the Liberal government adopted the theoretical basis of the new social technocracy as it was found in the thinking of Keynes and his kind. Peter Newman has observed that 'the pledge of massive intervention in the economy may have been Keynes' idea, but it paralleled exactly the notion of the country held in the minds and souls of Ottawa's senior public servants. They saw the Keynesian prescription as a way of purging capitalism of its defects without having to turn toward socialism ... Lord Keynes was their high priest, but pragmatism was their religion.'[8]

Among the legacies of the war was a 'crisis of conscience' related to the obvious inadequacies in the performance of the Canadian economy during the pre-war period. The 'crisis' was related also to the conviction that, morally, Canada should not regress into its previous economic state and that, technically, the weaponry was available to prevent such a regression. There was a very direct relationship between the Rowell-Sirois Report – the final summing up of the calamitous thirties – and the 'Green Books' of 1946 with their suggestions for unprecedented government interventions in the Canadian economy and society (all in the name of post-war reconstruction). In Canada, as elsewhere, the so-called welfare state was to be brought rapidly into being. Neither the rationale for the welfare state nor the measure of its success is at issue here. What is to be noted is simply the increasing importance which such a state inevitably attached to 'professional' judgments and 'efficient' administration.

The 'managed' society – even one as partially managed as that proposed in the Green Books, much less the one envisioned by the social engineers – requires both a high degree of professionalism and a capacity for taking corporate decisions. Neither of these conditions was provided for by the traditional political processes of parliamentary government which were characterized in Canada during this period by ministerial and departmental autonomy. Thus, the responsibility and the opportunity for orchestrating public policies and programs tended to be left to the administrative leadership of the senior bureaucrats – the mandarins.

The economic and social developments of the depression and war years had an enormous impact on the course of public administration in Canada and on the coming to full flower of the mandarinate. The administrative experience and technical expertise of public servants was invaluable during the depression and even more during the war when government responsibilities became increasingly numerous, complex, and critical. The number of public servants expanded dramatically; a more elaborate administrative apparatus was constructed; the prime minister and cabinet relied heavily on bureaucratic advice; and the discretionary decision-making powers of public servants were greatly extended. Prime Minister Mackenzie King encouraged the dependent relationship between mandarins and ministers by placing high trust in senior bureaucrats and permitting them to take a major part in the policy-making process.

The exercise of this growing bureaucratic, and still largely anonymous, power persisted after the war's end. In part this was because ministers needed the advice of public servants during the reconstruction period and in part it was because ministers had become accustomed to relying on bureaucratic advice. A small group of senior public servants – the mandarins – continued to occupy a central place in the policy-making process, especially between 1945 and the beginning of the Conservative government in 1957. The size of the group increased over time and has been estimated to have contained about a dozen members in 1945 and about three dozen by 1961.[9] The composition of the group also varied over time, but it tended to include the deputy heads and a few other senior bureaucrats from the most important departments, namely Finance, External Affairs, Trade and Commerce, National Defence, and Transport, as well as the secretary to the cabinet and the prime minister's principal secretary.

This 'mandarinate' contained the public servants who were the most highly respected and the most frequently consulted by the cabinet and the prime minister. Although, in their own right, they occupied strategic positions in the government, their interests and competence went beyond the boundaries of their own offices and even of their own departments. They had an over-all view of the broad sweep of government policies and thus served to co-ordinate policy among departments, especially through their common membership on inter-departmental committees. Their formal committee contacts were supplemented by a variety of other means of consultation, including close personal and social relationships. Lester Pearson noted in his memoirs that:

> The committee members were nearly always from the same group of senior civil servants who had become personal friends as well as official colleagues. Indeed they did a great deal of their work, and their thinking, in informal sessions over food or drink or both. The Chateau Laurier Cafeteria and, in

the summer, the Five Lakes Fishing Club became almost as important centres for discussion and decisions as the conference rooms in the East Block. This was a closely-knit group, and no government could have been more fortunate in the high quality of their service and in their devoted and untiring dedication. Nearly all of them were good friends of mine.[10]

This select group of senior officials by no means always agreed on policy proposals, but when they did agree they were able to exert enormous collective influence on their political superiors.

Occasionally, the veil of secrecy which obscured the influence of bureaucrats on major public events during the 1940s was lifted. On one of these occasions, W.A. Mackintosh, director general of economic research in the Department of Reconstruction and Supply, described in very frank terms his participation in the drafting of the White Paper on Employment and Income of 1945. This critically important statement on post-war economic problems and policies was published before the 1945 federal election. Mackintosh asserted that the suggestion that such a statement be issued was his own. He said that 'the White Paper as it appeared was written entirely by me except for two easily identifiable paragraphs added by Mr. Howe. The scope and pattern were mine.' When the draft White Paper came before a cabinet committee consisting of the three most powerful cabinet ministers, C.D. Howe, J.L. Ilsley, and Louis St Laurent, Mackintosh instructed the ministers in the meaning and implications of the document. Mackintosh commented that 'we spent the greater part of the day on it ... I required specific approval to each, or alternatively amended wording. By the end of the day, they were visibly wearied by my schoolmasterish drill, but they approved the text for formal acceptance by the Cabinet, having made no change of substance.'[11]

Like King, St Laurent trusted and depended on senior public servants. St Laurent's style of governing and his emphasis on efficiency permitted certain public servants to exercise influence on policy-making which exceeded that of many cabinet ministers. Policy proposals tended to be discussed between St Laurent and the minister involved and an agreement reached before cabinet consideration of the proposals. Thus, the proposals, which had been worked out primarily among senior public servants, were not subject to intensive examination by ministers of other departments. In this situation, the mandarins (e.g., Robert Bryce as deputy minister of Finance and

Mitchell Sharp as deputy minister of Trade and Commerce) not only sustained but enhanced the influence on policy development they had acquired during the King years.

The election of the Diefenbaker government in 1957, after twenty-two years of uninterrupted Liberal rule, broke the established and often intimate relationships which had developed between senior bureaucrats and their ministers. Peter Newman has noted that the mandarins 'who began to emerge as a cohesive establishment after the war ... prided themselves on their non-partisan approach in a highly political environment. But, given a choice, they much preferred the Liberals, partly because so few Conservatives showed enough trust in their impartiality to heed their counsel.'[12] Nevertheless, public servants were obliged to accept the new – and Conservative – order of things or to take their leave. Most senior officials adapted well but a few, including most notably Mitchell Sharp, departed after disagreements with their new ministers or with the Prime Minister.[13]

These developments seemed to call into question not so much the role of the mandarins as decision-makers but their relationship to the policy-making apparatus of a particular party. As early as 1955, J.E. Hodgetts, an especially astute observer of the Canadian political scene, expressed concern about the possible effects on the bureaucracy of changes in the governing party. He asked whether we could 'expect impartial service from the permanent servants or would we have to face some form of the American system of turning out the top-ranking officials?'[14] More pointedly, John Meisel concluded that much of the Liberal policy discussed during the 1957 election had been developed through the intimate co-operation of ministers and their senior officials.[15] And Pauline Jewett observed that the problem 'was not so much that the bureaucracy became "Liberalized" ... as that the Liberals became "bureaucratized".'[16]

Under the circumstances, it is not surprising that relations between mandarins and ministers during the Diefenbaker years were less intimate and less harmonious than those under the Liberal government. Bureaucrats had to serve ministers who, when in opposition, severely castigated the Liberal government's policies. In many instances, those policies had originated in or were strongly supported by the senior echelons of the bureaucracy. Even had this not been so, the suspicion would likely have lingered because of the personal relationships developed over time between ministers and senior bureaucrats.

It is fair to say that the adjustment of the mandarins to their new ministers would have proceeded more smoothly if Diefenbaker had not so mistrusted the public service and had not resorted so frequently before and after his election to public criticism of 'the bureaucrats.' While he was prime minister he often referred to the 'Pearsonalities' in the Department of External Affairs. It would be unfair, however, to lay all the blame on Mr Diefenbaker's doorstep. Some senior officials seemed to hold the view, largely as a result of their past influence, that they 'knew best' what should be done and how it should be done. Alvin Hamilton, Minister of Agriculture in the Diefenbaker government, complained about bureaucrats who poked holes in his unorthodox proposals. He noted that the bureaucrats 'give you good reasons why something shouldn't be done, but sometimes by God, you *know* that you're right and you resent their attitude of merely tolerating a minister.'[17] However, Howard Green, the Minister of Public Works, observed that it would have been 'quite impossible for a new government to have taken over ... without "great upset" if it had not been for the loyal cooperation given to us by the senior civil servants.'[18]

At the same time, it must be recognized that Diefenbaker himself has given conflicting evidence on this matter. In a conversation in May 1970, he asserted that, except for two persons, he had never found that the advice he received as prime minister 'was politically oriented in any partisan way or by the fact that the civil servants had been for years under Liberal Prime Ministers.'[19] But in his autobiography published in 1976, Mr Diefenbaker stated that, if he had been elected again as prime minister in 1965, 'there would have been some major changes made [in the public service]. It became obvious to me as soon as we were out of office in 1963 that there were quite a number of senior people in the public service, about whom I had not known, who had simply been underground, quietly working against my government and waiting for the Liberals to return to power.'[20]

In any event, there was no significant turnover of senior personnel. The bureaucrats in general remained in their positions, and the available evidence indicates that they continued to serve loyally and effectively the government of the day. No doubt this situation resulted in part from the indoctrination of the senior bureaucrats by Clark, Skelton, Norman Robertson, and others of similar influence as to the public servant's proper role in a parliamentary-cabinet system of government based on the Westminster model.

Another aspect of the relationship between the mandarins and political parties deserves attention. The extent to which some senior bureaucrats had become attached to the Liberal party must have seemed evident to Diefenbaker when he looked across the House at the new Liberal cabinet in 1962. Among twenty-five members of the cabinet, including Prime Minister Pearson, were nine former federal bureaucrats. Moreover, among this group of nine were several of the most powerful cabinet members in the Liberal government.[21] The constitutional implications of the transformation from influential mandarin to authoritative minister were demonstrated well by Mitchell Sharp. Following his appointment as Minister of the Department of Trade and Commerce, where he had served as deputy minister, Mr Sharp cautioned his officials: 'I knew most of you when I was with this department, and it seems a little strange now to be back as the minister. But *that's* what I am.'[22]

Mr Sharp's implicit assertion of the primacy in policy-making of ministers over bureaucrats became a frequently recurring theme during and after the mid 1960s, a period marked by a series of minority Liberal governments following elections in 1962, 1963, and 1965. Among the characteristics of periods of minority government are an increase in the influence of Parliament on the direction of public policy and an increased sensitivity of government to the suspended guillotine of the vote of non-confidence. Awareness of the partisan political ramifications of policy decisions appears to discourage bureaucratic intervention.

A review of the foregoing suggests that the period of time bracketed at its beginning by King, Skelton, and Clark, and at its end by Pearson, Bryce, and Robertson represents a kind of 'golden age' of the mandarin in the Canadian public service. In the period of the minority governments of the 1960s and on through the decade of the 1970s, their powers, as defined earlier in this paper, gradually declined. By the late 1960s, many had retired or had entered political life. It must be recognized that the bureaucracy of the 1960s and 1970s contained genuine luminaries (e.g. Reisman, Shoyama), all of whom within their own sphere exercised considerable influence both on public policy and public administration. However, they do not, as much as their precursors, appear as a *corps d'élite* which as a class dominated the public service and thereby exercised a profound influence on the shape and direction of public policy.

In part, this situation reflects the fact that the influence of the bureaucracy which has arisen from its control of information has to some extent been counterbalanced by the increasing use of competing sources of data and advice: advisory councils, task forces, consultancy reports, and the like. In part also it reflects the different ways of conducting government business as more policy issues have found their way into the realm of intergovernmental discussion and resolution by negotiation and agreement. Furthermore, recent reforms, and proposed reforms, in the structures and procedures of Parliament, cabinet, and even some of the central agencies have included among their avowed purposes that of consolidating the ultimate decision-making power in the hands of the politicians. From PPBS to the 'envelope system,' an expressed intention has been to create information systems and a decision-making apparatus to enhance political control of the bureaucracy. The Clark government was particularly vocal in its proclamations about the return of decision-making power to the politicians. Indeed, in respect of its diagnosis of the problems in the relationships between politicians and bureaucrats and of its remedial action, the Clark government resembled closely that of Diefenbaker.

While this brief record has traced, at least in outline, the rise and fall of the mandarin, it should not be interpreted as culminating in any major reversal of the more evident historical trend of increasing bureaucratic influence on the policy-making process. The institutional and environmental conditions which worked to produce the mandarin cannot be seen to have altered materially. There is little evidence that the elements of the administrative state that have come into being, particularly in the period since the Second World War, are likely to be substantially modified. Indeed, in some senses the gut issues of our time would seem to point towards more rather than less governmental intervention, and more rather than less technocratic (as opposed to political) influence in the operations of government as it faces such issues as inflation, unemployment, energy, and pollution. The strategic advantage of the bureaucrat that comes from control of the greater part of the necessary information sources (despite the counterbalancing effect of other sources) and his superior skill in the management and use of the information available make it inevitable that his profound influence in *all* aspects of government, including policy formulation, must continue.

At the same time, it seems unlikely that we will see the reincarnation of the mandarin of the 'golden age.' Three reasons for this are particularly relevant to our discussion.

First, there is the matter of size – the dominant characteristic of modern government. The sheer *volume* of transactions to be completed at all levels of decision-making is such that it quickly passes beyond the capacity of the lay politician who, with the best intentions in the world, can give only part of his or her time to the management of the Queen's business. Flora MacDonald, in her much publicized speech,[23] was correct in voicing her strong concern about the inundation of the ministerial offices. She was correct only to a limited degree in blaming the bureaucrats for flooding the system. But, for purposes of this discussion, it may be observed that the matter goes beyond the passage into bureaucratic hands of an increasing proportion of the responsibility for disposing of the public's business. Even at the level of the bureaucracy, the volume is so great as to make it impossible for any small group of the annointed – such as the mandarinate – to regulate its flow.

Second, the decision-making process in government (as in business) has become to a large extent a joint venture in pooled skills and knowledge. This has resulted partly from the unalterable advance of specialization and the continuous extension of the technical or professional nature of government decisions. (The purchase of fighter aircraft provides a recent and spectacular example of these developments). The mandarin in government, like the tycoon in business, has been replaced by the manager whose task increasingly is to tend to the welfare of the decision-making process rather than to make the decisions himself.

Finally, much of the rationalization of government procedures and operations has had the effect of constraining the decision-making activities of public servants. Indeed, the very purpose of this rationalization has often been to bring these activities within the framework of a more logical system designed to ensure a fuller measure of administrative responsibility. The years since the early sixties have been marked by considerable public suspicion and criticism of the bureaucracy and its works. From Glassco to MacDonnell, by way of PPBS and comprehensive auditing, governmental structures and systems have been designed to bring the whole decision-making framework under more careful and more open scrutiny. In respect of these developments, it is notable that the instruments devised to limit and channel the discretionary behaviour of the bureaucracy are for the most part administrative rather than political in their prescription, design, and application.

1 See Kenneth Kernaghan, 'Policy, Politics and Public Servants: Political Neutrality Revisited,' *Canadian Public Administration*, vol. 19 (fall 1976), pp. 432-56.

2 'Bureaucrats and Politicians,' ibid., vol. 15 (fall 1972), p. 426

3 *Debates* (House of Commons), 17 February 1941, p. 818

4 'The Bureaucratic Elite and Policy Formation,' in W.D.K. Kernaghan, ed., *Bureaucracy in Canadian Government* (Toronto: Methuen, 1969), pp. 82-3

5 J.W. Pickersgill, *The Mackenzie King Record*, vol. 1 (Toronto: University of Toronto Press, 1960), p. 633 (emphasis added)

6 Obituary, W.C. Clark, *Ottawa Journal*, 4 December 1952 (emphasis added)

7 See Kernaghan, 'Policy, Politics and Public Servants,' pp. 451-4.

8 *The Canadian Establishment*, vol. 1 (Toronto: McClelland and Stewart, 1975), pp. 330-6

9 James Eayrs, 'The Bureaucratic Elite and Formation of Canadian Foreign Policy,' in Kernaghan, ed., *Bureaucracy in Canadian Government*, p. 89. In *The Canadian Establishment*, Peter Newman provides a select list of 'the Ottawa mandarins' for the years between the late thirties and the late sixties; see pp. 435-7.

10 *Mike: The Memoirs of the Right Honourable Lester B. Pearson*, vol. 1, 1897-1948 (Toronto, University of Toronto Press, 1972), p. 196. For a similar statement see Sharp, 'The Bureaucratic Elite and Policy Formation,' p. 84.

11 'The White Paper on Employment and Income in Its 1945 Setting,' in S.F. Kaliski, ed., *Canadian Economic Policy since the War*, (Ottawa: Carleton University, 1966), pp. 15-16

12 *The Canadian Establishment*, p. 336

13 For separate and somewhat conflicting accounts of events leading to Mr Sharp's resignation, see Arnold Heeney, *The Things That Are Caesar's* (Toronto: University of Toronto Press, 1972), p. 150, and John George Diefenbaker, *One Canada: Memoirs of the Right Honourable George G. Diefenbaker*, vol. 2, *1957-1962* (Toronto: Macmillan, 1976), pp. 52-3.

14 'The Liberal and the Bureaucrat,' *Queen's Quarterly*, vol. 62 (1955), p. 182

15 *The Canadian General Election of 1957* (Toronto: University of Toronto Press, 1962), p. 38

16 'Political and Administrative Aspects of Policy Formation,' in T. Brewis *et al.*, *Canadian Economic Policy*, 2nd ed. (Toronto: Macmillan, 1965), p. 356

17 Quoted in Peter C. Newman, *Renegade in Power* (Toronto: Macmillan, 1963), p. 143

18 *Debates* (House of Commons), 18 December 1957, p. 2515

19 Thomas A. Hockin, ed., *Apex of Power: The Prime Minister and Political Leadership in Canada* (Scarborough: Prentice-Hall, 1971), p. 187

20 *One Canada*, vol. 2, pp. 53-4

21 These were Lester Pearson, Bud Drury, Maurice Lamontagne, Jack Pickersgill, and Mitchell Sharp. Pearson and Pickersgill had been ministers in previous Liberal governments.

22 Quoted in Peter C. Newman, 'Backstage in Ottawa,' *Maclean's Magazine*, vol. 76, no. 11 (1963), p. 3

23 Address to the Canadian Political Science Association, Montreal, 3 June 1980, reprinted in part under the title 'The Minister and the Mandarins,' *Policy Options* (September-October, 1980), pp. 29-31

ROCH BOLDUC AND JAMES IAIN GOW

Environment and Administration: Quebec, 1867-1980

We would like to bring together here two themes which are prominent in the work of J.E. Hodgetts – administrative history and the ecology of public administration. It will be argued that from 1867 until 1960 the Quebec administration, in spite of growth and change, was dominated by outside forces – political, religious, economic, and cultural. In the period since 1960 the administration has taken a much more active role in influencing the environment. As the number of its tasks increased, the administration grew rapidly and became more complex in its composition, its structures, and its methods. In recent times, the pace of change in the environment has increased the rate of change in the Quebec administration, but the administration is now clearly an actor in the political system, sometimes a force for change, sometimes a force against change. Political and economic agents in Quebec have adapted their intervention accordingly.

We present first a historical account of the 1867-1960 period which ends with some analysis of the place of the administration in its environment during that time. In a second part, changes in Quebec society since 1960 are related to changes in the Quebec administration and its more active role in that society.

Our version of systems theory is simple and formal: we consider the administration to be a subsystem of the political system. It may be identified as the personnel and the institutions which prepare and execute the decisions of the legislature and the cabinet. It has thus a formal existence and all factors external to it are considered to be part of the environment. We recognize that such an approach would not satisfy many definitions of a system. These latter extend to all elements interacting in such a way as to show interdependence and, therefore, include political leaders and organizations, client and other interest groups, suppliers, employee associations, and the like within the system.[1] While there is much merit in such an approach, it is not really possible to apply over a long period to an organization so complex as the Quebec administration. Moreover, in focusing on the administration as the system, we achieve a certain clarity and unity, while trying not to lose sight of its relations to other actors in the political, economic, and social systems. Our conception is therefore narrow in that it limits itself to the administration, but flexible in that it regards the administration as a very open, indeed porous, subsystem of the political system.

AN ADMINISTRATION DOMINATED BY OUTSIDE FORCES, 1867-1960

For almost one hundred years, the position of the Quebec administration with respect to the forces in its environment evolved very slowly. While it gradually assumed more and more tasks, it remained in a relatively weak position until the reforms of the 1960s. We examine briefly the growth of government activities and that of the administration before turning to the question of relations with the environment.

Over the first ninety years, the pattern of expenditure of the Quebec government varied considerably. A survey shows[2] that the most consistently important concerns were education and health, although the components of these also changed over time. The most spectacular but also the most fluctuating field of expenditure was that of capital investment in the area of transportation – railways in the nineteenth century and highways in the twentieth. Welfare expenditures were of little importance before the Great Depression; after some fluctuation in the post-war period they became an important part of the budget, running at over 10 per cent in the late 1950s. Since the beginning of the century, the relative importance of expenditure on justice and the debt service declined.

In the nineteenth century, a combination of laisser-faire philosophy, hard times, population exodus, and uncertainties about the division of powers in the new federation led governments to be cautious about increasing expenditures. In fact, the pattern of government activity is surprising.[3] In terms of organizational stability, budgets, and numbers of civil servants, the most important departments on a consistent basis were Public Instruction, Justice (court administration and prisons), and Lands and Forest (revenue collection). On the other hand, some of the basic functions of government were relatively neglected. The provincial police, created in 1870, was abolished in 1878 for reasons of economy and was only really restored towards the end of the 1880s. The revenue function was badly organized and it was not until 1888 that a revenue office was created in the Treasury Department.

The most important single item of public expenditure by Quebec governments in the nineteenth century was the subsidization of railroad building. When the federal government in 1873 settled a dispute between Ontario and Quebec over their respective shares of the debt of the United Canadas by assuming the whole of it at the federal level, the Quebec government felt free to turn to the bond market in order to finance railway construction in the province. The borrowing was heavy and probably beyond the means of the province for, at the beginning of the 1890s, the government was having difficulty borrowing new funds and debt service had reached the level of 33 per cent of total expenditure or over 40 per cent of ordinary expenses.[4] This experience was to leave its mark on the governments of the next period. It had almost no permanent effects on the administration, since most of the grants were made to private companies. When the most important line, from Quebec City to Ottawa via Montreal, ran into financial difficulties, the government did nationalize it in 1875 in order to ensure its completion. However, it was hardly completed and put into operation when the government sold it back into private hands at a considerable loss.

The years from 1900 to 1930 constitute a period of rapid economic growth, industrialization, urbanization, and, for the government, budgetary surpluses. Capital investment in railways gave way to important new expenditure programs for the construction of highways and of dams to regulate the flow of Quebec's rivers to hydroelectric power plants. In addition to these important undertakings of capital investment, the Quebec government was drawn, in the first third of the century, into new measures of regulation and social service. This pattern has been traced for the whole of Canada by J.A. Corry in his 'The Growth of Government Activities since Confederation,' written for the Rowell-Sirois Commission in 1939. New measures were introduced in Quebec, as elsewhere, for the regulation of trade, the quality of farm products, the stock market, and public utilities. Laws forbidding child labour and limiting the hours of work of women and young people were adopted and a Commission on Minimum Wages for Women was created (1925). A series of laws dealing with industrial accidents was also adopted culminating in the creation of the Workman's Compensation Commission in 1928. New campaigns were undertaken to combat smallpox and tuberculosis and a system of county health units was introduced. Also, in the first major change in the social welfare system since the days of New France, the Public Assistance Act of 1921 brought the government into the financing of public welfare services.

In good times this was the blend of policies which emerges: major capital projects in the hydro and highway fields, much new regulation of economic life, new social measures which, while not insurance schemes, were largely self-financing. Then, when the depression occurred in the 1930s, the Quebec government joined with the federal and municipal governments in trying to mitigate its effects. From 1930 to 1940 approximately $235 millions were spent, about one-third in various works programs and two-thirds in direct relief. Only 1 per cent of the total went to the Back to the Land Movement. Of this massive aid program, the Quebec government paid about one half, the federal government 27 per cent, and local governments 21 per cent.[5]

Maurice Duplessis is remembered for his autonomist policies. He strongly resisted federal intrusions into fields such as culture and higher education. In 1954 he restored the provincial income tax which the Godbout government had vacated in favour of the federal government during the Second World War. By taking this stand Duplessis forced the federal government to accord a certain abatement of federal taxes to Quebec residents.

The Union Nationale governments did introduce some important new policies. To aid his rural constituency, Duplessis brought in farm credit (1936), rural electrification (1945) and the farm products marketing board (1956). During his first mandate, he also had adopted some important welfare measures: old age pensions for the needy (1936), aid to the blind (1937), and aid to indigent mothers (1937). The first two of these were partly funded by federal programs. In the post-war years the Duplessis government introduced new programs creating technical schools and organizing apprenticeship centres. Highways continued to obtain a high priority during these years.

To a great extent the new province of Quebec inherited, in 1867, the machinery of government which it was to use for a very long time. As

J.E. Hodgetts has pointed out 'the bequests of the pioneer public service' of the United Canadas included a working system of governmental departments each directed by a permanent deputy head, a process of financial management with a cabinet committee on expenditures, the presentation of budgetary estimates, supervision of expenditure by an auditor, and, finally, an examining board to verify a minimum of qualification of candidates for appointment to the civil service.[6] Equally important as a heritage from Lower Canada were the decentralized systems of municipal government, school administration, and the administration of justice. Finally, although most of the civil servants of the United Canadas transferred to the service of the new federal government, Quebec and Ontario inherited the employees of the departments of Lands and Forests, Agriculture, and Education.[7]

Thus, although in 1867 an entire administration had to be created, the broad lines of administrative structures already existed and were maintained, just as pre-Confederation legislation was maintained in the new provinces until new laws were adopted.

The administration that evolved during these years was strongly decentralized and very open to outside influence. Decentralization was the prevailing doctrine and practice. Municipalities were charged not only with services to property, public works, and safety, but also with public health, labour relations, control of business, public relief of disaster victims and of the needy, as well as the promotion of agriculture and colonization. Not only was education in the hands of local school boards but, as of 1875, the position of Minister of Education was replaced by the Council of Public Instruction whose members were appointed along confessional lines and which was, in fact, governed by its two main committees, one composed of the Catholic bishops of the province or their representatives, the other by representatives of the Protestant community.[8] The Catholic church was strongly represented in education in other ways also, since many of the teachers belonged to teaching orders (and were not only very economical for their school boards, for they were also exempted from the general obligation for teachers to have a certificate of competence). Higher education in the French language was almost a monopoly of the church since the classical colleges and the principal university (Laval, which had a main campus at Quebec and a branch at Montreal) were either under the direct control of the church or of one of the religious communities. The church was in the same position in the field of social welfare, since most charitable institutions were religious organizations, and it was the leading force in land settlement, since the government basically limited itself to supporting *sociétés de colonisation* which were organized by parish and other religious groups as well as by certain municipalities. This practice of decentralization was important in other fields as well. The Minister of Agriculture had a rival for the direction of agricultural policy in the Agricultural Council which was composed of eminent farmers and agronomists appointed by the Lieutenant-Governor in Council.[9] When the first public health board was appointed in 1887 the law stipulated that at least four of its seven members be doctors.[10]

The civil service under this regime was open and vulnerable. In spite of the creation in of a Civil Service Board on the model of the Board of Examiners of the United Canadas, it appears that appointments were soon made without qualifying examinations and on the basis of political patronage.[11] However, it is also evident that changes of government (especially in 1887 and 1891) did not bring about widespread dismissals. Honoré Mercier, who was most candid about this, accepted the prevailing doctrine of the times that civil service jobs were a form of social welfare which it would be too harsh to withdraw on any large scale. Mercier did, however, have a law passed which removed the right of provincial civil servants to vote in federal or provincial elections, on the grounds that it was necessary to protect them from political pressure.[12] Even so, it should be noted that the Quebec service had among its numbers many highly qualified specialists who enjoyed, apparently, a high degree of job security.

In the twentieth century the civil service grew steadily. From approximately 600 employees in 1895, it grew to over 6,700 in 1933, to which should be added another 1,300 in public corporations. By 1959, these figures were about 28,000 members in the civil service, with another 7,000 in public corporations.

Most of the new functions assumed by the state in Quebec involved intervention in areas previously left to the decentralized sector. Two of the major instruments by which this was done were financial aid and technical decentralization. Financial aid was the trademark of the first highway construction programs and of the main social welfare activity under the Public Assistance Act. After the Second World War, the Duplessis government came to the aid of the school boards with grants under the Act to Ensure the Progress of Education (1946). Typically, these financial aid programs were administered from special funds not accounted for in the regular departmental budgets.

Technical decentralization was introduced largely in the form of regulatory commissions. Before 1960 relatively few public enterprises were created, a fact which shows the general trend of governmental intervention. All governments before 1960 thought that the state should aid private industry with large-scale development projects and with technical aid, but regulatory activities were preferred to competing with the private sector. Probably as much new governmental activity was assumed by new or existing government departments, but since these latter were forever being merged, subdivided, and rejoined, more absolute growth appears in the ranks of boards and commissions. With respect to the administrative system, few major changes were introduced during the long Liberal reign. In 1925, the Outside Service was integrated into the classification structure, thus bringing to an end a very disorderly situation for this large group of employees.

Control of appointments to the civil service followed a curious pattern. In 1926, all reference to the Civil Service Board disappeared from the law,[13] a gesture which was no doubt in accordance with practice, but which showed unusual candour at a time when the renewed federal Civil Service Commission was fighting its first battles. On his election in 1936, Duplessis fired many civil servants, thus breaking with the traditional pattern of patronage appointments without wholesale dismissals after a change of party.[14] When Adélard Godbout was elected in 1939, he brought back a certain number of the dismissed employees. Moreover, and this may have been in part because he was a former civil servant, he brought in the Civil Service Act of 1943 which provided for qualifying examinations for most positions.[15] When he returned to power in 1944, Duplessis obtained the resignations of the three Civil Service Commissioners and replaced them with a single Commissioner, his friend Ernest Laforce. The Commission thus became an instrument for personal control by the Prime Minister. However, the service had reached a size such that much of the work of the Commission was carried on without interference from above.

The administration remained paternalistic under Duplessis, as it had under all his predecessors except possibly Godbout. However it can be said that Maurice Duplessis was a gifted administrator. He was not a reformer; although he was elected under the banner of reform, his only gesture in this direction was to have passed a law forbidding ministers to sit on boards of directors of private companies.[16] He did create a centralized Purchasing Agency but it, like the Civil Service

Commission, simply served to increase his personal control of the administration. He appears to have understood administration very well and to have taken pains not to be restrained by any bureaucratic system. For example, although he created a committee in 1946 to revise the 1925 classification system, he saw to it that it never reported. Without a coherent and logical classification of positions competitive examinations for appointment to the civil service have little meaning.[17] His successor, Paul Sauvé, sought and obtained a new classification scheme from the Civil Service Commission within three months. Likewise, it was a source of complaint with the Federation of Catholic School Boards that most of their financial grants in the 1950s came from the surplus of the Education Fund which was distributed at the discretion of the cabinet.[18] These examples illustrate Duplessis' preference for discretionary powers.

In spite of its considerable growth and complexity, the Quebec administration, after ninety years, still remained in 1960 dominated by the forces in its environment. These were political, religious, economic, and cultural.

In politics this domination came from the party in power. An outstanding fact of political life in Quebec during this period was the domination by one party or another over long periods of time. From 1867 to 1896, the Conservative party was in power for all but five and a half years; from 1897 to 1936 the Liberal party was in power without interruption; and from 1936 to 1960 the Union Nationale governed for all but five years. This tradition of long periods in power by one party may have given some security to ordinary civil servants, but the precariousness of their position was seen when, under Honoré Mercier, they lost the right to vote in 1889 and when, in 1936, the first Duplessis government replaced considerable numbers with its own candidates.

The electoral system meant that there was considerable temptation to use the perquisites of office to enhance one's chance for election or re-election. Curiously, the administration seems to have become more vulnerable to pressure of this kind over time, rather than less as one would expect. The major political scandals of the late nineteenth century involved ministers, members of the Legislative Assembly, and party organizers rather than civil servants. The reason for this seems to be that the central administration was so little developed that ministers had a free hand in distributing such projects as the construction of the Parliament buildings or the Quebec City court house. In this century, however, the long period of uninterrupted Liberal government brought a number of senior civil servants into compromising positions with the government. The revelations before the Public Accounts Committee in 1936, so skilfully directed by the leader of the opposition, Maurice Duplessis, showed that many of them had profited personally from their positions. Several of them were forced into retirement by these revelations; others, as we have seen, were fired after the elections of 1936. In his turn, Maurice Duplessis used the new central agencies, the Purchasing Agency and the Civil Service Commission, to reward those deserving of party patronage. He also appears to have resorted, more consistently than his predecessors, to the practice of increasing government spending substantially in election years.[19] Thus, until 1960 the power of the party in office over the administration was very great.

The Catholic church was a formidable force in the environment of the administration during the entire period we have been discussing. The church was present both at the policy-making level and at the everyday level of practical matters. As J.-C. Falardeau put it, 'Historical circumstances having drawn the Canadian clergy into occupying successively all strategic positions in society, it remains omnipresent and associated with everything important which is considered, organized or happening.'[20]

The influence of the church was particularly strong in certain fields: education, social affairs, and colonization were matters which could not be touched by governments without the collaboration or at least tacit consent of the bishops and the clergy. Moreover, the church successfully associated itself with the first provincial professional associations of farmers, trade unions, and teachers. La Confédération des travailleurs catholiques du Canada (1922), l'Union catholique des cultivateurs (1924), and la Corporation des instituteurs et institutrices catholiques (1946) were all confessional bodies at their origins and for many years thereafter.

On the practical level, religious organizations owned and operated most French-speaking hospitals and welfare institutions. The entire public school system was confessional in its structures. The main path to university led through the collèges classiques which were mostly confessional. In 1950-1951, 38 per cent of the teachers in the Catholic school system were members of a religious order. The presence of the church, or of some of its leaders, might turn up at any level of administration. Certain appointments could be favoured or blocked.[21] The provincial corps of school inspectors found itself, in its efforts to improve the quality of lay teachers, accused of freemasonry tendencies, for long a very serious charge.[22] This last point helps to underline the advantages to political leaders of such a situation. Not only were confessional institutions vastly cheaper than fully funded public institutions would turn out to be, but any criticism of policy or practice in the fields reserved to the church could be construed and chastised as an attack on the Church.[23]

Equally important in the environment but less visible than political parties and the church was private enterprise. Let us note first, that the administration did not have to deal with the church and business at the same time. In fields where the church had the principle role, business was largely absent. It was only in the field of labour relations that the two had sometimes to be dealt with at once, and here the church was usually neutral, occasionally playing the part of arbitrator. However, it did happen that the clergy sided with the workers against private enterprise, as in the case of an episcopal letter of 1941 which concluded that working conditions in many establishments were absolutely revolting and that 'capitalism in our country exploits the workers who are insufficiently protected by our legislation.'[24]

In the main, however, the administration had to deal with either the church or business, but not both at once. For business, the longest fields of contacts were the Lands and Forests Department concerning the timber merchants, the Mines Service (later Department) with the mining companies, and the several administrations dealing with the private hydro companies. In these areas, the administration had a revenue-collecting function and a regulatory role, and it must be said that they were difficult to carry out efficiently. Not only was the prevailing philosophy that the role of the administration was to help business, but the specialists hired by the administration to deal with private enterprise in these sectors (forestry, mining, and electrical engineers) had the same training as their counterparts in private industry and indeed, their careers were often made up of periods in the employment of each sector. They were, therefore, dealing with people with whom they shared a common education, similar career patterns, and a common frame of reference. For these reasons and others the state in Quebec was not a severe regulator of these resource industries.[25]

Business was also present in the environment of the administration through its links with politics. The practice, before the Duplessis law of 1937, of ministers and members of the Legislative Assembly sitting on boards of directors is strong evidence of these links. Perhaps the most notorious area of such contracts was that of railway companies in the nineteenth century. The politics of aid to railway construction were all the more sordid because of the presence of ministers and members of the Assembly on the boards of many of the companies seeking subsidies.[26] In this century, the links between Premier Alexandre Taschereau and the world of high finance, particularly what was known as the Electricity Trust, were used against him by those who maintained that his government favoured the private hydroelectric companies against the ordinary people of the province.[27] In general, large and small businesses accommodated themselves to the patronage system of all governments of these ninety years, thus supporting an atmosphere of partisanship which impeded the development of an impartial administration.

A fourth factor in the environment which had a considerable impact on the administration was the division of Quebec society on language lines. By 1960 the presence of anglophones in the central administration was limited to three departments where they had traditionally been strongly represented. A study done of 60 per cent of the higher civil service in 1959 found that only 4.5 per cent of them were English-speaking and that they were concentrated in the departments of Finance, Mines, and Public Instruction. The greater impact of the cultural duality of Quebec came from the strength of English institutions in the decentralized sector. Aside from controlling the municipalities where they were in the majority, the English-speaking population had its own systems of school boards and schools, of colleges and universities, of hospitals and welfare agencies. It was used to considerable autonomy in all of these fields, autonomy which limited the initiatives which might be taken by the administration of Quebec.

Finally, it can be seen that the Quebec administration was condemned to follow changing economic conditions and technological change. Prosperity meant revenues to finance new initiatives; hard times, particularly the Great Depression, meant enormous responsibilities. Even more striking is the way that new policies and programs followed on technical innovations: the railways, hydroelectricity, the automobile all caused important changes in the administration as governments tried to meet their requirements and their consequences.

The Quebec administration of the late 1950s was thus very open indeed to the influence of the environment. It tended to be compartmentalized into specialized sectors, each with its links to its own clientele. There was no unified higher civil service but rather separate career patterns for specialists and professionals each in their own departments. The lawyers dominated at the Procurer General's Department, the doctors at Health, the accountants at Finance, the forestry engineers at Lands and Forests, and so on. This specialization had its good and bad effects. Among the good effects were the contacts that many specialists had with their counterparts elsewhere in the world. They attended conferences and made study voyages more often than might be thought. Moreover, they enabled the civil service to recruit many competent young people in spite of the low salaries of the time. Many of them taught part-time and they were able through these contacts to recruit some of their more able students.

However, there was little idea of public servants in the sense of belonging to a competent corps of relatively independent professionals. Faced with the dominant forces of political parties, the church and business, the Quebec administration adopted, of necessity, a style of accommodation to its various special publics, a style which would gradually change with the beginnings of technocratic approach in the 1960s. For the time, however, morale was not high in the civil service, and there tended to be an inferiority complex with respect to the larger, wealthier, and more powerful civil service at Ottawa.[28]

A MORE ACTIVE ROLE FOR THE QUEBEC ADMINISTRATION, 1960-1980

We wish to show now that the Quebec administration, while still very open to influence from the outside world, has taken a greater, more active part in shaping that world. We look first at the changes which have occurred in the socio-political context in the last twenty-five years, next at the change in the role of the state, and, finally, at the place of the administration as a result of these changes.

The context has to be divided into factors which have affected all western countries and factors which are more particular to Quebec. The familiarity and generality of the former should not blind us to their importance. Even the briefest reminder of some of these prodigious changes should convince us of this fact. It has been a time of great technical change stimulated by the scientific and technical rivalry of the United States and the Soviet Union in the post-sputnik era. Developments in computers and telecommunications have transformed our ideas about information, time, and frontiers. In economics, the emergence of giant multinational firms has been accompanied by that of trading blocs like the European Common Market and groups like the Organization of Petroleum Exporting Countries. New considerations have entered into economic analysis with new concerns such as ecology and, more recently, energy.

On the social and cultural fronts there has been a great shift in values and morals. On the one hand, the main thrust has been towards greater personal freedom in dress, social behaviour, and sexual morals. On the other hand, there have been certain religious and spiritual reactions, such as Vatican II, the popularity of various eastern religions, and different forms of Christian revival. Minority groups have demanded fairer treatment from the majority and feminists have been expounding a very different type of society, one based on equality of the sexes.

In politics, the rise of the Third World and the accompanying criticism of colonialism and racism had direct impact in Quebec where this language was used by many spokesmen for Quebec independence.[29] The rise of protest movements and the crisis of legitimacy had their counterparts in Quebec. It took a little longer in Quebec than elsewhere for disenchantment with the welfare state to set in, for it was only during the 1960s that the welfare state was really introduced into Quebec.

Turning to the more specific Quebec environment let us register some trends in population and economic matters before turning to the worlds of politics, religion, business, and culture. Some of the main trends in population change from 1950s to the 1970s are:[30]

1 continued urbanization, with the proportion of Québécois living in urban areas passing from 70 in 1956 to 80.6 per cent in 1971 with more than half of the total population in the Montreal region.

2 The dramatic fall in the birth rate from 28.3 per 1000 in 1959 to 14.2 in 1974. This change took Quebec from the highest birthrate in the country to one of the lowest in a very few years.

3 The rapid rise in the rate of attendance of young people at schools, particularly post-secondary institutions and universities. By the mid

1970s a much more highly educated and skilled labour force was available in Quebec than was the case in the late 1950s.
4 The labour force was not only larger and better educated; it was composed increasingly of women: their share of the whole went from 25 to 45 per cent in twenty years.
5 The structure of the labour force has been transformed. The primary sector has lost ground (reduction of 34,000 jobs from 1966 to 1976), the manufacturing sector has grown slightly (50,000 jobs in ten years), and the tertiary sector has risen sharply (435,000 jobs). More and more, in Quebec as elsewhere in Canada, the economy is becoming a service economy.

Guy Rocher has suggested that for the first sixty years of the century structural changes were predominant but that since 1960 cultural changes were more important in Quebec.[31] One of the biggest of such changes was in the attitude towards the state. It was now seen as a lever or an instrument to be used for the collective defence and advancement of the francophone population in Quebec. We shall return to the changes in political life of these years below, but let us note here how changes in the vocabulary of these years reflected a rising nationalist sentiment. The needs of the French language had already made it customary before 1960 to refer to the leader of the provincial government as 'le premier ministre' and 'the prime minister.' There was a desire in that expression to show that the provincial leader was in no way inferior in status to his federal counterpart. In the 1960s Jean Lesage began to speak of the state of Quebec in pursuit of his 'politique de grandeur.' Then, in one of the most successful feats of nationalist persuasion, the word 'Québécois' was substituted for 'Canadien' to refer to a French Canadian of Quebec. Before 1960, to many people in the province, 'un Canadien' was a French Canadian, whereas an Anglo-Canadian was referred to as 'un Anglais.' These changes reflected a focusing of aspirations on the government at Quebec. In terms of party politics, these were years of instability, with the eclipse of the Union Nationale, the rise and fall of the Créditistes, and the emergence of the Parti Québécois. This instability affected the government: four changes of party in office occurred in sixteen years.

The second great force which we identified in the pre-1960 environment of the administration, the church, was reduced in a few short years to the position of a silent observer of the Quebec scene.

Its control over educational, hospital, and charitable institutions was almost completely replaced by that of the state. The number of lay teachers continued to grow at the expense of the members of religious teaching orders. The secularization of social and economic life was striking during these years. Each of the major interest groups referred to above abandoned its religious affiliation: the CTCC became the CSN (la Confédération des syndicats nationaux) in 1961; the CIC became the CEQ (Corporation des enseignants du Québec, 1967, and then Centrale de l'enseignement du Québec, 1972); and the UCC became the UPA (Union des producteurs agricoles) in 1972.

With respect to business, there was not such a dramatic change. Private enterprise was still welcome in Quebec under all governments but there was a clear desire to regulate private business more than in the past and, even, in limited fields to rival it through the use of public corporations. Another effect on business of governmental action came through the strengthening of the trade union movement through the unionization of the public sector employees. Their subsequent experience in negotiating with the government was a factor in their radicalization in the late 1960s and early 1970s. Finally, the introduction of measures destined to make French the language of work helped to demonstrate that many young Québécois were not opposed to making their careers in business, as had been often supposed; they simply wanted to do it in French. By the end of the 1970s, more people were studying business administration proportionately in Quebec than in any other province in Canada.[32]

With respect to the cultural environment, two trends are worth mentioning. With the Quiet Revolution there was something like a release of cultural energy in Quebec which was manifest on all fronts – newspaper, magazine, and book publishing, television, theatre and cinema, music and record publishing. Then, the anglophone population has seen its influence reduced, first by the centralization which has diminished the importance of all decentralized sectors, municipal, school, and social services.[33] Also, the various language laws, of which more below, have restricted the use of English and thus the prospects of anglophones in business, education, and the public services generally.

It is difficult to describe adequately the remarkable growth of the state and of the governmental apparatus in Quebec since 1960. We shall highlight some of the major innovations in policy before looking at the place of the public sector in the economy and the changed role of the state.

Perhaps the most important change since 1960 is the emergence of the state as the dominant force, if not a monopoly, in the fields of education, health, and welfare. The entire educational system was restructured: secondary schooling was made compulsory (1961), a new network of regional school boards and of regional comprehensive high schools was introduced (1964-66), a new post-secondary level of free public education was introduced with the creation of the collèges d'enseignement général et professionnel (CEGEPS) in 1967, and university education was transformed by government financing of new construction projects and most operating costs, loans and bursaries to students, and a new public university, l'Université du Québec, with campuses in five centres around the province (1968). In health, the major new programs were hospital insurance (1960), medical assistance for those receiving welfare payments (1966), and health insurance (1970). In welfare, Quebec went its own way in 1965, introducing its own Quebec Pension Plan at the same time as, and in place of, the Canada Pension Plan. In 1969, the Social Aid Act replaced seven existing laws with an integrated approach to welfare, based on the family. Finally since 1971 a network of local community service centres has been gradually introduced, offering a variety of services and referring those needing more specialized care to the appropriate institutions.

These three fields had in common several features. First, they were and are expensive; since the mid 1960s they have together accounted for over 60 per cent of the annual expenditures of the province. Next, the restructuring was carried out by a new department whose role was to plan and co-ordinate activities in its sector, the Department of Education (1964) and the Social Affairs Department (1970). Finally, while these departments continued to operate through the decentralized sector, they introduced laws and regulations which greatly increased their control over school boards, colleges, universities, hospitals, and welfare agencies and institutions. The main weapon in this exchange was the budgetary control which accompanied the various grants, subsidies, and other forms of financing of the decentralized sector.

In the economic field, the governments have continued the tradition of major public investment programs. The highway system has been greatly extended, particularly by the introduction of autoroutes. With the nationalization of hydroelectricity in 1962, Hydro-Québec launched several huge development projects, the best known of which was on the Manicouagan River. Since 1971 Hydro-Quebec has been associated with the James Bay Development Corporation in the massive development projects of that region.

Other signs of government intervention in the economy may be found in the proliferation of public corporations since 1960. Two of the best known are Hydro-Quebec and La Caisse de dépôt et de placement. In the former case, the 'nationalization' by purchase of shares of the seven remaining private electrical power producers and distributors gave the existing Hydro-Quebec a monopoly in the distribution of electricity and paved the way for the investment projects already mentioned. The Investment and Deposit Fund, created in 1965 to receive and invest contributions to the Quebec Pension Plan, has become the depository of all government funds of this sort, so that in 1979 its total available capital was almost $10 billion. Equally important is the fact that the fund has invested 32 per cent of its available resources in Quebec government bonds thus reducing the dependence of the government on the 'syndicat financier,' that is, on the group of banks and brokers who have traditionally handled the sale of Quebec bonds.[34] In addition to these two and the James Bay Development Corporation, since 1960 new corporations have been created in the fields of resource exploration and development, industrial development, steel production, agriculture, housing, co-operatives, cultural industries, television broadcasting, and auto insurance.

In the case of regulation of the economy, the initiatives since 1960 have tended to strengthen and complete measures already introduced in the past, rather than to innovate completely. The Labour Code had been revised three times since 1960. Successive governments have tackled the difficult problem of labour relations in the construction industry with indifferent success.[35] New legislation on health and safety in the workplace was adopted in 1979. Control over the marketing of farm products was extended from dairy products to potentially all others. Rent control was generalized and made more severe. In a new departure, the Parti Québécois government introduced compulsory public automobile insurance in 1977.

A brief idea of some other fields of new activity may be obtained from a partial list of new government departments or major administrative units: cultural affairs, intergovernmental affairs, communications, New Quebec (the northern territories of the province), regional planning and land use, the office of the French language, environmental protection, sports and leisure, energy.

The sum of all these activities has been rapid growth of the public sector in Quebec. The Quebec government expenditure budget has increased twenty-five times from 1959-1960 to 1979-1980 (from $600 million to $15 billion). The expenses of all governments in Quebec have risen from 25 to 45 per cent of the Quebec gross domestic product. This is less than the governmental share in the Maritime provinces but higher than that of any province to the west.[36] The share of the public sector in the total capital expenditures rose from 30 in 1963 to 45 per cent in 1978, the latter figure well ahead of the national average of 31 per cent. We will deal in more detail with the growth of the civil service below, but let us note here that the entire public sector in the late 1970s was composed of 320,000 people, representing 15 per cent of the labour force in Quebec and their salaries consuming half of the governmental expenditure budget.[37]

Beyond the quantitative changes, important qualitative changes must be noted in the role of the Quebec state. Since 1960, governments have been trying to orient and direct the economy, to manage the framework if not the detail of economic life.[38] For a short time the Lesage government considered introducing a type of economic planning in the manner of French planning. Lacking the necessary control of its economy and the necessary technical instruments, it abandoned this hope in 1964. However, central government planning has continued first in the Council of Economic Orientation and, since 1969, in the Office of Planning and Development on a wide variety of subjects, most notably regional development and the planning of governmental activities.

One sign of this new desire has been the proliferation of research and consultation activity. It began under the Lesage government which created a record number of royal and other commissions of inquiry.[39] Almost invariably these commissions reported that Quebec had no policy in the area under study and recommended that steps should be taken to adopt one. At this time, or soon afterwards, the various government departments created planning divisions and one or more advisory bodies. While commissions of inquiry have not entirely disappeared, under the Parti Québécois government new forms of planning and consultation have been introduced. The standard pattern involves the introduction of a policy paper, followed by consultations, often in parliamentary committee. Other forms of consultation have been used recently, including tripartite economic 'summit' conferences with business and labour representatives and constant consultations of Quebec municipalities on such matters as fiscal and regional reforms.

It must be recognized, too, that this new role reflected a widespread feeling that only through the state could the Québécois protect and develop their position in the Quebec economy and society. This theme was already present in the speeches of Jean Lesage, who spoke of using the state as a lever for the advancement of society and who presented the nationalization of the private hydroelectric companies as a measure to make the Québécois 'maîtres chez nous.' Then the Laurendeau-Dunton commission's studies and reports revealed the full extent of the economic disadvantage of being French Canadian in Quebec.[40] The first language legislation, adopted by the government of Jean-Jacques Bertrand, led to the collection of statistics on the choices of immigrants about the language of education. They showed that in Montreal, 90 per cent of immigrant families chose to send their children to English-language schools. In view of the declining birth rate these figures were dramatic in their impact. The Bourassa government, with its slogan of 'cultural sovereignty,' tried to solve the problem with Bill 22 which opened the English schools only to those who already spoke the language adequately. This law created considerable controversy without satisfying either the nationalists or the English-speaking population. The French Language Charter adopted by the Quebec government in 1977 makes French the language of work and government, with specific exceptions, and limits education in the English language to children whose parents have received their schooling in the Quebec English school system or who are clearly on temporary assignment to Quebec.[41]

In short, what inspired the extraordinary growth of the government sector in the last twenty years was a new conception of the role of the state in Quebec society, one which was far removed from Professor Corry's factors of executive branch expansion. Where he found a pattern of limited state intervention in reaction to new problems created by industrialization, urbanization, and the expansion of trade, since 1960 the new middle class has come to power in Quebec and it has sought to use the state in a positive manner to achieve social and economic goals.

To see how this growth of government activity affected the Quebec administration, one must look at the structures and processes of the administration and its human resources. Mention has already been made of several of the new structures, new departments, public corporations, and planning bodies. To this should be added the increasing complexity of structures, particularly of the functionally decentralized sector. In a study done in the early 1970s, André Gélinas found some 130 autonomous bodies in this category, 90 per cent of which had been created or transformed since 1960.[42] Thus in the last twenty years, the Quebec administration has seen the creation of new, or the transformation of the existing, departments and the grafting on to them of a variety of autonomous bodies.

An area which has been completely transformed since 1960 is that of financial management. In 1960, Lesage brought with him his experience as parliamentary assistant to the Minister of Finance at Ottawa. He quickly had the Treasury Board reorganized along lines similar to those of Ottawa, giving it for the first time a formal decision-making power in the authorization of expenditures. At the same time the post of Comptroller of the Treasury was created, with functions very similar to those of the federal comptroller at that time, ensuring a central control of financial commitments as well as prior control over expenditures. The final touch to this reform was not completed until 1970 when the Auditor General of the province ceased to share this task of prior authorization, being limited henceforth to post-auditing of the public accounts on behalf of the legislature.

The Financial Administration Act of 1970[43] also revised the functions of the Treasury Board, making it the general manager of the administration, exercising the powers of the Lieutenant-Governor in Council in virtue of the Civil Service Act, the Civil Servants' Retirement Plan, and so forth. To ensure co-ordination, the Civil Service Minister was made a member of the board and his deputy minister was appointed associate secretary of the Board. Under the new organization, program budgeting was introduced in 1972 for the entire administration. More recently, some units have introduced zero-base budgeting, but this has not been tried across the board.

The period since 1960 is even more fertile in personnel administration in the Quebec civil service.[44] Since these are too far-reaching to be presented otherwise, we merely list them in roughly chronological order:

1 Beginning in 1960 competitions were introduced in place of qualifying examinations for most positions in the civil service. This meas-

ure was made possible by the preparation of a new classification plan during the short mandate of premier Paul Sauvé in 1959, the plan being the first general revision since 1925. It was based on the American or 'position plan' approach.

2 The Civil Service Act of 1965 made the Civil Service Commission the personnel manager of the government and introduced collective bargaining with the right to strike for the great majority of Quebec's civil servants.

3 The gradual restructuring of the management function in the next three years culminated in the creation, in 1969, of the Civil Service Department which received the dual mandate of preparing government personnel policies and taking charge of its labour relations in the role of employer.

4 Under the impetus of collective bargaining also, the classification system was reformed in 1966-67. The new system did a great deal to rationalize the career structure of the civil service. In particular, it identified and regrouped two functions which had been previously considered almost case by case: senior executives and their assistants ('les cadres supérieurs et les adjoints aux cadres') and the 'professional' civil servants, that is, university graduates in the civil service. In the case of the latter group, features of the career system used in France and Britain were introduced. The following year competitive examinations for promotions and a performance evaluation system were introduced.

5 A new emphasis on personnel training was made, leading to the creation, in 1969, of l'Ecole nationale d'administration publique as an affiliated school of l'Université du Québec. Up to this time, training of middle management had been achieved in part by sending officers to l'Ecole nationale d'administration at Paris. From 1964 to 1968, forty young men were sent to ENA from Quebec; ten years later ten of the twenty-five deputy ministers were ENA graduates.

6 In 1974, a code of ethics was adopted concerning conflict of interest, political participation, and so on. The Civil Service Act of 1978 altered the situation with respect to political participation by allowing civil servants to stand for election and, if successful, to retain the right to rejoin the civil service after either one term or not more than five years as a member of Parliament or of the National Assembly.

7 The structural reform which began in 1969 was continued by the new law of 1978 which puts the planning function in the hands of the Minister of the Civil Service, while giving operating responsibilities to the deputy ministers of each department and leaving to the Civil Ser-

vice Commission adjudicative and auditing functions. The selection process is now the responsibility of the Office of Recruitment and Selection which may, in turn, delegate a number of its powers to deputy heads. This pattern, which is very similar to that adopted in Britain after the Fulton report, had originally been proposed in 1969 but was not adopted then.

The effect of these developments on the civil service may be seen in the figures. The civil service has grown from about 30,000 persons to 60,000 between 1960 and 1980. This gives an annual rate of growth of 4.5 per cent as compared to 12 per cent for the 'professionals' and 13 per cent for senior management. In the late 1970s, however, under the pressure of severe financial constraints this growth has stopped.

This is a much more technocratic civil service than was that of 1959. The ratio of professionals to ordinary civil servants has risen from 1:15 in 1959 to 1:3 in 1978. It is important to see also how the background preparation of higher civil servants has changed. From 1959 to 1975 business administration graduates have increased their place among the 'cadres supérieurs' from 11.7 to 39.1 per cent. The second most important group, engineers, have fallen in importance from 37.5 in 1959 to 14.7 per cent in 1975, while the social science group rose from 4.5 to 16.5 per cent. This 1975 profile is very similar to that of the senior executive group in the United States' civil service.[45] The Americanization of the Quebec civil service may also be seen in the evolution of ENAP and by the fact that the MBA is a much respected diploma in the Quebec civil service, even by those who have a MPA from ENAP.[46]

With respect to senior civil servants, one must ask if it is not they who have profited the most from the Quiet Revolution and its sequels. This is the thesis of Hubert Guindon who notes the importance of the public sector as a source of careers for the educated middle class.[47] The higher civil service has been most dramatically changed. It is younger, more mobile, less experienced than the traditional elites. This applies to the deputy ministers also. There were as many deputy ministers appointed from 1960 to 1978 as there were from 1867 to 1960, about one hundred for each period. The duration in office of a deputy minister has fallen from about fourteen years in the period 1945-70 to three or four years in the late 1970s. A new group has experienced rapid growth at this level: assistant deputy ministers have increased in number from 14 in 1959 to 88 in 1978.

For the mass of civil servants, the period has meant improving conditions of work, thanks, in good measure, to the work of the civil servants' unions, le Syndicat des fonctionnaires provinciaux du Québec and le Syndicat des professionnels du Gouvernement du Québec. Each round of negotiations has seen more strike activity, the most important being that in 1972 of the 250,000 employees of the Common Front of civil servants, teachers, and hospital and other public sector employees. One of us, who lived through that event, has concluded that in matters of this kind, the more you grow, the more vulnerable you become! In the eyes of many, public sector negotiations have become a no-win game for governments. In spite of a special study which it commissioned on the question, the Parti Québécois government was no more successful than its predecessors in avoiding prolonged and fruitless negotiations in 1978. Indeed, it adopted the unprecedented measure of passing, in November 1978, emergency legislation outlawing a general strike by the Common Front before it had occurred. Many of the party's leaders felt that the labour situation in the public sector was responsible in part for the sweep by the Liberal party of the three by-elections held at that time.

So the result of the trends of the past twenty years has been the creation of a technocratic administration which has adopted rationality as its goal. While some ideas have been imported from France (economic planning, the 'corps' approach to classification, and ENAP) and some even from Britain (the Civil Service Department), most ideas for achieving this goal have come from the United States (sometimes via Ottawa, but often direct). Program budgeting, zero-base budgeting, management by objectives, group dynamics, organizational development, policy analysis, and performance evaluation, these and many other reforms have been introduced on a broad or a narrow range.

At the same time, the administration has become more politicized, most notably through the processes of unionization and collective bargaining. The union movement in Quebec was radicalized in part through its contact with governments in this relationship.[48] Many phenomena which were considered to be merely administrative in the past have now become political either because they are the object of negotiations (for example, maternity leave or job security) or else, as a result of negotiations, they are subject to arbitration where they were once matters of unilateral decision.

To conclude this survey of changes since 1960, we turn now to some ways in which the environment has had to adapt to the new Quebec administration. This is most noticeable in the political sphere, but we also look at that of economic interest groups and even the role of individuals as relating to the administration.

In politics the changes are multiple. To keep some kind of control over the administration, governments have had to streamline their activities and procedures. The reinforcement of the Treasury Board and the creation of the Comptroller of the Treasury represented the intention of the government to have its own civil servants to watch over the others. In 1968, the post of secretary general to the cabinet was created, making the top civil service job one of general supervision and co-ordination rather than simply one of clerk to the Executive Council.

The biggest change in this area has come, however, from the restructuring of cabinet. Under the Bourassa governments (1970-76) a new committee structure was developed, which included a cabinet committee on priorities. The Parti Québécois, immediately on assuming power, implemented a new structure designed to give the government much greater control over planning and co-ordination of policy and its execution. Six positions of minister of state were created and confided to senior party members: Social Development, Cultural Development, Economic Development, Regional Development, the Status of Women, and Parliamentary and Electoral Reform. These ministers of state together with the prime minister, the Minister of Intergovernmental Affairs, and the Minister of Finance make up the cabinet committee on priorities. They also chair cabinet committees in their respective fields. Although it appears cumbersome, this new system seems to work well, for two main reasons. First, Prime Minister Lévesque has consistently applied the new rules, so that ministers of operating departments may not ordinarily have access directly to cabinet in plenary session without passing through the appropriate committee. Moreover, each minister of state has a small support staff under the direction of an associate secretary general of the government. This has resulted in a flexible system of shared responsibility wherein the cabinet committees, the ministers of state and their staffs, the Treasury Board and its staff, and the responsible departments are all involved in new policy developments.[49] It is perhaps not surprising that the Parti Québécois, with its group of former senior civil servants in the highest posts, should have introduced this scheme to keep the administration in its place, although the plan was not in the party program at the time of the 1976 election.[50]

The National Assembly has also had to reorganize itself to adapt to the new administration. In the early 1960s the estimates were still considered in committee of the whole (Ways and Means) and the Public Accounts Committee very seldom met. In the late 1960s the committee structure was completely revised with a standing committee being created for each executive department or group of departments. These committees debate the estimates for their respective departments and certain, but not all, bills emanating therefrom. In addition to the Public Accounts Committee, a Committee on Financial Commitments has been created. Each recognized party represented in the National Assembly receives a grant for research purposes. We are far from the investigative staffs of American Congressional committees, but these changes reflect the attempt of the Assembly to strengthen its position in its task of supervision of the administration.

Party politics, too, have been changed by the evolution of the administration. For one thing, patronage is much less available to the government than it was before 1960. The implementation of the merit system has almost eliminated patronage from the ordinary selection process for the civil service.[51] A good deal of discretion remained in the awarding of contracts until 1976, but the Parti Québécois has adopted stricter measures for this purpose. The Parti Québécois has been in a good position to implement this and other reforms, such as the control of election financing, since it has been from the beginning a party based on widespread participation, mainly financed by individual members' contributions. Moreover its methods put it in a stronger position than most parties on being elected, for it had behind it years of study and debate by its members, with the result that the party had an elaborate and precise program which it wanted to implement.

The second main impact of the growth of the administration on political parties in Quebec concerns the political impact of collective bargaining. On the one hand, there are the civil servants and the members of the public services who negotiate with the government every three years. More than 320,000 employees and their families represent considerable voting power, a fact which was not lost on either side during the 1980 referendum on sovereignty-association.

On the other hand, the public opinion polls have repeatedly shown that the public is, by a large majority, opposed to the right to strike in the public service. It is for this reason that we referred to this above as a no-win situation for the government.

Other governments have also been affected by the changes in the Quebec administration. As early as 1964, federal ministers and civil servants were aware that they were dealing with a much stronger, better prepared Quebec delegation whether it be in direct relations between the two governments or in federal-provincial conferences. The competence and quality of the Quebec delegation was still being remarked on by participants in and observers of the constitutional conferences of 1980.[52] At another level, local governments have had to adjust to the new position of force of the Quebec administration. For municipalities, it has meant adapting to a much reduced role in local society. For school boards, hospitals, and welfare organizations, the process has been more like nationalization so that they may hardly be considered as local governments now. Here the frontiers of the system have changed, extending themselves to include units which were previously outside it.

Interest groups and other economic agents have adapted to the new administration in much the same way as they have all over the western world. For the last twenty years at least they have found it more profitable to intervene with the administration rather than turn to the legislature for help.[53] The tremendous growth of advisory bodies has opened structured links between these groups and the administration. Indeed, through membership on these bodies, and by the distribution of grants of all kinds, the administration is able to favour or punish existing or new groups trying to be heard. Some groups which were previously autonomous have now come under greater governmental surveillance. Such is the case of the professions since the adoption in 1973 of the Code of Professions and the creation of the Office of Professions. Other groups, notably the public sector unions, have achieved greater power through the right to negotiate with the state. Business accommodates itself to the inevitable: for instance, only two large companies refused to create the 'francization' committees required by the French Language Charter, and they did so on the grounds that they were obviously French (La Presse and La Banque Provinciale).

Finally, individual citizens, while benefitting from the new range of governmental services, are often overwhelmed by their contacts with the administration. The Citizen's Protector, or Ombudsman, provides one channel for them to seek equitable solutions to their difficulties. However, lacking access to senior officials and ministers, ordinary citizens will use disruption of the work of administration offices by occupations, sit-ins, and the like in order to obtain attention.

CONCLUSION

It has been our thesis that the Quebec administration, for all its growth and development, was largely dominated by the forces in its environment from 1867 until 1960. Since that time, the administration has not only undergone a prodigious growth, but its position in society has changed qualitatively. Being given a role of managing and orienting social and economic life in the name of rationality has greatly strengthened its position in its relations with governments, legislatures, parties, and interest groups. While there has been some reaction in Quebec opposing the extent of the intervention of the administration in social and economic life, there has not as yet been a serious threat to its position. Rather, other forces seem to have adapted to this position and tried either to profit from it or to limit their losses.

1 Such a definition is implicit in Herbert Simon's theory of equilibrium in *Administrative Behaviour*, sec. ed. (New York: Free Press, 1957), chap. VI. Recently, Vincent Lemieux has shown that a structuralist-systemic approach to the study of social affairs in Quebec requires the inclusion in the system of decentralized institutions and their clients: *Les cheminements de l'influence* (Québec: Les Presses de l'Université Laval, 1979), chap. 10. Our definition is similar to that of J.E. Hodgetts in *The Canadian Public Service: A Physiology of Government, 1867-1970* (Toronto, University of Toronto Press, 1973), chap. 2, 'The Public Service and the Powerful Persuaders.'

2 J.I. Gow, 'Les dépenses du gouvernement du Québec (1867-1970) comme indicateur d'activités étatiques,' Département de science politique, Université de Montréal, juin 1980, 46 p.

3 On the constraints felt by Quebec governments of the period see J.I. Gow, 'L'administration québécoise de 1867 à 1900: Un Etat en formation,' *Canadian Journal of Political Science*, vol. XII, no. 3 (September 1979), 587-94.

4 As of 30 June 1897, the consolidated net debt of the province was $24 million; the amount spent on railway subsidies from 1874 to 1897 was $26 million. *Quebec Yearbook, 1921*, p. 394

5 *Rapport général du ministère des Travaux publics du Québec*, rapport du Président du Bureau de reconstruction économique 1940-1941, pp. 92-104

6 J.E. Hodgetts, *Pioneer Public Service: An Administrative History of the United Canadas, 1841-1867* (Toronto: University of Toronto Press, 1955), pp. 274-80

7 Marcel Hamelin, *Les premières années du parlemantarisme québécois (1867-1878)* (Québec: Les Presses de l'Université Laval), 1974, pp. 35-6

8 Quebec Statutes 1875 (31 Victoria), chap. 10

9 Quebec Statutes 1869 (32 Victoria), chap. 11

10 Quebec Statutes 1886 (49-50 Victoria), chap. 38

11 Gow, 'L'administration québécoise,' 605-6

12 Quebec Statutes 1889 (52 Victoria), chap. 6

13 Quebec Statutes 1926 (16 Geo. V), chap. 14

14 There is some disagreement over the extent of these firings. Those who lived through the period can recall many, but Conrad Black suggests that there was no 'wholesale house cleaning.' *Duplessis* (Toronto: McClelland and Stewart, 1977), pp. 118-28

15 Quebec Statutes 1943 (7 Geo. VI), chap. 9

16 Quebec Statutes 1937 (1 Geo. VI), chap. 51

17 See the remarks of an experienced civil servant, Stanislas Vachon, *Le service civil de la province de Québec vu de l'intérieur*, Charlesbourg, n.d. (ca. 1960), pp. 14-17.

18 'Mémoire de la Fédération des Commissions scolaires catholiques de la province de Québec à la Commission royale d'enquête sur les problèmes constitutionnels,' 1954, p. 141

19 Gow, 'Les dépenses du gouvernement du Québec,' pp. 34-6

20 J.-C. Falardeau, 'Rôle et importance de l'Eglise au Canada français,' in *Esprit* (Paris), Aug.-Sept. 1952, pp. 214-29 (our translation)

21 T.D. Bouchard tells in his memoirs how his appointment as chairman of Hydro Quebec was blocked by Cardinal Villeneuve in spite of the sympathy which Premier Godbout had for him. *Mémoires*, vol. II (Montréal: Beauchemin, 1960), pp. 172-9

22 Gérard Filteau and Lionel Allard, *Un siècle au service de l'éducation, 1851-1951, l'inspection des écoles dans la province de Québec* (Québec 1951), mimeo, vol. 1, p. 110

23 G.E. Lapalme, *Le vent de l'oubli: Mémoires*, vol. II (Montréal: Leméac, 1970), pp. 116-17

24 J.-P. Lefebvre *et al.*, *En grève* (Montréal: Editions du Jour, 1963), p. 46
25 Louise Toupin, 'L'intervention du premier ministre Taschereau dans l'industrie du papier journal, 1928-1935,' master's thesis, Université de Montréal, 1972, pp. 55-92; and Richard Brunelle, 'Histoire de l'administration québécoise: le secteur minier,' Département de science politique, Université de Montréal, 1972, pp. 91-106
26 Jean Hamelin et Yves Roby, *Histoire économique du Québec, 1851-1896* (Montréal: Fides, 1971), pp. 129-30
27 See *Le cathéchisme des électeurs* (1935) re-edited by Les Editions Albert St-Martin (Montréal, 1974), arts. 33-50, pp. 7-8
28 When Roch Bolduc returned to Quebec in 1952 after post-graduate studies in political science at Chicago, he made the rounds of the departments and met with most of the deputy ministers. Not one of them recommended that he stay in Quebec, but several suggested that he go to Ottawa to make his career!
29 For example, Pierre Vallières, *White Niggers of America* (Toronto: McClelland and Stewart, 1971); André d'Allemagne, *Le colonialisme au Québec* (Montréal, Editions R-B, 1966).
30 *Annuaire du Québec (1977-1978)*, pp. 285, 362, and 722
31 Guy Rocher, *Le Québec en mutation* (Montréal: Hurtubise, 1973), pp. 13-32
32 Pierre Laurin, 'Le Québec et le monde des affaires,' *Le Devoir*, 1 Feb. 1979, p. 5
33 Dominique Clift and Sheila McLeod Arnopoulos, *The English Fact in Quebec* (Montréal: McGill-Queen's University Press, 1980), chap. 7
34 Caisse de dépôt et placement du Québec, *Annual Report 1979*, pp. 24-5. If the bonds of Hydro Quebec and others issued or guaranteed by the Quebec government are included, the government's share of the holdings of la Caisse amounts to 49 per cent.
35 See the *Rapport de la Commission d'enquête sur l'exercise de la liberté syndicale dans l'industrie de la construction* (Cliche Report) (Québec: Editeur officiel, 1975).
36 Gouvernement du Québec, *Bâtir le Québec: énoncé de politique économique* (Québec: Editeur officiel, 1979), pp. 38-41. This figure includes federal, provincial, and local expenditures.
37 *Discours sur le budget* given by Jacques Parizeau March 25, 1980, Québec, ministère des Finances, 1980, pp. 14-16 and *Rapport Martin-Bouchard*, Commission d'étude sur la révision du régime des négociations collectives dans les secteurs public et parapublic (Québec, 1978), pp. 17-21
38 An interesting testimony on this new role comes from *Le Rôle de l'Etat* (Montréal, Editions du Jour, 1962), being the proceedings of the annual conference of l'Institut canadien des affaires publiques.

39 Jean-Charles Bonenfant, 'Les Commissions d'enquête du Québec,' *Annuaire du Québec, 1972*, pp. 36-72

40 Kenneth McRoberts and Dale Posgate, *Quebec: Social Change and Political Crisis*, sec. ed. (Toronto, McClelland and Stewart, 1980), p. 127

41 Quebec Statutes 1977, chap. 5

42 André Gélinas, *Organismes autonomes et centraux* (Montréal: Les Presses de l'Université du Québec, 1975), p. 134

43 Quebec Statutes 1970, chap. 17

44 J.E. Hodgetts and O.P. Dwivedi, *Provincial Governments as Employers* (Montreal: McGill-Queen's Press, 1974), say (p. 22): 'The rapidity of changes experienced by the Quebec central personnel agency (the Civil Service Commission) and the heavy work load thrust on it have no parallel among other provincial jurisdictions in Canada.'

45 Roch Bolduc, 'Les cadres supérieurs quinze ans après,' *Canadian Public Administration*, vol. 28, no. 4 (winter 1978), pp. 618-39. Comparable figures for the United States may be found in *Executive Personnel in the Federal Service*, by the U.S. Civil Service Commission (Washington: Government Printing Office, Nov. 1977), p. 45.

46 Alain Baccigalupo, *Les grands rouages de la machine administrative québécoise* (Montréal: Les Editions de l'arc, 1978), pp. 67-8, reproduces the report of this study which originally appeared in *Le Soleil*, 20 March 1975.

47 Hubert Guindon, 'Social Unrest, Social Class and Quebec's Bureaucratic Revolution,' *Queen's Quarterly*, vol. LXXI (summer 1964), pp. 150-62. On the younger group of technocrats, see J.-J. Simard, *La longue marche des technocrates* (Montréal: Editions Albert St-Martin, 1979).

48 A somewhat extreme version of this thesis is presented in Diane Ethier *et al.*, *Les travailleurs contre l'Etat bourgeois, avril et mai 1972* (Montréal: L'Aurore, 1975).

49 Ministère du Conseil exécutif du Québec, *Rapport annuel 1978-1979* (Québec, 1979). This is the first report ever made of the activities of what is, in effect, the prime minister's department. See also Louis Bernard, 'Les mécanismes centraux de coordination au Québec,' text of a communication given at the 'Colloque international de l'ENAP sur l'administration publique: perspectives d'avenir,' 30 May 1979.

50 Lionel Ouellet, 'L'appareil gouvernemental et législatif,' in Gérard Bergeron et Réjean Pelletier, *L'Etat du Québec en devenir* (Montréal: Boréal Express), pp. 61-108

51 Vincent Lemieux et Raymond Hudon, *Patronage et politique au Québec, 1944-1972* (Sillery, Boréal Express, 1975), p. 69, and Hodgetts and Dwivedi, *Provincial Governments as Employers*, pp. 20-2

52 See Peter Desbarats, *The State of Quebec* (Toronto: McClelland and Stewart, 1965), chap. 9; *The Globe and Mail*, 13 Sept. 1980, 'Faceless Men Hold Key to Provincial Relations.'

53 André Gélinas, *Les parlementaires et l'administration au Québec* (Québec, Les Presses de l'Université Laval, 1969), p. 207; Pierre Fournier, *The Quebec Establishment* (Montréal: Black Rose Books, 1976), pp. 70-8; and Raymond Hudon, 'Les groupes et l'Etat,' in Bergeron and Pelletier, *L'Etat du Québec*, pp. 263-84

JOHN W. LANGFORD AND NEIL A. SWAINSON

Public and Quasi-Public Corporations in British Columbia

... choose cautiously and confide liberally ... LORD MACAULAY

Of the wide variety of 'structural heretics' which he has exposed to students and practitioners of Canadian public administration over the years, Professor Hodgetts has probably lavished his most critical attention on public corporations.[1] His writings on them focus most persistently on the difficulties of identifying and classifying such corporations, the historical problem of why they have been employed as vehicles of public policy, and the nature of their internal organization. These subjects are treated, largely, as prefatory material to the major issue of determining the appropriate control, scrutiny, and accountability relationships amongst public corporations, the government, and Parliament.

As Allan Tupper has recently suggested, Professor Hodgetts' preoccupations concerning public corporations can be construed as a rather narrow selection from the wide spectrum of political and economic topics which now appear to be relevant to a full understanding of the public corporation.[2] Nevertheless, as Tupper also notes, modern governments have not succeeded in dealing with the issues of political control and accountability very well, and – in Canada particularly – the question of how best to administer public corporations to assure efficient and effective performance within the boundaries of responsible government remains an important contemporary issue. Moreover, it is an issue which is still being successfully argued largely within the confines of the questions and ideas raised by Professor Hodgetts in his earliest analysis of the problem. We would like to take this opportunity to review and comment upon part of his analytic framework and upon some of the questions and hypotheses which he developed, and to illustrate briefly how these, lifted out of the federal setting in which he largely conducted his investigations, can be applied to the examination of public and quasi-public corporations in a provincial setting – in this case, British Columbia.

IDENTIFICATION AND CLASSIFICATION

Traditionally, the identification of public corporations was not even recognized as a problem, and classification was seen to be a rather obscure exercise whereby public corporations are divided on the basis of some vague principles into rough groups to which regimes for control and accountability are applied.[3] The classification exercise – as practised in the federal Financial Administration Act, for instance – has tended to be a smokescreen designed to allow the government to apply to any particular corporation whichever regime it desires.

Two factors have cast doubt on this traditional approach in recent years. First the variety of public corporation 'types' has increased significantly as the scope of government's corporate involvement in the society and the economy has grown. This has led to serious problems related to the identification of public corporations and their differentiation (particularly at the margins of the public corporate sector) from private sector organizations. The days when all public corporations were wholly owned entities incorporated under their own statutes are over. It has become more and more common to find corporations which have been created by the government under general companies legislation (often without reference to the legislative body), corporations which have entered the public realm by virtue of the government's purchase of all or some of their shares, and corporations which are dragged into (or are close to) the public corporate sector by virtue of a continuing financial involvement by government in their affairs. At the federal level the majority of the government's corporate entanglements are indirect (i.e., subsidiary or associate corporations of other public corporations), established on a partial ownership basis (with private investors, other provinces, or states), or based on a sponsorship or membership relationship whereby the government funds and oversees the management of non-profit entities. Both of these latter corporate types are strongly in evidence at the provincial level. The net effect of this trend towards corporate diversity has been to obscure the boundary of the public corporate sector and to introduce 'identification' as a major new activity which must be carried out before classification takes place if the latter activity is to be comprehensive.

The second factor – related to the first – is that classification itself has changed character as an organizational activity. Most governments are now involved with a selection of corporations with widely different characteristics. Some of these differences (e.g., the degree of government ownership) can be significant in the consideration of appropriate regimes. Moreover, there has been a more general acceptance of the idea that useful relationships might be drawn between the characteristics of a corporation and the environment in which it operates and the regime of control and accountability which is applied to it, if the latter is to serve the seemingly conflicting needs of ministerial responsibility and accountability, on the one hand, and efficient corporate performance on the other.

Recently, Professor Hodgetts has become concerned about the problem of investigating the margins of the public sector. He was a strong supporter within the Lambert commission of research designed to analyse and define the new complexity of the federal public corporate sector as a basis for a comprehensive identification exercise. He also supported an approach to classification which recognized it as a significant and necessary step in the building of regimes of control and accountability. The commission's final report discusses not only 'wholly-owned corporations,' but also 'subsidiary and associated corporations,' 'shared enterprises,' and 'quasi-public corporations,' and breaks new ground by laying down recommendations with respect to regimes for all these categories. As a result of this work it seems unlikely that the importance of identification and classification will be as underestimated in the future as it has been in the past.

It is possible that the identification and classification of public corporations will prove to be an even more difficult brace of tasks at the provincial than at the federal level. In British Columbia, one gets no statutory help with respect to identification or classification from anything analogous to Ottawa's Financial Administration Act. Similarly, no government agency has traditionally been held responsible for producing and maintaining a list of all corporations in which the government is involved as an owner, member, or regular provider of funding. However, the government clearly is concerned about this problem, and in August 1980 put forward a discussion paper and draft financial administration act which appeared to presage the establishment of a wide-ranging definition of the public corporate sector, and a classification system based on the characteristics of public corporations and the environment in which they operate.[4] The discussion paper included a tentative list of some 170 'public bodies' which suggests that the public and quasi-public sector in British Columbia is as complex and varied as its federal counterpart and that, in absolute terms, it may even prove to be significantly larger.

In British Columbia, as elsewhere, public corporations have been created in a number of ways. There are currently 18 wholly owned corporations which have been created by statute (including the very large BC Hydro and Power Authority), and a number more which have been incorporated under the provincial Company Act or corresponding federal legislation (e.g., BC Steamship Co. Ltd.). During the 1970s a further contingent (e.g., Ocean Falls Corporation) gained their public status through government purchase of all of their outstanding shares. Subsidiaries and associated corporations of wholly owned corporations seem to be a rather insignificant feature of the BC public corporate sector by contrast with the federal situation.

It is noteworthy that there has been no spate of Company Act incorporations in BC; indeed the first authority to create Crown corporations in this way for specific purposes was only conferred on three ministers, by statute, between 1973 and 1975. A number of these powers were used to create corporations, some of which still exist. All of the powers themselves still exist, although some have been relocated in restructured ministerial statutes. In any case, in British Columbia, as in Ottawa, ministers have tended to view the Crown as possessing all of the rights of a legal person, and, on occasion, have sought incorporations under the Company Act without explicit statutory authorization.

While there are a substantial number of wholly owned public corporations in BC, there are very few shared enterprises. The most prominent example of this corporate type was the BC Resources Investment Corporation – in some respects a provincial counterpart of the Canada Development Corporation – with a growing number of subsidiary and associated corporations. Until early 1981, the BC government had a direct ownership position in BCRIC on a minority basis (4.65 per cent), but these shares have since been transferred to a quasi-public cancer research foundation.

The BC public corporate sector contains at least two other types of corporate entity which employ significant amounts of provincial government funds and for which some degree of accountability is owed to the responsible ministers and the legislature. The first type, which is directly delegated authority under acts of the legislature, includes boards of school trustees, public hospitals, the universities, and colleges. The second type is an extremely varied and apparently numerous collection of ostensibly private corporations – some profit-oriented and created under provincial company law, and others 'non-profit' and created under the BC Society Act. These 'quasi-public' corporations are most often involved in the provision of social services, research, and promotion functions, and the government is often their major – if not their only – source of funds in the form of *per diem* fees, annual grants, or contracts. Although there are estimated to be over a thousand such corporations, as yet no reliable count is available. In addition, the nature of the government's legal relationship with corporations of this type has never been closely analysed.

Clearly if the identification exercise was vigorously pursued in BC, the provincial government would inevitably have to contemplate the development of a sophisticated public corporation classification scheme. While it is well beyond the ambitions of this paper to design a classification system for BC public corporations, the above analysis of the identification question suggests the outlines of a system which would resemble that proposed for the federal public corporate sector by the Lambert commission. Tentatively, it would appear that one should at least consider distinguishing the following four categories: wholly owned corporations; shared enterprises; non-commercial corporate instruments (e.g., public hospitals, school boards); and quasi-public service corporations. The lumping of all wholly owned corporations together raises immediately a pet peeve of Professor Hodgetts – the grouping of so-called 'convenience' or 'branch' corporations with public corporations that appeared to be performing 'tasks akin to private sector entrepreneurial undertakings in a market setting.'[5] It might be necessary to create a further category for such corporations (e.g., the BC Buildings Corporation, BC Systems Corporation) or – as Hodgetts would prefer – contemplate their return to branch status within an existing ministry.

RATIONALE FOR CREATION

Under the guise of what today passes for the 'rationale for creation' question, Professor Hodgetts addresses two closely related issues: why has the public corporation become such a common means to increase the scope of government activity as a supplier of goods and services, and why has a public corporation so often been used instead of a department or some other organizational form? Hodgetts has argued strongly that the basic explanation for the growth of the public corporation at the federal level is not to be found in a single 'unifying philosophy' endorsing nationalization or, for that matter, efficiency. He views the development as 'piecemeal and pragmatic.' Not unreasonably, he associates this pragmatism with the distinctiveness of the discrete corporation, with the simple legal 'convenience' of employing a corporation to carry out a task in a specific set of circumstances, with the utility of the form as a vehicle for geographically decentralizing government operations, with the public corporation's potential for politically neutral administration, and, often, more significantly, with its organizational appropriateness for the pursuit of business activity. He demonstrates that, generally, federal public corporations have started as 'fresh ventures' designed to bridge 'gaps,' thus largely avoiding direct competition with existing private enterprises, but occasionally operating parallel to the private sector (e.g., CBC, Air Canada.)

These arguments have provided the foundation for some fascinating developments with respect to the rationale question in recent years. Government initiatives during the seventies, in the energy field for instance, have rather outflanked the Hodgetts' generalization concerning the non-competitive role of the typical federal public corporation. While the hypothesis concerning the pragmatism of the federal approach to the use of the public corporation has not been effectively challenged, this line of reasoning has been found to have its limitations within a number of provincial jurisdictions because of the perceived direct, or contagion, impact of socialist political parties favouring nationalization and public ownership. On the other hand, the recent use of joint ventures and quasi-public corporations for promotion and service delivery at both levels of government has tended to reinforce the sense that governments see the corporate organization as a flexible instrument to be employed in a wide variety of forms and settings.

There have been recent attempts to flesh out the 'pragmatism' concept with a complex analysis of more specific pragmatic rationales for resorting to government ownership. One thinks quickly, for example, of the use of the public corporation to preserve and, it is hoped, revitalize the sick industry, often in a politically crucial environment, and of the attempt to regulate natural monopolies – in the context of the availability of other instruments of governmental intervention, such as the regulatory agency or the subsidy program.

This determination to better understand the broad appeal of the public and quasi-public corporation has also led to some detailed efforts to analyse its specific institutional and legal characteristics. The ideas being developed in this area represent distinct advances on the characteristics originally explored by Professor Hodgetts. For example, he has tended to focus very extensively on those features of the public corporation which flow from its resemblance to its opposite number in the private sector (e.g., on its capacity as an instrumentality to attract private businessmen to its executive) and on its potential managerial autonomy from partisan politics and bureaucratic procedures (e.g., in fiscal management and labour relations.) Some of the more recent emphasis, on the other hand, has shifted to such matters as the potential for policy co-ordination among public corporations, their suitability when related to the pursuit of a terminal as opposed to an on-going function, their capacity to underscore symbolically certain governmental concerns and values, and their advantages as instruments wherewith to monitor the activities of the sector in which the corporation operates. Such additions to earlier perspectives in the 'rationale for creation' theory open up the prospect of re-examining in more detail the historical record of public corporation creation both at the federal and provincial levels.

When Professor Hodgetts' insights on the emergence of the Crown corporation in federal Canada are applied to the province of British Columbia, the resulting impression over-all is that they appear to fit very well. There are exceptions: for example, the far-western province has never assigned regulatory as well as operational responsibilities to any of its public corporations, and relatively more of them emerged from existing instruments than was the case nationally, at least until the beginning of the last decade. Over-all, however, the *majority* of the province's corporate creations have been utilized for highly pragmatic reasons, and certainly have not reflected a commitment to a nationalization ideology as such. They have been used to fill gaps, to induce a degree of managerial freedom already referred to (sometimes for cabinet-level as well as executive personnel), to by-pass roadblocks and accelerate action, even on occasion to forestall private sector action. They have been turned to as well as a device wherewith to facilitate and guarantee the borrowing of other public bodies, to receive grants from the agencies of other governments, and to hold real property assets. And so the list continues. There has never been a major public debate in BC, by the way, on the suitability of the public corporation as opposed to the government department as the operational home for state developmental entrepreneurial and social welfare activities. As we shall see in a moment, most of BC's public corporations are very recent creations in a province which has simply accepted a positive assessment of their potential from other jurisdictions which faced 'instrument choice' questions earlier.

The province's pragmatic approach to the creation or acquisition of the public corporation was well reflected in the initial stages of their development, first during the years prior to 1950, and then (between 1952 and 1972) during the long administration of Premier W.A.C. Bennett. The very first public corporation, the Pacific Great Eastern Railway (renamed BC Rail in 1971) was acquired by a very reluctant provincial government in 1918 under circumstances strikingly similar to those leading to the emergence of the Canadian National Railway at virtually the same time. The second corporation, the British Columbia Power Commission, on the other hand, was established in 1945 by a Liberal-Conservative coalition government quite deliberately prepared to expand the public sector to increase the supply and availability of electric power to much of rural and non-metropolitan British Columbia beyond the levels attained by private and municipal effort.

During the W.A.C. Bennett years, the public corporation format was turned to on at least six significant occasions by a notably non-predictable but highly flexible administration. Two of these new corporations, established in 1963 and 1967, were little more than legal shells for departmental authorities designed to facilitate school district and regional hospital district borrowing. One began life in 1953 as a toll-bridges and highways authority. Subsequently it had devolved on it, in 1960 and 1962, responsibility for a new coastal ferry fleet; it was transformed into a ferry authority in 1964, and disbanded and folded into a line department in 1968. A further corporation, the BC Harbours Board, was established in 1967 to alter the course of port development in the province and to prod both the CPR and the federal government in the process. By far the most dramatic of this administration's public corporate creations, of course, stemmed from its nationalization of the BC Electric Company, the province's largest private utility, in 1961, when inaction by that company threatened to frustrate provincial government power planning. Almost equally dramatic – in the face of the subsequent legal challenges to this take-over – was the scrambling of the assets of the BC Electric with those of the BC Power Commission in a 1962 amalgamation, out of which emerged a further public corporation, the BC Hydro and Power Authority.

Inevitably the coming to power of the New Democrats in British Columbia in 1972 marks a break in this story, for, while they shared with their predecessors an acceptance of the mixed economy and also were pragmatists, they were ideologically committed to expanding the public sector, and did so significantly during their forty months in office. In the process they almost quadrupled the number of significant wholly owned provincial Crown corporations, established via statutory enactment, Company Act incorporation, or purchase. In addition, they made important investments in a number of food processing industries, purchased outright some small operations in the public transportation field, acquired the bulk of the shares in a property development company, and over 79 per cent of the equity in Canadian Cellulose Ltd., a major entity in the province's forest industry. Statutory approval was also obtained for the creation of a state-owned trust company, and a transit company, but these had not emerged before the government fell in December 1975.

In the NDP years – as in all the others – the creation of Crown corporations was often the result of an amalgam of motives. The nationalization of an entire industry – automobile insurance – and, in effect, the creation of the Insurance Corporation of BC in 1973 had been a campaign commitment. But the investments made in a number of agricultural enterprises, for example, had a different background; they reflected, in most cases, simply a desire to turn around ailing industries or to encourage the innovative. There certainly was a pro-nationalization dimension to the take-over of four significant forestry operations, but these actions also were derived in part from a desire to reduce or forestall non-resident resource ownership and to acquire benchmarks in that industry. In at least three cases, furthermore, the creation of Crown corporations involved – as the acquisition of the PGE had done in 1918 – a determination to preserve industries or communication links facing closure when these were deemed to be of crucial regional/community significance. In this era we also see at work the developmental objective so frequently identified by Professor Hodgetts as operative federally. One public corporation established during these years, of course, the BC Development Corporation, was explicitly charged with its pursuit.

The election of a Social Credit government in December 1975 inaugurated the final stage (to date) in the evolution of the public corporation in British Columbia. The new administration was very much in the tradition of the national governments surveyed by Professor Hodgetts up to 1970, in that it had strong ideological reservations concerning a competitive role for state-owned enterprise. Thus the agricultural corporations, parts of the public transportation companies, and the property development company[6] acquired during the NDP years were disposed of. Statutory authority for the existence of another was revoked.[7] Interestingly enough the administration used its best known corporate creation (the British Columbia Resources Investment Corporation), which briefly was wholly owned by the province, as an instrument to return the assets which the New Democrats had acquired in three forest companies, plus a 10.78 per cent interest which they had purchased in the Westcoast Transmission Company, back into the private sector. This transfer was effected via a distribution of shares to all residents of the province, and the sale of additional shares in BCRIC, again to British Columbians.

Otherwise there are three features of this government's approach to public corporations which warrant a mention. It has retained – with modest revisions – some of the most highly visible of the New Democrats' creations,[8] and placed much emphasis on strengthening their management. Practically also, it has found the public corporation to be an extremely useful instrument; in its first five years in office, it created at least ten of them, counting BCRIC. Two with project development objectives have been established with time limits in their mandates. In a search for operational fiscal responsibility and (still unrealized) harmonious labour relations it has returned its coastal ferry fleet to a corporate umbrella. Three corporations have been established to deal with urban transit and inter-city bus operations. Two of these last involve, in part, former subsidiary operations of BC Hydro, and one (the Urban Transit Authority) is a classic example of a public corporation established both to co-ordinate the activities of two levels of government (here provincial and local), and to limit the responsibility of one (the province). The other three recent corporations have been much closer to line departments. Two, indeed, the BC Buildings Corporation and BC Systems Corporation, owe their existence in large measure to a belief that, in the interest of promoting operating efficiency and facilitating the determination of the relative merits of policy options, distinct corporations can be effective vehicles from which to apply to line departments the 'charge back' cost of providing essential support services. Finally, the government has made limited use of the shared corporation (most notably in the process of privatizing BCRIC) and has begun a process of recognizing and rationalizing the use by various ministries of quasi-public corporations largely in the social services area. In part, the government's use of both of these corporate models reflects the force of pragmatism, manifested, for example, in attempting to garner votes through share 'give-aways' and in the employment of appropriate private organizations for service delivery. It also reflects the force of ideology which favours the limitation of the size, if not the scope, of government, the distribution of share-ownership amongst the citizenry, and contracting for services from private suppliers.

In summary, there is evidence of the operation of both a nationalization ideology and the efficiency ideology but, on the whole, the rationale for the creation or employment of public corporations in BC over the last sixty years can be captured within an expanded definition of Professor Hodgetts' notion of pragmatism. However, there are obvious exceptions in which the pragmatism rationale derived by Hodgetts from federal experience either does not apply or is insufficiently developed to capture the subtleties of the BC scene. For example, the capacity to move operational headquarters away from the capital city, and the desire to create a politically neutralized administrative instrument (save perhaps with respect to the Power Commission prior to 1959) have not been significant considerations leading to the creation of public corporations in this province. The creation of the British Columbia Ferry Corporation in 1976 was the end product of a complex evolution which began with the employment of the public corporate form in 1960, in part to forestall service interruption caused by strikes. There also may well be something unique in the establishment of the BC Buildings Corporation, which seems to have emerged from a government's conviction that attaining a desired level of operating efficiency required both dismantling a long established department and creating a replacement corporation without transferring to it the great bulk of the original departmental staff.

THE INTERNAL ORGANIZATION OF THE CORPORATION

Recognizing that a perceived need for collegial rather than hierarchical leadership has often been a key consideration in the choice of the corporate form to deliver public policy, Professor Hodgetts has attached a great deal of importance to the internal organization and operation of public corporations, and has laid special emphasis on the place of the board of directors within these organizations. Indeed, to date, most of the pioneering work on the internal structure of the public corporation has been focused almost exclusively on the appointment and membership of such boards, as well as on their formal powers. In what follows we continue this with reference to British Columbia, restricting our examination to that group of corporations which is wholly owned. A fascinating research enterprise to come lies in the analysis of the composition, organization, and behaviour of the boards of non-commercial corporate instruments, joint ventures, and quasi-public corporations in British Columbia.

Professor Hodgetts early noted that the boards of federal Crown corporations are commonly appointed by the Governor-in-Council (in a few cases by ministers), commonly 'at pleasure,' and normally with no requirement that they be 'representative.' These observations apply equally well to the wholly owned corporations in the province of British Columbia where all board appointments are made by the Lieutenant-Governor-in-Council, and all in fact are 'at pleasure,' although often now for two or three year terms as well. The boards of a small group of financing authority corporations are a variant, in that their members are specified by statute. As well, in this province at present there are no statutory requirements for geographic, employee, or clientele group representation on such boards, although the concept has been intermittently debated, most recently in a January 1981 report of the Legislative Committee on Crown Corporations.[9] Some geographic representation is in fact secured on some boards, but the amount is limited, in view of the size of the province and the regional concentration of its population. Where such representation has been practised, furthermore (as has been the case with the Ferry Corporation), the result has been a clouding rather than a clarification of the goals towards which the board is expected to direct its senior management. The closest that any corporate organization is required to come in incorporating 'consumer representation,' by the way, is a Users' Advisory Committee of representatives of government departments called for by the constituent act of the BC Systems Corporation.

As Professor Hodgetts recorded for the federal scene, so in British Columbia Crown corporate boards vary greatly in size. On the whole they are small. The largest is BC Hydro's, at fifteen; most of the rest contain between five and nine members.

In his examination of specific appointments to boards, Professor Hodgetts notably has voiced strong reservations concerning the federal custom of placing senior public servants (and for that matter, management representatives) on them. He acknowledges the practice followed in a number of provinces of placing the designated minister on the board (often as chairman) and remains non-commital concerning it. On the basis, however, of his negative reaction to other practices which tend to dilute the role of the board as a buffer between the management of the corporation and the government, one might safely infer that he would not favour the adoption of this practice either. For Hodgetts the genuinely independent board represents the quintessential feature of the public corporation; its proper constitution and unfettered operation are amongst the most fruitful expressions of Lord Macaulay's dictum – which he is fond of quoting – 'to choose cautiously and confide liberally.'

In contrast to federal experience, and if we exclude from our examination for the moment the significant number of public servants who serve – especially in the health and welfare field – on the boards of quasi-public corporations in British Columbia, the province has not made a practice of placing many senior departmental personnel on corporate boards. British Columbia, on the other hand, has had a long standing tradition of placing ministers on the boards of public corporations. The custom dates from the acquisition of the PGE, whose presidents over a continuous stretch from the mid-thirties until 1976 were the province's premiers. (The current premier no longer serves.) The practice was not applied initially to the board of the Power Commission, whose non-partisan direction was emphasized at the time of its creation. This state of affairs ended in 1959 when two ministers were added to the commission after a major dispute had emerged between the commission's general manager and the provincial government. Almost without exception, Crown corporate boards since have contained at least one cabinet representative; some have carried two, and a very few three. Four corporations, which in federal parlance would be classified as departmental, have no staffs (the School Districts, Regional Hospital Districts, and Educational Institutions Financing Authorities, as well as the Provincial Rental Housing Corporation) and are dominated by ministerial members. Again, in line with the policy of some other provinces, British Columbia has been prepared to make ministerial board members into board chairmen on occasion. The PGE, by the way, had no chairman until 1976, and ICBC had a minister by statute concurrently both chairman and president for the first four years of its existence. A few ministers still occupy the chairman's seat, although not for the largest corporations, and it is worth recording that the present administration has indicated its intention of abandoning the practice.

Implicit in Professor Hodgetts' emphasis on the board of directors (which is carried through to the Lambert commission recommendations) is an acceptance of the classic doctrines concerning the key role which a board plays in conducting the business of the corporation. One of the shortcomings of this doctrine, and certainly of much earlier work on this subject, is that it is not based on much empirical data concerning the actual operation of modern corporations, public or private. Recently, this gap has begun to be filled by studies examining the internal workings of corporations. These studies are now suggesting, indeed, that the board often is not as pivotal a decision-making forum within the corporation as it might be, and that, in the public sector particularly, boards have suffered both from the politicization of the appointment process and from poor definitions of their tasks vis-à-vis management and the government. The Lambert commission's findings do suggest that many federal corporate boards have severely limited roles and that often governments, when appointing boards, have not chosen 'cautiously.'

What evidence is available concerning the power of the boards of public corporation in British Columbia does suggest that it also is limited. It is not constrained generally by statute, however; the constituent acts do appear to devolve basic responsibility for direction and management squarely on them. At the same time they do not always go as far as the Lambert commission suggests in allowing them to select the chief executive officer entirely without cabinet involvement, and the board chairmen with such cabinet approval. In practice all chairmen are designated by the Lieutenant-Governor-in-Council, and in practice, if not in law, chief executive officer selections are cleared with the cabinet or premier, either directly or via cabinet board members. The admittedly very incomplete evidence available does suggest that the typical public corporation board in British Columbia relies very heavily on its chief executive officer, whether on or off the board, especially for the identification of major policy options. It is equally difficult to be precise about the role played on boards by cabinet members, although it is not insubstantial. This matter is dealt with in the next section.

Finally, it is worth noting that quite a number of the (especially newer) corporations' boards have adopted administrative practices endorsed by Professor Hodgetts and the Lambert commission. Audit committees made up of external directors are now common, and some of the largest corporations have developed and make extensive use of corporate strategic plans. And a number of boards have adopted specific codes of ethics for the guidance of board members and corporate personnel.

Executive officers in British Columbia's public corporations prize, as do others elsewhere, their freedom from many of the organizational and personnel management constraints facing the departmental bureaucracy. The province's public corporations are not subject to its Public Service Act, and their managers are free to develop their own organizational structure, incentive, and classification systems. Innovation in their personnel administration has not been common, however, anymore than it has been, as Professor Hodgetts observes, at the corresponding federal level.

All but the smallest of the corporations employing a handful of employees regularly bargain with highly organized labour forces under the province's Labour Code, often via several unions concurrently. The four largest (BC Hydro, BC Rail, ICBC, and the Ferry Corporation) have all faced major strikes within the past decade. While the first three of those corporations maintain their own pension and benefit plans, virtually all of the other statutory corporations have taken advantage of provisions in their constituent acts to opt under the coverage of the very attractive package of pension and other employee benefits made available to the province's public servants, and some of the other corporations are moving to follow their example.

CONTROL, SCRUTINY, AND ACCOUNTABILITY

Professor Hodgetts' major contribution to the study of public corporations has been his framework of analysis and hypotheses on their control and accountability, and their scrutiny by parliament. The essence of his views on wholly owned corporations – the classic Crown corporations at the federal level – is implicit in his emphasis on the primacy of the board. In his view, the wholly owned public corporation is directly delegated the responsibility by Parliament (or with Parliament's indirect blessing in most cases) to manage an enterprise, and the necessary balance of powers and disclosure must be established to allow the designated minister to exercise his ultimate policy responsibility for the corporation without impairing the capacity of the corporation to conduct its managerial tasks in a business-like manner.

Over the years this basic philosophy has led Hodgetts to oppose the gradual encroachment of bureaucratic power over both policy direction and the management practices of wholly owned public corporations and to argue for the revitalization of the board of directors in the control and accountability regimes. In the earlier years, Hodgetts focused largely on financial controls and accountability along the traditional lines outlined in the federal Financial Administration Act of 1951. More recently, emphasis has been shifted to policy control or 'direction.' In the Lambert commission's final report we find a discussion of a comprehensive regime of control, formally establishing the balance of powers and disclosure amongst parliament, central government agencies, departmental bureaucracies, and the boards and managements of a corporation across the widest spectrum of corporate activities including mandate setting, strategic planning, budgeting, subsidiary creation, borrowing, financial and personnel management, and performance evaluation. In contrast to the recent federal government proposals, the tendency in the Lambert report is to place more formal power in the hands of the corporation board and the senior management of corporations.

Again here, as with the Hodgetts' approach to the internal organization of the public corporation, the emphasis is on the formal powers and roles of the various actors involved in the direction and management of the public corporation. While formal legal regimes are required, there is a growing realization that (at least in logic) they should only be established after detailed empirical studies of the existing inter-relationship between parliament, the various involved government agencies (Ministry of Finance, Treasury Board secretariat, the designated minister and his departmental bureaucracy, etc.) and the boards and senior managements of the public corporations. Only through such studies of the existing formal regimes and informal networks do we get an accurate reflection of what is possible in management terms – as opposed to what is desirable in terms of the classic definition of the 'arm's length' relationship and the accountability demands of responsible government.

With the publication of the final report of the Lambert commission, the Hodgetts' framework for control and accountability has been extended, at least in a preliminary manner, to the world of shared enterprise and quasi-public corporations. A natural extension of the Hodgetts' vision of the public corporation would be to push this work further, both in terms of an empirical understanding of the shared enterprise and quasi-public corporate phenomena and a more detailed set of regimes for their control and accountability. The framework of analysis (focusing on mandate, direction, control, and accountability) which emerged from the royal commission's work provides an excellent foundation for both empirical investigation of existing regimes and the design of new ones.

Where the BC government is clearly starting from scratch in the area of identification and classification, it has, by necessity, an established heritage of experience in dealing with the control and accountability of the wholly owned group within the public corporation sector. While not all of this experience has been positive, the BC government has recently taken initiatives with respect to the legislative scrutiny of a small group of wholly owned corporations which are significantly in advance of developments elsewhere in Canada.

With reference to the Hodgetts' framework for control and accountability, it is clear that in BC formal control over wholly owned corporations has been – for the most part – of the financial variety. Moreover, there would appear to be little enough of that which is effectively exercised on a regular basis. The financial controls applied to wholly owned corporations have not followed uniform or consistent patterns, but have varied in the light of such considerations as the political sensitivity of the functions involved, the personalities of key ministerial and senior corporate personnel, and the workload and general administrative and financial philosophy of successive governments.

In virtually all cases, the approval of the cabinet or of a committee of cabinet is required for corporate borrowing. Furthermore, as the Minister of Finance in the majority of cases is designated as the corporations' fiscal agent, his ministry has drawn unto itself the approaches to the market, or to provincial or Canada Pension funds, which the raising of capital requires. Some corporations must receive the approval of the Minister of Finance before investing surplus funds. Another way of making this point is to observe that, in effect, all of the Crown corporations have to receive a cabinet clearance for their capital budgets. This is true, as well, at least in so far as ministerial approval is concerned, for the two major corporations which have managed to acquire resources without formal borrowing, through the use of the sale and leaseback of assets. Only two Crown corporations (by statute) are required to obtain cabinet approval of their operating budgets, and this form of independence the rest now jealously guard. Four of the largest, however, either by statutory requirement or board decision submit all or part of the tariffs and fees which they charge for their services for cabinet approval. Changes in BC Hydro's rate structure, in addition, in 1980 were made subject to approval by a newly established British Columbia Utilities Commission. There has been some tension between the province's Ministry of Finance and the senior corporations over the ministry's role in the borrowing of funds, but to date the ministry has not been prepared to devolve this function directly upon them.

Most of the statutes establishing corporations require that they maintain accounting systems satisfactory to the Minister of Finance or to the designated minister, require the filing of accounts with the Treasury Board, and authorize the Minister of Finance to have the Comptroller General investigate a corporation's financial affairs. In practice, while some corporations have been constrained in this fashion, those which have wished to establish their own distinctive internal accounting systems have been able to do so. Interestingly enough also, all save one of the Crown corporations are now audited by private auditors, whose appointments are made variably by boards or the cabinet on board recommendation, often with the concurrence of the Auditor General or, still in a few cases, with that of the Comptroller General.

Financial controls excepted, by far the most significant cabinet supervision of these Crown corporations in British Columbia is effected through their boards. The cabinet, as we have seen, appoints all board members (at pleasure), establishes their tenure, and fixes their remuneration. Formally, neither the cabinet nor designated ministers possess an explicit directive power, although the cabinet normally has a capacity to refine the implementation of constituent acts by regulation. In practice, however, the cabinet's wishes are relayed directly by ministers, as most Crown corporate boards possess one ministerial member, and a few have contained two or more. It is difficult to assess in other than general terms the impact which cabinet ministers have had in corporate decisions. For obvious reasons, where they relay a cabinet perspective on an issue such as capital borrowing or charges on which the cabinet has an effective veto, their leverage is immense. The strength of a minister's own personality can be a factor of real significance, as also are the general confidence of the cabinet in the board, and the sensitivity of the issues at stake, not least because of the position of the government in the electoral cycle. On the other hand, especially within the last decade, as the legal liability of directors for board decisions has mounted, governments in the province have had some difficulty in recruiting technically qualified directors of the calibre desired. Indirectly, as a consequence, real limits have emerged on cabinets' abilities to dominate boards whose members have tended increasingly to emphasize their own independence, who have not been loath to point out that the capacity to veto is not necessarily the same thing as the power to direct, and who in some cases appear to have insisted that cabinets acknowledge in practice an obligation to compensate corporations for the costs incurred with the adoption of cabinet vetted decisions. As board meetings are privileged, it is not possible to determine categorically whether any of the major ones today are dominated by ministerial personnel as was the PGE/BC Rail board prior to 1976, but the evidence suggests that this era, very real to that date, is now passing. Still, just as the cabinet has not removed all ministerial representation from BC Rail's board (which the Mackenzie royal commission advised it to do in 1976[10]) so, by the simplest of linking mechanisms, it continues to be alerted to impending board decisions, and often is consulted about them, when they are likely to arouse substantial controversy.

One major constraint on corporate boards which tends to increase cabinet supervisory authority stems from the fact that in British Columbia, as elsewhere, legislatures and cabinets together have never cleared up the ambiguities in the objectives of some corporations. Much of this ambiguity stems from almost inevitable conflict between the values or goals toward which the Crown corporation is directed. Cabinets in this province, understandably enough from their perspective, like to preserve the right to reorder the weights attributed to those goals over time. This flexibility is most in evidence with respect to those corporations created under the Company Act. Since October of 1973, there has been no listing of corporate objectives in the memorandum, which with articles and a registrar's certificate, gives effect to incorporation in this province. Thus a Crown corporation once established in this way, unless constrained by some formal agreement with executive government, is potentially an extraordinarily wide ranging instrument – and one in which the legislature often has no opportunity to approve or even to scrutinize its goals or objectives.

With reference to the Hodgetts' framework, it seems clear that, to date, the BC government has not yet even contemplated the assignment of a number of powers and duties which in other jurisdictions have gained recognition as essential components of a comprehensive regime of control and accountability. There is, for instance, no obligation on the part of the wholly owned corporations to prepare multi-year financial plans for government approval. The issue of the government's general power to issue formal policy directives has not been dealt with in the context of the confusion generated by the position of ministers on boards. And, the government has not as yet found it necessary to equip itself with a general power to control the creation or acquisition of subsidiaries and associated corporations by its wholly owned corporations. On the accountability side, despite some pressure from the provincial Auditor General, the government has not worked out the degree to which it wants to push its wholly owned corporations beyond the reporting requirements of a corporation in the private sector to include regular variance and project reporting and effectiveness evaluations.

Not surprisingly, in this context, the government has not come to any decision, to date, on the wider questions of the control and accountability of those members of the public or quasi-public corporate sector which are not wholly owned. This situation, as we suggested earlier, is generally far more significant at the provincial level than the federal because of the apparently vast number of quasi-public corporations employed by provinces to deliver program services to the public. At the moment, at least one ministry in the BC government has worked out an innovative and comprehensive contracting system as the control and accountability linkage with corporations of this type, but this approach has not been universally adopted across the government. The government has also experienced the classic 'catch-22' dilemma associated in other jurisdictions with the relationship between governments and shared enterprise corporations. As recently as February 1981, despite the fact that it had divested itself of over 95 per cent of its shares of BCRIC, thereby relinquishing its capacity to control any aspect of the corporation's activities, the government was still viewed by the public and the opposition in the legislature as being responsible for the behaviour and performance of the corporation. The problem of reconciling the government's objectives, the legitimate interests of other shareholders, and the expectations of the voters with respect to shared enterprise corporations has yet to be resolved at the federal or provincial levels. The Lambert commission report provides one of the few available attempts to design a regime which deals with these potentially conflicting pressures, and further developments of this regime may provide the framework for a solution to these problems in BC.

Finally, we come to the difficult issue of the appropriate place of the legislature in the control and accountability framework. Beyond the rather limited role of the legislature in the establishment of the mandates and control and accountability regimes of those corporations created by statute, the essence of legislative control is the capacity to ask significant questions, the right to expect reasonable answers, and the impact which, via the doctrine of anticipated reactions, this sequence of events can have on patterns of administrative behaviour. It has been very much a part of this province's political experience since 1871, but until recent years it had a singularly modest impact on the province's public corporations.

First, we should note that the British practice of accompanying the presentation of a corporation's report with a short ministerial statement, and then following it up with a lively debate, has never been part of this province's legislative tradition. Such reports are regularly tabled without comment.

The written question responded to by a written reply has long been used in the province's legislature; it has frequently been and still is addressed to a probing of the affairs of public corporations. The oral question is crucial as well, but was not allowed in a daily question period until the spring of 1973. Until that date oral questioning on public corporate affairs was normally possible only when the estimates of designated ministers were being dealt with in the Committee of Supply. The grilling then on corporate affairs was frequently intense. Still the interrogation was truncated. Until 1973 it was never carried over to any of the legislature's committees, which did not review public corporation reports. Further, the corporations' financial statements were not included in the public accounts. Since 1973 they have been, and the reports, along with senior officers of the public corporations, have been available to the Public Accounts Committee for examination. Note must be taken also of the creation of a special standing Committee on Crown Corporations by the William Bennett government in the light of an electoral commitment to heighten corporate accountability. We shall return to it in a moment.

Three observations in the meantime can be made quickly on the questioning vis-à-vis corporations as practised in the legislature over the years. First, it has tended to cluster on the larger and more controversial entities; the smaller ones have frequently been ignored. Second, during the last decade, if allowance is made for the increased number of days in which the legislature sat, and for the increase in the number of public corporations, the general attention devoted to the corporations in oral and written questions actually declined. This trend may well have been accentuated by the creation of the new legislative committee. And finally, there has been a gradual increase in the number of questions focused on public corporate policy, and on corporate-government relations, rather than on their day-to-day corporate operations.

The creation of the Committee on Crown Corporations, which has been operative since the spring of 1978, has clearly been a significant development. The committee has a paid staff (of about six analysts), may meet between as well as during sessions, and enjoys the powers of the Speaker and the legislature to compel attendance at its hearings and the production of records. The staff play a facilitative role but do not take part in the interrogative process directly, and try to avoid dictating the committee's reports. The committee's chairman is not a member of the opposition, as the latter group had wished. Initially, a good many of the public sessions of the committee were marked by sharp partisan exchanges. Over-all, however, especially since 1979, a committee perspective on non-partisan lines does seem to have begun to emerge, as the twenty odd members of the legislature who have served on this body have clearly learned a good deal about the world of public corporations. In the face of some initial opposition (from the corporations) they have extended their already broad mandate well beyond that of reviewing annual reports. Their perspective has become prospective as well as retrospective; thus they are deeply concerned about long-range planning and are pleading for a clarification of some corporate mandates. A review of some of their recent reports, indeed, suggests that they are now much more sensitive than they were earlier to the problems which corporations face; some of these reports, indeed, are light-years ahead of the treatment recently accorded Crown corporate affairs either in the legislature or the media.

The Lambert commission suggested, succinctly, that the essence of parliamentary review in this field is that Parliament receive appropriate accounts of Crown agency activities, and periodically be able to re-examine the mandates and objectives of these bodies.[11] This is precisely what the Committee on Crown Corporations has been trying to do, for the four corporations with which it currently deals.[12] Over-all, however, the legislature's record on this front is a mixed one. As we have seen, its general questioning has left a good deal to be desired, and its other committees – notably the Public Accounts Committee, whether on its own or conjointly with the province's Auditor General – have not, to date, dealt with the balance of the Crown corporations, let alone the shared enterprises (or the mostly unrecognized quasi-public corporations) in any systematic way.

CONCLUSION

The Hodgetts approach to the study of the public corporation began with and is still rooted in a conviction that it is helpful to obtain the clearest possible picture of the anatomy and physiology of a governmental organization before examining it, from other perspectives, to refine one's understanding of its use and behaviour. In earlier pages we have referred to some of the additional questions being raised today concerning public corporations, in an attempt to understand in Marshall Dimock's apt phrase, this 'genus of great variety and versatility.' Applying Professor Hodgetts' analytic approach to British Columbia has reminded us also how little we know concerning the susceptibility of public corporations to pressure groups, concerning their own behaviour as pressure groups, concerning the informal linkages of their boards with managements, overloaded cabinets, the bureaucracy and the legislature, concerning the impact which some of these corporations have had on the society which they serve, and concerning, for instance, the risks which some have incurred for the state. All these, and more, are legitimate subjects for further investigation. Indeed, such a list is very much in keeping with a parallel enumeration of challenging topics for inquiry advanced by Professor Hodgetts in the introduction to his *Canadian Public Service*.

The authors wish to express their thanks to the research and secretarial staff of the B.C. Government Research Project and the President's Committee on Faculty Research and Travel at the University of Victoria for assistance in the preparation of this paper.

1 See his 'The Public Corporation in Canada,' in *The Public Corporation: A Comparative Symposium*, W. Friedmann ed. (Toronto: Carswell, 1954), pp. 51-92; *Pioneer Public Service* (Toronto: University of Toronto Press, 1955); 'The Public Corporation in Canada,' in *Government Enterprise: A Comparative Study*, W. Friedmann and J.F. Garner eds. (London: Stevens, 1970), chap. 12; *The Canadian Public Service* (Toronto: University of Toronto Press, 1973), chap. 7. For further evidence of Professor Hodgetts' views, see Royal Commission on Government Organization, *Report*, vol. V, *The Organization of the Government of Canada* (Ottawa, 1963), pp. 58ff; and Royal Commission on Financial Management and Accountability, *Final Report* (Ottawa, 1979), Part IV.

2 'The State in Business,' *Canadian Public Administration*, vol. 22 (spring 1979), pp. 124-50

3 For a more detailed discussion of the evolution of the problems of identification and classification, see J.W. Langford, 'The Identification and Classification of Federal Public Corporations: A Preface to Regime Building,' *Canadian Public Administration*, vol. 23 (spring 1980), pp. 76-104.

4 Government of British Columbia, Ministry of Finance, *Discussion Paper: A New Financial Administration Act* (Victoria, August 1980). Due to a vigorous lobbying effort by the affected parties, that part of the draft legislation related to the identification, classification, and control of public bodies was dropped from the Financial Administration Act passed in 1981. The future of the government's initial proposals on identification and classification is unclear at this point.

5 Royal Commission on Financial Management and Accountability, *Final Report*, p. 439

6 The Dunhill Development Corporation, subsequently part of the Housing Corporation of British Columbia

7 The Crown Development Corporation

8 Such as the BC Development Corporation and the Insurance Corporation of British Columbia

9 *Inquiry into the British Columbia Ferry Corporation: Interim Report*, January 1981, p. 60

10 Royal Commission on British Columbia Railway, *Report*, vol. 3 (1976), p. 156

11 Royal Commission on Financial Management and Accountability, *Final Report*, p. 412

12 One of the five corporations referred to it, the Housing Corporation of British Columbia, has been dismantled.

RICHARD SCHULTZ

Regulatory Agencies and the Dilemmas of Delegation

In *The Canadian Public Service*, one of Ted Hodgetts' central themes is the innovative and adaptive capacity demonstrated by the Canadian bureaucracy in the face of complex physical, economic, technological, cultural, and political changes. One of the marks of this capacity is the creation of what he described as 'a veritable jungle of quasi-departmental agencies' whose members he tersely designated as 'structural heretics.'[1] The resort to these heretics was viewed as a response to the twin problems of overloaded conventional departments and the assumption of new governmental functions. Solutions to problems often, however, have a remarkable facility for creating new problems in their wake and the creation of structural heretics offers no exception. The purpose of this chapter is to analyse one of the central contemporary public policy problems associated with one variant of the heretics, namely the independent regulatory agencies. In particular, we shall concentrate on what Hodgetts perceived to be a major negative consequence of the creation of non-departmental forms, the fact that 'the conventional channels of ministerial responsibility and control are clogged up and obscured, while parliamentary supervision and public comprehension are correspondingly diminished.'[2]

THE NATURE OF THE PROBLEM

Although there has been continuous railing, over the last fifty years, in the United States about the 'headless fourth branch of government' that regulatory agencies constitute, similar concerns in Canada are much more recent. It has only been in the last decade that regulatory independence, and the concomitant limitations of political control, have emerged as significant topics of political debate. A number of reasons can be advanced to explain why regulatory independence has become an issue. Some stress 'environmental' factors such as inflation undermining the quiet life of regulators and the regulated; others emphasize that agencies have been caught up in the general trend towards political activism which, in the regulatory context, was translated into determined participation by consumer and environmental groups and other interests which hitherto had been largely under-represented in the regulatory process. While such explanations have merit, I believe a more fundamental issue is involved. The independence of regulatory agencies has become a political issue because of the recognition that such agencies share that central characteristic which Emmette Redford maintains is the distinguishing feature of the modern liberal democratic state: 'Policy is made for and applied to us by minorities composed of men occupying strategic positions in specialized organizations, operating only in part under directives from organizations directly representative of the people.'[3] Regulation, as a sub-set of administration, has increasingly become a political function and the regulatory process a central component of the larger political process. Such features are, as Redford indicates, endemic to modern public administration and not unique to regulatory agencies. It is the independence of regulatory agencies, however, which provides a particular degree of insulation shielding such agencies, in unique ways, from political control that raises a special set of problems of coping with this variant of the administrative state.

In part, the problem of political control arises because regulatory agencies increasingly have come to play what can only be described as a political role. In this they have been caught up in the general shift, typical of contemporary bureaucracy, from what Redford characterized as a 'directed' to an 'adjustive' role.[4] The former involves 'overhead direction of activity setting the preconditions of administration on the basis of some measure of consensus on what will be expected of it.' Adjustive activity, on the other hand, entails 'an extension of the political process of adjusting among interests.'[5] Redford maintains that when administration is involved in the adjusting of choices and brokerage of interests, it is 'in this aspect of its performance, political.'[6] It must be emphasized that Redford does not suggest a dichotomous relationship between directed and adjustive activity. Rather, he stipulates that administration is both and that a continuum links the two types of activity which can be found in most forms of administration, often simultaneously.

For our purposes, the argument is that in recent years the regulatory process has increasingly provided a forum in which adjustive activity, at the expense of directed activity, has come to be central. The primary reason for this can be readily identified. Contemporary legislative statements of purpose do not effectively or meaningfully confine or structure agency discretion. They do not establish significant boundaries. Statutes, because they contain neither unambiguous goals nor precise directions for their attainment, ineluctably transfer much of the goal-setting process from the legislature to administration, in this case, independent agencies. The result, as Stewart has claimed, is that 'the exercise of agency discretion is inevitably seen as the essentially legislative process of adjusting the competing claims of various private interests affected by agency policy.'[7] We would amend this only to add 'public' interests such as departments, crown corporations, and provincial governments to the competitive process. In the next section we shall provide examples that illustrate this problem.

While the trend for regulatory agencies to play an increasingly adjustive role is significant in itself, its importance is greatly enhanced because of the transformation in the role of regulation in our political system. Regulation, as a governmental activity, has come to rival, and in some respects eclipse, the traditional spending and taxing powers of government as a means by which governments seek to influence, direct, and control economic and social behaviour. It is our contention that the initial function of regulation, assigned either to the cabinet before the turn of the century or to an agency such as the Board of the Railway Commissioners, was primarily a policing responsibility. The role of the regulator was to supervise specific aspects of the behaviour of designated interests in order to subject such behaviour to a reasonably precise and narrow range of public goals. As society's designated 'economic policeman' the functions of regulators were limited in scope, reactive in process, and remedial or grievance-solving in character. Regulation as policing was primarily negative and proscriptive. This is not to suggest that regulators, when performing a policing role, did not exercise discretion, for they surely did. Rather it is to argue that this discretion was substantially constrained by the nature of the purpose of regulation and, as such, was comparable to that of the 'policeman on the beat.' It was also constrained by a reasonably precise, in *contemporary* terms, legislative mandate. Although an injunction to determine 'just and reasonable' rates may, today, appear ambiguous, at the time the parameters for such a determination were known because the words were 'freighted with meaning,' to use Friendly's term, by both historical interpretation and contemporary context.[8] Accordingly, the adjustive role of regulators when performing a policing role, while not unknown, was minimal.

The initial negative policing function of regulation has evolved over the last eighty years to include *additional* positive, prescriptive functions as well. One such function is that of promotion where the role of regulation is to protect and enhance the security or health of the industry being regulated so as to satisfy, ostensibly at least, public goals. A promotional role has normally been associated with a power to license entry into a field of endeavour, i.e., to control the number of entrants or to determine conditions of operation. Such a regulatory role has traditionally been associated with broadcasting and some forms of transportation such as airlines and trucking. For our purposes, the significance of a promotional role is found in the inevitable broadening of the range of interests involved in the regulatory process. Traditionally, as the statement cited above indicated, the regulator stood between the regulated and the public seeking to balance the interests of both. With a promotional role, to the traditional relationship was added one of standing between regulated parties as well. Broadening the range of interests represented and, hence, expanding the issues involved, invariably substantially altered the function of regulation and hence its political significance. The scope of regulation was broadened considerably to include not simply a limited range of behaviour but the very existence of economic actors. Regulation would not just be reactive but was assigned to play a more activist gate-keeper role. Furthermore, by assuming a more positive function, regulation as promotion was being transformed from an individual grievance-settling to a more generalized problem-solving activity.

Although the adoption of a promotional role for regulation was the first step in changing regulation from a negative to a positive instrument of governing, the more fundamental change came when regulation began to be employed as a planning agent. Regulation as planning involves a public role in setting objectives for a regulated sector of economic activity, establishing priorities among objectives, assigning responsibilities to the individual regulated entities, co-ordinating their activities, and resolving any disputes within the regulated sector. Regulation as planning entails a comprehensive expansion in the scope of regulation and an initiating rather than reacting role. Finally it entails the subordination, although not necessarily the elimination, of grievance-settling by generalized problem-solving.

In emphasizing the evolution in the nature of the function of regulation we are not suggesting that each change has entailed a complete break with the prior variant of the regulatory function. If anything, the change has involved an additive process. Promoting has supplemented policing while planning has been added to both. Normally, the most recent purpose will be the dominant one although this has not occurred in all instances. In any event, regardless of the mix found in each agency at a specific time, most of the contemporary agencies perform all three functions.

In short, it is our argument that regulatory agency independence has emerged as an issue of political debate in large part because of the fusion of two separate developments. The first is the *political* – i.e., adjustive – role that regulatory agencies now play in the administrative system. They have been delegated substantial discretion that permits, and indeed requires, them to make choices between competing interests. The second development is the political significance of the function of regulation in our system of governing. As the regulatory function evolved, it increasingly assumed political relevance that transcended the traditional rationale of insulating politicians from controversial, no-win political issues. Today, in areas of fundamental importance – telecommunications, transportation, energy – regulatory agencies can make decisions that may have an enormous impact on the allocation of resources, on the organization of production and consumption, and on the distribution of income. The fact that these agencies are empowered to make such decisions, free, to a very large degree, from authoritative, effective political control and direction is the reason for the contemporary debate.

Although we are linking the adjustive role with the planning function as the main explanation for the attention paid to regulatory independence, we would not insist on an automatic, strict congruence of the two, or conversely of directed regulation with the policing function. There are examples of regulation which combine an adjustive role with a policing function and, in theory at least, one can conceive of a mix of directed and planning regulation. The trend in the development of Canadian regulatory agencies, however, has certainly been in the direction we have emphasized, namely to combine a planning function with an adjustive role.

SOME ILLUSTRATIONS

It is our argument that regulatory independence has become a political issue because regulatory agencies today perform politically significant political roles. In this section we wish to support this argument by providing three illustrations of regulatory agencies involved in such activities. We will cite the relevant statutory powers and then, in a very summary fashion, refer to some of the major adjustments and political conflicts that have been involved in the exercise of such powers. The examples involve the regulation of railways, broadcasting and telecommunications.

In 1967 with the enactment of the National Transportation Act, Canadian railroads were substantially deregulated.[9] The effect of this was 'to free the Canadian railways to compete forcefully in their markets, to adjust almost all freight rates by commercial and competitive conditions, and to act like other firms in competitive industries.'[10] In terms of freight rate regulation this meant the removal of legislative restrictions on railway rate-setting practices including provisions that prohibited 'unjust discrimination' or 'undue preference.' The only exceptions when the NTA was introduced in Parliament were provisions protecting 'captive' shippers where the railways were in a monopoly position or protecting competing modes of transport from 'predatory pricing' by the railroads. As a result of pressures from western governments and members of Parliament, a further protection was included when the NTA was before the House of Commons.[11] This protection is found in s.23 of the NTA and is commonly referred to as the 'public interest' protection clause. S.23 provides that where 'a person has reason to believe' that any act, omission, or the effect of any rate '*may prejudicially affect the public interest*' (emphasis added) in respect to rates or conditions for carrying traffic within, into or from Canada, that person may appeal to the Canadian Transport Commission for redress. To obtain redress, a 'prima facie' case must be established before the CTC will undertake any investigation. In any investigation, the Commission is enjoined to consider, but is not limited to, the following factors:

1 whether the rate creates 'an unfair disadvantage beyond any disadvantage that may be deemed to be inherent in the location or volume of the traffic, the scale of operation connected therewith or the type of traffic or service involved':

2 whether the rate creates 'an undue obstacle to the interchange of commodities between points in Canada or an unreasonable discour-

agement to the development of primary or secondary industries or to export trade in or from any region of Canada or to the movement of commodities through Canadian ports';
3 whether control by or the interests of another mode of transport may be involved.

One would be hard put to conceive of a more 'adjustive' role assigned to a regulatory agency involving historically one of the most controversial issues in Canada, railway freight rates, than this section. To paraphrase James Landis, the addition of s.23 to the NTA, turned over the whole burning issue of freight rates to the CTC and has resulted in the CTC, rather than Parliament or cabinet, becoming the focal point for all the pressures and counter-pressures that have kept freight rates in the centre of political debate in this country for the past century. The CTC became the forum for the 'ideological' freight rate battles, to use Darling's phrase, about regional development and exploitation.[12] Although there seems to be little appreciation of the root cause of the problem, interpreting and applying s.23 has become the central issue in battles between western governments, the federal government, shippers, and the railways. The record of the CTC on s.23 cases has not been a happy one with cases taking, on average, two and a half years to 'resolve.' The delays, the costs, and the controversies that have resulted from the CTC's difficulties with s.23 were central to provincial governmental criticisms of the CTC and to the federal government's receptivity to demands that the NTA be substantially amended.

In 1968, in recognition of the complexity that had emerged in the broadcasting system in Canada, a new regulatory agency was created, the Canadian Radio and Television Commission (CRTC).[13] This agency was delegated the responsibility to license all radio, television, and cable television companies operating in Canada and the purpose of such licensing was to achieve the objectives of the broadcasting policy enunciated in s.3 of the Broadcasting Act. Although this section contains ten objectives, we need only cite five:
1 the Canadian broadcasting system should be effectively owned and controlled by Canadians so as to safeguard, enrich and strengthen the cultural, political, social and economic fabric of Canada (s.3(*b*));
2 the programming provided by the Canadian broadcasting system should be varied and comprehensive and should provide reasonable, balanced opportunity for the expression of differing views on matters of public concern, and the programming provided by each broad-

caster should be of high standard, using predominantly Canadian creative and other resources (s.3(*d*));

3 the national broadcasting service should contribute to the development of national unity and provide for a continuing expression of Canadian identity (s.3(*g*));

4 where any conflict arises between the objectives of the national broadcasting service and the interests of the private element of the Canadian broadcasting system, it shall be resolved in the public interest but paramount consideration shall be given to the objectives of the national broadcasting service (s.3(*h*));

5 the regulation and supervision of the Canadian broadcasting system should be flexible and readily adaptable to scientific and technical advances (s.3(*j*)).

The extracts from the Broadcasting Act provide an excellent illustration not only of a regulatory agency being assigned a planning responsibility, but of an almost open-ended licence to engage in adjustive activity. In seeking to satisfy the statutory policy objectives, the CRTC is confronted, continuously, by a vast range of interests that must be accommodated by the choices made by the commission. Among the more notable obvious competing, or at a minimum not obviously compatible, interests are the public and private networks, traditional and non-traditional broadcasters (i.e. cable and pay-TV), federal and provincial governments, Canadian cultural and advertising 'constituencies.' The CRTC record of performing both planning and brokerage functions is replete with major conflicts involving public-private, federal-provincial, and Canadian-American disputes. The five-year deadlock over the introduction of pay television which has not yet been broken is exceptional only because of the all-encompassing range of interests demanding to be 'respected.' With the development of new technologies, the complexity of, and the necessity for, an adjustive process can only increase.

Earlier we indicated that, while not automatic, there has been a correlation between the degree of regulatory discretion and the nature of the regulatory function. This means that the more positive the role of regulation the greater the likelihood that the regulator will play an adjustive rather than a directed role. Our last example illustrates that it is possible to combine the policing function with an adjustive role. This example involves the CRTC which, in 1976, was delegated regulatory authority over telecommunications and renamed the Canadian

Radio-television and Telecommunications Commission. The specific telecommunications regulatory powers are found in the Railway Act[14] and the primary power, found in s.321, requires the CRTC to ensure that the rates charged by the carriers are just and reasonable and without unjust discrimination or undue preference.

Until 1976, the regulatory agency had a traditional perspective as to the meaning of 'just and reasonable' and 'unjust discrimination.' This perspective was based on the lengthy history of telephone rate regulation and, although regulatory discretion was part of that history and the regulatory agency did play an adjustive role, both the discretion and the adjusting were narrowly constrained. This changed dramatically with the CRTC which adopted the widest possible interpretation of its policing responsibilities. In a magisterial statement, reminiscent of Chief Justice Marshall of the US Supreme Court, the commission declared, before its first case, that

> The principle of 'just and reasonable' rates is neither a narrow nor a static concept. As our society has evolved, the idea of what is just and reasonable has changed, and now takes into account many considerations that would have been thought irrelevant 70 years ago, when regulatory review was first instituted. Indeed, the Commission views this principle in the widest possible terms, and considers itself obliged to continually review the level and structure of carrier rates to ensure that telecommunications services are fully responsive to the public interest.[15]

The commission also declared that 'the public interest requires that [telecommunications] services should be responsible to public demand over as wide a range as possible, and equally responsive to social and technological change.'

In making these declarations, the CRTC was clearly responding to interests which felt themselves inadequately or insufficiently represented because of the CTC's narrow perception of its adjustive role. It is also clear, however, that, in part because it was accustomed to such a role under the Broadcasting Act and because it no doubt, as economists would say, wanted 'to differentiate its product,' the CRTC was intent on playing a substantially enlarged adjustive role in the policing of telephone rates and services. To this end, the CRTC was prepared to encourage and, where necessary, generate additional interest participation in the regulatory process. By so redefining its regulatory role, the very nature and scope of telecommunications regulation was radically transformed. This occurred, it should be noted, without the slightest change in the statutory basis for such regulation.

EXISTING CONTROLS AND THEIR INADEQUACIES

We have argued that independent regulatory agencies today play very significant political roles within our administrative system and have provided several examples that illustrate such roles. The independence of such agencies, of course, is relative and not absolute. There are political controls that should permit politically responsible authorities to provide appropriate direction to limit agency discretion. In this section we wish to establish that existing controls are clearly inadequate for the nature of the task of control that exists today. In an earlier period when the agencies' adjustive capacity and demands were more restricted and the regulatory function more narrowly circumscribed, available controls may have been appropriate and sufficient. This is no longer the case.

There are two categories of control mechanisms, direct and indirect, whereby the government can provide policy direction to regulatory agencies. The indirect mechanisms include the government's power to appoint the members of the agencies, especially the chairmen, and approve the annual budgets. Although the evidence is sparse, there have been instances when these powers were used to indicate directions for the agencies. The replacement of the chairman of the CRTC, even though the incumbent had most of his term remaining, by the Clark government in 1979 is one example of the use of the appointment power. Similarly, in the early 1970s, the government signalled its intentions to the National Energy Board concerning its policy advisory role by severely cutting back allocations for designated 'policy' positions. Notwithstanding these examples, and they are probably exceptional, the appointment and budgetary processes are inadequate mechanisms for exercising political control over agency adjustive roles. They are far too blunt and time-specific and insufficiently discriminating to address directly the substance of a policy. At best they can only suggest the general direction or approach the government might favour and, accordingly, can have little overall impact on the adjustive activities of the agencies.

The direct mechanisms of control are three-fold. The first is the approval of agency regulations which provide one of the means by which the agencies may openly articulate some of their policy positions. Political approval of regulations by either cabinet or the appropriate minister is, in principle, not an insignificant mechanism. The government was able, for example, to develop its own policy on natural gas exports and not rely on the National Energy Board licensing because it was empowered to issue regulations that the board had to implement. In general, however, the regulation-approval mechanism has two serious defects. In the first place, unless the political authorities are empowered to issue regulations on their own, there may be no means by which an agency can be compelled to develop regulations if it chooses not to. Secondly, the regulations of two of the most significant agencies, the CTC and CRTC, do not require political approval. The second control mechanism is the directive power whereby the political authorities may issue a policy direction to an agency which is required to follow such direction in its decision-making. Again this power in principle is significant but less so in practice. At present the government is empowered to issue directions to Atomic Energy of Canada on any matter, and to the CRTC on three very specific areas.

The most serious disputes exist today over the third control mechanism which has come to be designated the 'political appeal' power. By virtue of this power, agency decisions can be vetoed, or even, in the case of the CTC, be changed by cabinet. Some have argued that the existence of such a political power over individual decisions renders the designation 'independent' meaningless. This is a great exaggeration. Notwithstanding such a power, the agencies continue to exercise a substantial degree of discretion and independent decision-making capacity. The cabinet legally cannot order an agency to hear an application, cannot order an agency to stop a hearing or not to listen to a party, cannot dictate an agency's reasons for a decision and, as indicated in all but one case, cannot substitute its decision for that of an agency. Cabinet's appeal power should be seen to be similar to that of a superior court over a junior court and, in fact, is less. That a superior court can overturn a lower court's decision does not render the concept of an independent judiciary meaningless.

In any event, there is considerable doubt about the efficacy of the political appeal provision as an effective means for limiting and structuring agency discretion. Except for the CTC, the government can stop agency actions but cannot positively direct it. At best, such negative controls can only transmit a message that may be received by the agency. Even where the government can change the decision, the power is application-specific and there is no guarantee, as one minister of transport learned, that the agency will regard the government's decision as a binding precedent for future decisions.[16] More generally, the weakness of the appeal provision as a means for providing policy direction results from the fact that it was conceived in a much earlier era when discretion was significantly confined by both statutes and tradition. It was much easier in an earlier period to identify when 'principles not in accord with public policy have been applied' or when it was 'manifest that the board has proceeded upon some wrong principle,' and thereby justify political intervention.[17] If agency policy-making was expected to be exceptional. so was government intervention – only six appeals from decisions of the Board of Railway Commissioners and its successors were allowed between 1904 and 1961.[18]

It is worth noting, in this regard, that as the function of regulation initially evolved to include a promotional as well as a policing role, the government was not satisfied with the efficacy of the political appeal mechanism. In both broadcasting and airline regulation the government, determined to protect its interests in the crown corporations which were to dominate the two sectors, reserved ultimate licensing powers to itself and circumscribed the respective regulatory agencies' discretion in other ways. The government was intent on ensuring that it, and not an independent regulatory agency, would play the decisive policy role.

Today when regulation is an even more multifunctional governmental instrument, the government has less control powers than it possessed previously. It has delegated the licensing powers to the agencies and yet the political appeal mechanism, if insufficient in itself in the earlier era, is clearly inadequate today. Agency policy-making, because of the lack of effective statutory guidance and the adjustive role for agencies, has become the norm. A control device, even without the problems cited above, designed for exceptional circumstances when policies and principles were generally clear and clearly stated, can hardly be expected to be more than minimally effective. The record of the past decade offers ample evidence that this expectation has not been disappointed.

IMPROVING POLITICAL CONTROL: SOME ALTERNATIVES

There is general agreement today that existing control mechanisms are inadequate for their contemporary tasks. A host of governmental reports, legislative proposals, and academic and popular criticism attest to this agreement.[19] What is lacking, however, is a comparable degree of unanimity on how to resolve the problem. In this section, we will analyse three possible major solutions that have been advanced. Our goal is not to be definitive in our treatment of these proposals, but rather to emphasize their major characteristics as well as some of the trade-offs and dilemmas that confront those who wish to ensure that the political decision-maker is effectively subject to political control.

To deal with the central problem, there are only, as Redford points out, two basic alternatives.[20] One is simply to avoid the problem of excessive discretion while the other is to find mechanisms for effectively confining it. The first proposal incorporates the former solution and recommends that the problem can be resolved by the abolition of regulatory agencies and the substitution of reliance on market forces to perform agency functions. It should be apparent that such a proposal is unlikely to be premised primarily on the principles of effective control, but is derived from criticisms about the growth of government intervention in general and excessive, inefficient and/or ineffective regulation in particular. Nevertheless, a proposal for agency abolition or deregulation is not without relevance to our concerns, because there are examples of government regulation which have been identified as not performing their economic functions while creating problems of political control. The deregulation of railway rate regulation in 1967 is an example that can be cited as satisfying both economic and public administration rationales, although, as noted, it is only a partial example because of the last minute addition of s.23.

Although additional candidates could be readily found, agency abolition, as Stewart notes, for a variety of reasons cannot offer a universal prescription. One of the more important objections is the belief that 'deregulation may in practice merely lead to a transfer of discretionary power over policy from administrative agencies to large and highly organized private interest groups.'[21] It is worth noting, however, that in recent years a practice closely akin to agency abolition, at least in effect, has been introduced in Canada. The federal government has been both less inclined to assign new regulatory functions to agencies over which it apparently perceives it has limited or ineffective control and also, and this is perhaps more the case, and more prepared to 'hive off' regulatory functions and assign them to 'quasi-regulators' who are not given the statutory independence of traditional regulatory agencies.[22] This has occurred in the transportation sector with the creation of the Prairie Rail Action Committee to handle the branch-line abandonment program and the Grains Commissioner with responsibility for facilitating the transportation of grain from western Canada. Similarly, in the energy field, the Northern Pipeline Agency and the Petroleum Monitoring Agency have been established. While creation of these agencies can be defended in terms of unique tasks, one cannot ignore the fact that actual or potential traditional functions, normally assigned to independent agencies, are now assigned to less independent bodies. The government has evidently decided that one answer to problems of political control is to avoid them by employing instruments other than independent agencies for regulatory functions.

The other two proposals attack the problem of limited control by seeking to confine the scope of independent decision-making. One would do this by reducing the opportunity and scope for agency discretionary decision-making by specifying in detail the policies to be implemented. Theodore Lowi is the most prominent advocate of this solution, and although he predicates his argument on the American constitutional doctrine on non-delegation, the principle of opposition to 'blank cheque' delegation is relevant to Canadian circumstances, even if the doctrine is not.[23] Lowi's position is summed up in the following: 'A bad program is a government response to an urgent demand that expresses the appropriate sentiments (for example, "put an end to poverty") but does not direct the coercive powers of the state clearly and effectively toward the pathology that activated the demand.'[24] His main concern is the modern predicament of 'statutes without standards, policy without law' for such characteristics result in excessive discretion being conferred on non-elected authorities responsible for 'implementing' statutes and policies.[25] His solution, as indicated, is to insist on 'clear standards of implementation' in all statutes that delegate power to administrative agencies.

While personally sympathetic to such a proposal, I believe that the battle for detailed specification of policy in statutes is largely lost. The overwhelming consensus is that such action is neither desirable nor feasible. It is thought to be not feasible because those who make the laws cannot resolve all the policy issues and conflicts in order to specify, to any significant degree, the subject matter of those laws; and it is seen to be not desirable because it would deny the appropriate degree of flexibility that is deemed to be necessary in modern administration. Notwithstanding this opposition to Lowi's solution, there may be a middle ground that is possible. I have argued that the degree of adjusting of competing interests by regulatory agencies is highly correlated with the nature of the regulatory function. Accordingly, while it may not be a viable alternative to confine discretion in general, à la Lowi, by attacking the adjustive dimension directly, perhaps it is possible to confine it to a particular set of activities that may be more narrowly circumscribed. In other words, discretion could be reduced, not by more explicit statutory direction, but by returning the function of regulation to its original role – that of policing behaviour – rather than the contemporary variant of prescribing norms and goals for behaviour. Such a solution, admittedly only a partial one, would recognize the continued need for regulatory agencies which the 'abolition of agencies' proposal could not, but incorporate the goal of confining discretion, albeit in a more limited manner than Lowi would advocate.

The third proposal entails neither the structural changes nor the fundamental reorientation that are required by the other proposals. This proposal recognizes that in many instances statutes do not and cannot provide effective policy guidance that will limit the discretionary power of regulatory agencies. The proposal calls for statutory provisions that will enable the cabinet to issue 'policy directives' to agencies regarding the implementation of the policy objectives contained in the statutes. By such a power, the cabinet would be able, where necessary, both to rank alternative and potentially competing goals as well as to offer interpretations of such goals, and the agencies would be required to consider such directives as authoritative and binding as the statutes themselves. There would be safeguards to limit the directives to general policy matters and the government would be prohibited from issuing directives that dealt with individual adjudicative cases before the agencies.

In principle, this proposal has been endorsed by the Lambert Royal Commission on Financial Management and Accountability, the Economic Council, the Law Reform Commission, provincial governments, and a host of academic and other commentators. Notwithstanding this general agreement, there is also widespread concern about the implementation of the principle.

At the heart of such concern is an aspect of the regulatory process which Hodgetts identified as a commonplace feature of contemporary Canadian public service, namely the growth 'in the *direct* exchanges between the public service and its clients ... that supplants or supplements the conventional, indirect methods of routing demands through the more visible, representative institutions.'[26] The qualified support for the directive power is based on a critical comparison of the client exchange practices, not of regulatory agencies vis-à-vis cabinet and Parliament, but of the former vis-à-vis traditional departmental structures. It is believed that regulatory agencies, today at least, are far more responsive to a more diverse cross-section of interests than are departments. The thrust of the argument is that the bureaucratic process is far too confidential and dominated by the norms of clientelism than is the contemporary regulatory process. The regulatory process, for both statutory and judicially enforced reasons, is increasingly far more open and to a far more diverse group of affected interests than the departmental process. The concern is that a directive power which does not incorporate a role for both agency and public input 'publicly inputted' may lead not to political control, except in a very nominal sense, but to bureaucratic, i.e., departmental, control. Such a result will simply transfer the discretionary adjustive process from what is, comparatively speaking, largely a public process, whatever its flaws, to a private process. The fact that this essentially private process may occur within the public sector does not make it any more democratic or subject to greater political control. Indeed it may be less. Numerous proposals have been made that reflect such concerns which would statutorily require agency, public, and parliamentary roles in the directive process.[27] If such amendments were made to the governments' various proposals, the concept of a policy directive could be a very useful contribution to the regulatory process by introducing a significant tool for political control which respects the interests of all the major interests.

CONCLUSION

Ted Hodgetts concluded *The Canadian Public Service* with a warning that recent developments within the public sector 'may well turn on its head the master-to-servant relationship which has been the essence of responsible government and of the liberal democratic state.'[28] Some would argue that this has already occurred in the regulatory system and that elected authorities have lost effective political control over independent regulatory agencies. There is much merit in such a conclusion. We have attempted to account for this development and our analysis has emphasized the importance of transferring a political role – an adjustive role – combined with a political function – planning – to the regulatory agencies. We have sought to illustrate the problem of defective delegation associated with ineffective political controls that are inappropriate for the dimensions of the current problem. There are a number of solutions to the dilemma of independence and political control. Developing appropriate solutions that will incorporate respect for the legitimate interests of all the participants in the regulatory process will require all the adjustive, balancing skills that, as we have contended, have become integral to that process.

1 *The Canadian Public Service* (Toronto, 1973) p. 143
2 Ibid.
3 *Democracy in the Administrative State* (New York: Oxford University Press, 1969) p. 196
4 Ibid., p. 199
5 Ibid., p. 188
6 Ibid., p. 194
7 Richard B. Stewart, 'The Reformation of American Administrative Law,' *Harvard Law Review*, vol. 86 (1975), p. 1683
8 Henry J. Friendly, *The Federal Administrative Agencies* (Cambridge: Harvard University Press, 1962) p. 13. For supporting Canadian evidence see Howard J. Darling, *The Politics of Freight Rates* (Toronto: McClelland and Stewart, 1980).
9 *RSC* 1970, c.N-17
10 T.D. Heaver and James C. Nelson, *Railway Pricing under Commercial Freedom: The Canadian Experience* (Vancouver: Centre for Transportation Studies, UBC, 1977), p. 9
11 Martin W. Westmacott, 'The CTC, Freight Rates and the Public Interest,' in K.M. Ruppenthal and W.T. Stanbury, eds., *Transportation Policy: Regulation, Competition and the Public Interest* (Vancouver: Centre for Transportation Studies, UBC, 1976), p. 61
12 Darling, *The Politics of Freight Rates*
13 *RSC* (1970) c.B-11
14 *RSC* (1970) c.R-2
15 *Telecommunications Regulation – Practices and Procedures*, 20 July 1976, p. 3
16 Hudson Janisch, *The Regulatory Process of the Canadian Transport Commission* (Ottawa: Law Reform Commission of Canada, 1978), p. 119

17 Currie quotes these statements from Privy Council decisions on appeals. See A.W. Currie, 'The Board of Transport Commissioners as an Administrative Body,' in J.E. Hodgetts and D.C. Corbett, eds., *Canadian Public Administration* (Toronto: Methuen, 1960) p. 229

18 Arthur R. Wright, 'An Examination of the Role of the Board of Transport Commissioners for Canada as a Regulatory Agency,' *Canadian Public Administration*, vol. VI (1963), p. 385

19 See, for example, Royal Commission on Financial Management and Accountability, *Final Report* (Ottawa, 1979), chap. 18; Economic Council of Canada, *Responsible Regulation* (Ottawa, 1979), chap. 5; Hudson Janisch, 'Policy-Making in Regulation,' *Osgoode Hall Law Journal*, vol. 17 (1979), pp. 46-106; and Richard Schultz, *Federalism and the Regulatory Process* (Montreal: IRPP, 1979), chap. 5.

20 Emmette S. Redford, 'Regulation Revisited,' *Administrative Law Review* (1976), p. 562

21 'The Reformation of American Administrative Law,' p. 1693

22 See Janisch, 'Policy-making in Regulation,' pp. 89-92.

23 *The End of Liberalism*, 1st ed. (New York: Norton, 1969), esp. chaps. 5 and 10

24 Lowi, *The Politics of Disorder* (New York: Norton, 1970), p. 59

25 Lowi, *The End of Liberalism*, p. 155

26 *The Canadian Public Service*, p. 346 (emphasis in original)

27 As in Lowi, *The End of Liberalism*

28 P. 353

A. PAUL PROSS

Space, Function, and Interest: The Problem of Legitimacy in the Canadian State

The administrative state is more than simply a polity in which 'administrative organizations and operations are particularly prominent.'[1] Bureaucracy is indeed its most prominent feature and the dominance of bureaucracy is rightly the pressing concern of those who study the administrative state.[2] But if we wish to fully understand the state in this guise, we must be careful not to be mesmerized by the machinery of government; its growth, its power, its perversion. We must pay nearly as much attention to the environment of the bureaucracy and the ties that link them as we do to the workings of the administrative state itself.

Obviously such studies will add depth to the results of research into the conduct of public administration, but there are more profound reasons for looking at the administrative state in context. We enrich our understanding, but we also come to appreciate how the bureaucratic institutions of the administrative state affect the other significant institutions of the polity. Thus we avoid the danger of apostrophizing bureaucracy as Louis XIV apostrophized himself, and in observing the relationship between prominent institutions we develop a keener sense of the health of the political community. As particular institutions lose power and others gain we can determine whether the transfer and adaptation of functions is advancing or bringing about the deterioration of the political condition.

At a fairly pedestrian level this leads us to ask whether new institutions fully serve needs that were met by earlier forms. Then, if they do not, we can ask whether such needs have to be served or whether society has moved beyond them. By way of illustration, we can open up an issue that will concern us throughout this discussion. It may be that the administrative state performs some aspects of policy communication in a fashion that is vastly superior to the way in which political parties perform those same functions. On the other hand, other aspects of policy communication once prominent in party business may now be neglected because they are excluded from the bureaucratic world-view and because the party system has lost the capacity and the desire to put them forward. If significant portions of the community feel that their interests are detrimentally affected as a result, the administrative state may face more than a trivial lapse of the nerves of government. It may find that the public has come to doubt the capacity of government to meet its need; that the public has come to question the legitimacy of its government.

It is the argument of this paper that problems of this sort are inherent in the modern administrative state: specifically, that the growth of the administrative state has fostered important changes in the way the public communicates with government, so that quietly, inexorably, rapidly the processes of policy formation have adapted themselves to the sectoral lines of communication that best serve the modern machinery of government. As they have done so, political parties have declined in policy influence, leaving behind a vacuum that has been filled only partially by the elaborate networks of interest groups which have come to serve both as communicators of policy needs and goals and as legitimizers of government action. The Canadian experience of this process, it is contended, differs a little from that of other industrialized democracies by virtue of the intense particularism which invades all aspects of political life in this country. Even so, the decline of the party system and its supersession by sectoral politics presents a major dilemma for all who are concerned about democratic government in Canada, not least for Canadian public servants who are both progenitors and victims of the new order.

We shall begin our discussion by looking at the political rather than at the administrative aspects of policy communication, for the condition that concerns us has its roots in the failure of traditional party systems to keep abreast of changes in the structures of modern society.

FUNCTIONALISM AND THE DECLINE OF PARTY POLITICS

The decline of politics has been a matter of immense concern to the twentieth century. Most frequently we have worried about the diminished part that legislatures play in the modern state,[3] and in casting about for explanations of this decline we have tended to accuse the party system of matricide. Political parties, the argument goes, adapted too well to mass society. In responding to universal suffrage they evolved organizations that relied increasingly upon the vote-catching power of the leadership. Thus party power fell into the hands of its leaders, and the rank and file of elected members became the obedient herd, voting as the whips dictated and – despite brave talk of caucus influence – having virtually no effect on policy-making. These tendencies in the mass party were exacerbated by the media which, in seeking the ultimate simplicity of centralized communications, focused literally on the leader, transforming all but the closest advisers into nonentities.

The rise of the mass party only partially explains the decline of Parliament. After all, party organizations themselves do not seem to have been beneficiaries of these changes. They frequently have experienced the same sense of powerlessness that afflicts parliamentarians. This has been the case particularly in Canada where, despite a surge of reform sentiment in the nineteen-sixties and early seventies, party contributions to policy appear to be quite limited and riding organizations seem to prefer to direct their energies to delivering the seat and distributing patronage, rather than acting as policy advisers to members.[4] In displaying such realism, party members demonstrate that the mass party is less a contributor to the reduced influence of parliament as it is another victim of more profound forces in the evolution of western society.

Like the institution of Parliament itself these forces are rooted in the division of function which has propelled industrialized society for the last several centuries. Industrial society 'is a society based on large-scale industry, predominantly concerned with the performance of that industry and therefore with the corresponding organizational requirements. It is an urbanized society of nuclear families and mass culture. Its division of labour is increasingly determined by its technology, as also is its accumulation of capital and its search for a calculus of rational choice.'[5] Parliament unfortunately is ill-suited to acting as a forum for exercising choice in the mode of rationality demanded by industrial society. This is because Parliament is built on an anachronistic view of how politics is joined to economics in the processes of public policy formation. For the basis of the modern parliamentary system is the single-member constituency and the assumption that the individual member can successfully mediate between the demands of the general will and the specific needs and wishes of his constituents. Such assumptions were appropriate to the early nineteenth century when the emergent industrial fabric of the west was composed of innumerable relatively small enterprises which, though increasingly interdependent, were rooted in and dependent upon specific localities. The political economy of this period found representative government and the single-member constituency quite appropriate to its needs.

Not so the political economy of the late nineteenth century and our own time. The complex corporate industrial structure of this era demands far more of government than did its predecessor. The distributive politics of the earlier period has consequently given way to a redistributive and regulatory politics in which governments must be increasingly responsible for both supply and market management. The effect of such complexity upon policy-making is to render local institutions virtually ineffectual in the face of the sweeping regional, national, and international considerations which influence the modern political economy.

We see an early illustration of this point in the experience of a northern Ontario community which at the turn of the century had grown up around the logging and sawmill industries, industries whose demands for timber holdings were individually relatively small and were generally processed in consultation with local riding officials of the party in power. The advent of the pulp and paper industry changed that way of doing business. Pulp mills required very long-term leases of timber-lands that were extensive enough to ensure a perpetual supply of pulp wood on a sustained yield basis. It became quite common to lease concessions of several thousand square miles – often exceeding the extent of any one constituency. Consequently the promoters of pulp and paper companies insisted on dealing chiefly with the centres of power. They argued that their affairs were associated with the province as a whole and not with any locality, so that in their dealings with government they bypassed the local party machine. Furthermore, the spokesmen for these concerns usually, though not always, represented large corporations or groups of important financiers, and they were accustomed to dealing with governments rather than with the intermediaries that lesser men had to contend with. As one commentator on this transition in the forest industry remarked:

They were, however, different types from the original loggers and the lumber magnates. Vast capitalization was required to set their pulp and paper mills into operation; financing and investment bankers became powerful factors in their setup. The days of the individual leader and that of partnership had passed away. The corporation was here to stay.[6]

As a result, though local political organizations sometimes played a significant role in the decision-making process, power necessarily resided almost exclusively in the hands of the party leaders. The impact of this development is illustrated in this letter written to an Ontario MLA in February 1926 by a riding official in Northern Ontario protesting the apparent allotment of three townships to a pulp and paper company:

When in Nipigon you announced the deal that Hon. G. Howard Ferguson has promised to the people of Nipigon, that the townships of Booth, Purdon and Ledger would be open for settlement in the near future.

Nipigon as you will remember gave the largest proportionate Conservative majority in the last elections in your constituency.

Is that the reason why the interests of the people of Nipigon *are first to be sacrificed* by our Provincial Prime Minister? Do you expect me as President ... to be forced by unprecedented nasty dealings apparently going on with the knowledge of the Prime Minister favouring the Nipigon corporation to the exclusion of everybody else – do you expect me to be forced to announce that Hon. Howard Ferguson, whom I praised to my friends before the last election, is a man who does not honour his given word? If your Nipigon association can't trust in the word of our Prime Minister, can't have faith in the promise of the first citizen of the province, then who are they ever to trust in the future?

I sincerely hope that such despicable action has not been confirmed, as yet, and that you will find some means to prevent it, so that I will not be made a liar among my political friends, in having advocated the interests of the Conservative party.[7]

The importance of the centralizing trend, and its consequent weakening of local party organizations, is underlined by the increasing frequency with which local and regional interest groups applied public pressure to government. In this sense, the rise of businessmen's organizations in small towns may be attributed to the weakening of the party machine as the petitioning agent of regions and localities.

Replacing the party machine at the local level was an increasingly technically oriented bureaucracy whose influence depended on a degree of centralization of authority. Thus, for example, as professional foresters made steady progress towards positions of influence in Ontario's timber administration, they found that one of the major barriers to the reforms they sought lay in the role and structure of the field service.

> By tradition local officials had always been appointed on the patronage system. Thus a man appointed as lands agent in a small town probably owed his job to the kind offices of some politician or prominent business man. As a consequence, he and his job formed part of the local political machine; he was accustomed to pin his trust on the local barons, deferring to their wishes even before those of his nominal employers in Toronto.[8]

A shift to professional administration would frequently have much to do with the decline of the influence of local party officials. These local oligarchs were the enemy of the forest reform movement and they were attacked by invoking the need to 'get a technical umbrella over the field staff'[9] by appointing men with professional qualifications to key positions in the field. The traditional political influence of local barons had to be sidestepped and the recruitment function centralized in Toronto. As well, a reorganized field service had to be built around regional foresters who were selected 'partly on the basis of their personal capacity to serve as a "barrier" between the district foresters and the outside pressure groups.'[10]

Thus we see both corporate power and bureaucratic power gradually eroding the influence of local bodies in the direction of local affairs. Not only was the local political party a leading casualty in this decline; so was local influence itself. Nor was Ontario's experience unique. Studies of other forest industries elsewhere describe similar evolutions of central management.[11] It was an evolution which linked the decline of traditional rural economies to the falling away of the vigour and influence of local party organizations.

The pattern has been noted by others. Galbraith, for example, has commented on the relationship between the growth of public and corporate bureaucracies and the decline of local party organization and influence. For him the rise of the technostructure, the expert bureaucracies of the public and private sectors, spells the decline of patronage, at least on a small scale: 'For direct political action the technostructure is far more circumscribed than the entrepreneur.'[12] While more dependent on the state than the entrepreneur, or even the entrepreneurial corporation, the mature corporation, as Galbraith calls the complex, often multi-national, private sector organization, derives benefits from the state that are of a different order. Though the need for specific resources has not disappeared and the passions of regulators must still be thwarted, the benefits of economic planning – the supply of trained manpower, 'the regulation of aggregate demand, and ... stability in wages and prices'[13] – are far more important. To ensure an acceptable configuration of macro-economic policies the corporations must bend their energies to wooing the technicians of the new industrial state, rather than bribing 'the archaic survivors of an earlier era.'[14] The harmony that is fostered between the mature corporation and the modern state is born of a similitude of structure, personnel, goals, and process, not of the purchase of decisions. Indeed, 'there is, to speak loosely, no decision available for purchase. There is, instead, a process of decision-making in which many people participate over a long period of time.'[15] The political party that is 'above all a fighting organization'[16] is reduced to impotence in the face of such sophistication.

In short, during the twentieth century it has become steadily more apparent that systems of representative government built on the concept of the single-member constituency do not answer the needs of modern communities. They fail because modern economics integrates communities in a manner never before possible. Local politics is no match for the politics of regionalism, nationalism, and ultimately internationalism. The politics of the larger unit manipulates the resources of the smaller unit and integrates them with the resources of other equally impotent localities leaving little room for the intervention of community politics with its strong note of partisanship and its tendency to systems of patronage. Where the spatial orientation of the legislative system once provided an adequate base for lines of communication between polity and government, now it is inadequate. Roger Williams quotes an editorial in *The Times* which expresses in a particularly apt way the bafflement that is created by this decline of traditional party politics:

Many advanced states are experiencing the same kind of gap between public opinion and the machinery of government. A paradox of the modern technological society is revealed: the society creates problems so complex that they can be handled only by those with specialist skill and intricate knowledge, and at the same time it produces people who are in general more highly educated and enquiring than previous generations. It centralizes decision-making but spreads the desire to make decisions. How can democracy in this predicament satisfy both the need for greater efficiency and the need for wider participation?[17]

The decline of party politics creates two central problems for the polity. First, and most important, the legitimacy of policy decisions are cast in doubt. That is, the object of representative government is to ensure that the legislature is equipped to consider the public interest from a local as well as national perspective. Thus the sovereign people confer legitimacy on the acts of government. Thus also, the people have a right to assume that their representatives have a role to play in the policy process. If that role is reduced to the merely symbolic, it is inevitable that the public will come to question the legitimacy of the acts of government and eventually the legitimacy of the regime itself.

The second problem is the one that we shall address here and it derives from the fact that governments cannot afford to be without their lines of communication with the polity. If the party system no longer provides effective policy communication, then some other system has to be developed. In western industrialized countries that system has been built around the functional orientation of administrative agencies. As we have just noted, and as Morstein Marx has expressed it, 'the development of the administrative machinery of government to its contemporary size corresponds broadly to the evolution of the industrial order.'[18] Government agencies have developed as they have in the twentieth century because the public sector has had to respond with specialist solutions to the specialized needs of modern business organizations. In so doing, governments have created new patterns of policy communication that have in many instances proven far more effective than traditional party lines of communication. This is not a new observation. In the early 1950s Paul H. Appleby quoted Charles Wiltse making this very point:

It is only with the rapid spread of industrialism coincident with and subsequent to the Civil War that representation in Congress ceased to be in effect functional. The railroad and the telegraph served to break down sectional barriers, and economic and cultural interests thereafter cut too sharply across state lines to be adequately represented on a geographical basis. At the same time, the impact of technology forced Congress to deal with the highly complex problems of a rapidly changing economic and social structure. The law making machinery was unequal to the task, the trained expert was introduced, and executive and legislative functions tended to merge. Thus the purposes of functional representation came to be accomplished through the creation of administrative agencies.[19]

Functional representation, however, goes beyond the creation of administrative agencies. It involves as well the elaboration of complex networks of pressure groups. Pressure groups are many things to their various clients and opponents. To their members they are voluntary associations, built to help them achieve, in common with others, some personal goals. Usually their 'pressure group' role is a minor and often distasteful aspect of their work, a necessary evil if the common interest is to be protected and promoted. To outside observers, however, pressure groups perform several important functions in the political system. They play para-governmental roles by regulating some groups and professions or by administering certain kinds of services like children's aid. More importantly they legitimate government policy by publicly supporting it. Most important of all, they provide a vital communication function by serving as a link between the administrative agency and its functional constituency.[20] It is in this capacity that the pressure group has come to be seen as the rival of political parties, for not only are most pressure groups capable of providing agencies with the detailed information needed for policy-making and regulation, but they communicate in the specialized language of bureaucracy. This is a language that political parties will only learn at the cost of a fundamental change in nature.

The importance of this communication function has been noted internationally. The British remark on the extent to which agencies rely on their coteries of interest groups to provide specialized information.[21] The British, but more especially the Americans, have also expressed concern that 'policy segmentation' has led to the creation of sub-governments comprised of agencies, influential groups, and sometimes key politicians.[22] The present writer has identified similar configurations in Canadian policy-making.[23] These tightly knit but informal groups are considered by those who have studied them – Lowi being the foremost and most outspoken[24] – to have undermined the system of government upon which most western democracies have been built. As Richardson and Jordan put it:

> As governments seem to be drawn closer to the group system as a means of determining public policy outcomes, observers have become concerned that our traditional notions of democratic representative government seem to have been abandoned ... [F]or ... Britain (though we believe it is true for virtually all Western democracies) the traditional model of Cabinet and parliamentary government is a travesty of reality ... Politics, in a sense, has gone underground.[25]

Thus representative government gives way to functional representation, and 'politics goes underground.' In its place the administrative state creates the special-interest state. The special-interest state is a polity in which policy communication is so arranged that interests are first and foremost identified and drawn into communications with government, not through their geographic or spatial affiliations, but through their specialized contact with a functionally oriented arm of government. It is a state in which the term 'pressure group' takes on a new meaning. No longer are such groups merely peripheral adjuncts of the political system through which particular interests lobby for special favours. Rather they occupy a central role in policy communication and legitimation. They become the principal channels through which governments elicit public opinion and, in order to ensure that they are effective communicators, governments encourage their development with financial assistance, regulatory persuasion, and formal recognition as participants in advisory bodies and at policy conferences. Sinclair comments on this relationship in the American context:

> The central fact of bureaucratic lobbying is the clientele orientation of government agencies ... Government agencies consult regularly with relevant interest groups for several reasons. The development of new programs must anticipate the reactions of those people most directly affected, and often interest groups are the only source of this information. The next step – selling new programs to the upper levels of the bureaucracy and relevant congressional committees – requires strong clientele-group support. Finally, implementing new policies requires the cooperation of those being regulated or served by the program. For their part, consultation at the planning stage means that interest groups obtain a chance to influence the shape of a policy before it 'goes public' in Congress.[26]

Thus, for governments such efforts pay off in an improved capacity to communicate with fragmented publics and the assurance that the support of a broadly canvassed special public confers legitimacy on government action in the eyes of the general public. For the participating groups the benefits are obvious, but for the general public there can be less satisfaction. The policy communities which develop in these surroundings may exclude the weak, or the unorganized, from policy discussions[27] and they will do all that they can to ensure that policy changes are treated as technical or routine changes, thereby providing against wider participation and against the full review of policy.[28] In this way the public interest is either perverted or becomes the residual of group interests, and the public finds that it has no effective, long-term way of controlling its own administrative creations. In other words, the public discovers that what it thought was democracy has become that excess of pluralism which has engendered so much criticism and so much alarm in recent years.

The emergence of the special-interest state confronts industrialized democracies with a central tension of over-riding importance: the state's legitimacy is built upon the spatial orientation of traditional representative government, but its effectiveness rests on a functional approach to policy communication. Upon their success in coming to terms with this inherent conflict depends the future of western democracies. Canada is no exception.

THE FEDERAL PUBLIC SERVICE AND THE SPECIAL-INTEREST STATE

Canada has approached the special-interest state more recently and less obviously than other countries, particularly the United States. This is because the particularism of the Canadian political system imposed on the Canadian public service a degree of political involvement in administration that was unusual. This was first remarked by Sir George Murray in his famous 1912 study of the civil service when he pointed out that Canadian cabinet ministers 'have too much to do, and try to do too much.'[29] Hodgetts has argued that the harried life of the senior Ottawa policy-maker stemmed in part from the institution of regional representation in the federal cabinet, an institution which forced senior ministers in particular to manage not only their own departments but to concern themselves with the activities of other agencies in so far as those activities affected their region. Since these regional concerns involved more often than not patronage, ministers and often the entire cabinet frequently found themselves immersed in the petty detail of administration.[30] This was a source of anguish to innumerable consultants from Murray to Glassco who argued that it prevented the cabinet from considering the broader issues of policy, but it did serve to impose on public policy-making an awareness of the geographic imperative in Canada and it gave the cabinet a sense of being in control of its bureaucracy, a sense that it could 'work' the public service. So strong, in fact, was that sense that a prime minister like Mackenzie King frequently revealed an intimate understanding of the inner workings of the federal agencies. A 1923 intervention into a dispute between the Department of Trade and Commerce and the Dominion Bureau of Statistics illustrates both King's knowledge of the persons involved and his sense of control:

> I have come to think that the trouble is not so much with the [Civil Service] Commission as with the officers of the Trade and Commerce Department. There is a certain jealousy between O'Hara and Coates [Dominion Statistician] which I think you should know about and which, I think, you should look carefully into. Unless the embarrassments which have grown out of this personal feud or whatever it may be can be overcome, it is my intention to ask Council to transfer the Statistical Branch to some other Department and take it from O'Hara's control.[31]

This sense of control survived well after the Second World War and is evidenced by the persistence with which senior public servants argued that they played only a limited role in policy formation. As late as the mid 1960s, Mitchell Sharp insisted that 'civil servants do not make policy, all rumours to the contrary notwithstanding.'[32] By this time, however, such assertions were more and more open to challenge. In 1957 Hodgetts noted that 'the increasing importance of the civil service in the realm of policy has been the occasion for violent diatribes and anxious reassessments of the role of bureaucracy in a democracy.'[33] Though referring to a debate that was occurring in many countries, Hodgetts did not exclude Canada from this experience. Writing from the vantage point of Queen's University when that institution enjoyed a particularly close relationship with the senior federal civil service, Hodgetts suggested, as an example of bureaucratic influence, that the Financial Administration Act of 1951, 'was essentially a product of the experience and detailed knowledge of many civil servants.'[34] Although such influence was a product of forces beyond the control of the federal 'mandarins' –

Hodgetts argued that they had had influence thrust upon them by virtue of the fact that others lacked the expertise either to appreciate the need for choice or to make informed judgments – it is worth noting that the power and significance of men like Graham Towers and Clifford Clark was becoming known and appreciated beyond the limited circle in which they moved and worked.[35] In a sense, the spread of that understanding was as sure a sign as any of the drift of power from the political to the administrative arena, of Canada's approach to the special-interest state.

The process, of course, had begun many decades before. In a sense, if we accept the argument that the structure and role of government responds to the challenges of the community at large, we can argue that the 'powerful persuaders' emanating from the economic life of the country had set the process in motion even before Canada was officially baptised as an independent entity.[36] It is useful, however, to set aside for the moment our awareness of the pressures created by the world outside government and to look instead at the internal developments that have helped transform our processes of policy communication. These we can categorize as changes in personnel policy, changes in structures and ultimately, and most recently, changes in process.

If we wish to pinpoint a specific event in a long, generally imperceptible process of change we should probably fix on the introduction of the merit system. That event brought about the end of the system of patronage appointments which, as Hodgetts and his colleagues have remarked, did so much to tie Ottawa to constituency interests across the country.[37] In effect, it cut one of the most important ties between the party system and the day-to-day life of the community. Scholars in Canada and elsewhere have rightly hailed the implantation of the merit system as a great step forward in the development of modern government, but we should be aware that, like most benefits, the system has imposed costs, some of them profound. The merit system is founded on the principle of appointment through competitive examination, but it involves far more. In particular, it requires the precise delineation of positions and the determination of the qualifications needed by aspirants to those positions: in short, a classification system. Merit and classification together invoke technocracy.

Technocracy does not fit easily into a political system that is governed by geography. It resists the forces of localism, which it denigrates. Parochialism and particularism, it argues, are inefficient and outmoded and must be weeded out. Its distaste is reflected in Polsby's words: 'devolved authority presumably means that public administrators must temper the norms of professionalism and neutral competence with the norm of attentiveness to the needs of communities.'[38] We have seen in our earlier illustration of the decline of local party influence in northern Ontario, how a 'technical umbrella' was used to cut back patronage appointments in the field and to shield field officers from local pressures. Other studies, notably Herbert Kaufmann's study of the US Forest Service, have described similar developments elsewhere.[39] The federal government was influenced as much as any by the trend to professionalism.

A professional perspective is a functional perspective and as professionals became influential in the Canadian public service the agencies they populated began to change structurally to mirror that perspective. The restructuring of the federal public service following the First World War hastened this development, and the Second World War put it firmly in place. Gradually, for example, the Department of the Interior – beloved of theorists as an outstanding example of organization by place – was reduced in scale and influence, its role in part taken over by provincial governments, but also by functionally oriented agencies like Agriculture. Its modern manifestation, Indian and Northern Affairs, though powerful, is a shadow of the old department and very much threatened by both the home-rule aspirations of northern communities and the functional imperatives of other agencies like Environment and Energy, Mines and Resources who question its capacity to administer in the north the specialized legislation for which they are responsible elsewhere in Canada.[40] The decline of this department is yet another illustration of the trend in Canada towards functionalist systems of administration and policy-making and away from areally or spatially oriented systems.

It is worth noting, in this context, that the only other federal department specifically designed to provide programs that are geographically defined was the recently restructured Department of Regional Economic Expansion, a department which was often viewed in Ottawa as a pariah, but which served, primarily, an area of the country in which the traditional party system still flourishes. It is tempting to suggest that this department survived by accommodating its policies to this party system, but a more subtle explanation is probably nearer the mark: that there is an integral relationship between the structure of the market economy in Canada's depressed regions and the characteristics of the policy system there.[41] The market economy uses the party system for policy communication whilst the predominant mode elsewhere in Canada is the functionalist or technocratic. Any development agency working on the borderline between the market economy and what Galbraith calls the planning system[42] thus is inevitably drawn into a closer relationship with party organizations than would most functionally oriented agencies. It will be interesting to see how the reconstituted department copes with this phenomenon.

With these exceptions the trend to professional, functional administrative structures was most marked, at both the federal and provincial levels, in the years following the Second World War. The Glassco reforms of the 1960s consolidated these processes. They led to the clarification of central agency powers and established the professional character of departmental management. The first had effects which we shall refer to shortly; the second brought the relationship between ministers and their departments more in line with what has come to be seen as accepted practice in parliamentary democracies. It is not the function of ministers, Glassco argued, to work their departments, but to see that they are competently worked.[43] In accepting that argument and in implementing it, however imperfectly, the federal cabinet loosened yet another of its ties to the party system of earlier years. Just as the inherent regionalism of the spoils system had been undermined by merit, so the residual regionalism of political plum pudding was demolished by cost-benefit analysis and the centralization of supply and service functions. The inadvertent localism of graft and corruption has not entirely disappeared – the unsynchronized structure of the Canadian economy keeps it alive – but it is increasingly peripheral to the main business of public policy.

The most recent step towards functional domination of policy communication, and possibly the step which has had the greatest effect on the development of the special-interest state in Canada, has been the reorganization of central policy structures which has occurred at Ottawa and most provincial capitals in the last fifteen years. One might have expected these changes to have enhanced the capacity of senior policy makers to take a broad view in decision-making, and to some extent perhaps they have. However, in an admittedly speculative argument, we would suggest that improved co-ordination and review of policy at the centre has been offset by other factors. Not the least of these has been the bureaucratization of the cabinet. Mitchell

Sharp has remarked that he 'couldn't imagine ministers of [St Laurent's] day agreeing to read the numerous and voluminous cabinet papers we are presented with from week to week.'[44] Reorganization of cabinet procedures has, in his view, ensured that ministers are better informed than in the past on the broad spectrum of public policy, but at the cost of spending innumerable hours reading briefing notes and, by his calculation, some 'twelve to fifteen hours a week in cabinet or cabinet committees.'[45] This suggests that cabinet has won a degree of independence from bureaucratic manipulation, but in the process ministers have become bureaucrats themselves. Sharp himself admits that 'ministers have had to spend a good deal more of their time in Ottawa and in cabinet and cabinet committees than they would prefer, perhaps to the detriment of the political interests of the government and the party.'[46]

The sea-change that politicians undergo as they become ministers must surely mean that they become less and less capable of appreciating the local needs and aspirations that have been the well-spring of party influence. Increasingly they are oriented to the demands of the special interests of their policy fields.

Perhaps a more potent consequence of central agency restructuring has been the effect it has had on policy competition between agencies. Again we have to speculate, but not unjustifiably. In the first place, it seems clear that cabinet 'prima donnas' are defunct. Perhaps occasionally a Romeo LeBlanc can run his department in the old style, but in general the Jimmy Gardiner's and the C.D. Howe's are out of place in today's cabinets. If personal influence can no longer protect and promote departmental initiatives in the bear-pit of co-ordinated policy making, then departments must find other ways of winning their way. One of the more effective of these, we suggest, has been the cultivation by agencies of friendly interest groups who can make common cause with agencies in appearances before parliamentary committees and in the specialized and general press.

Some aspects of this relationship were suggested by Hodgetts as early as 1957 when he asked whether some Canadian agencies should be compared to the major American agencies, as

> really glorified pressure groups in their own right, acting on behalf of a special clientele which was largely responsible for their creation in the first place, and which looks to these departments for favours and sympathetic consideration whenever its own vital interests are at stake. To what extent would this

prove true in the case, say, of our own Departments of Veterans Affairs, Labour, or Agriculture? What is the impact on D.V.A., for example, of the Canadian Legion when reinforced by a parliamentary committee made up entirely of ex-servicemen and further buttressed by a staff largely recruited from the same source? What are the relations between the Canadian Federation of Agriculture and the Department of Agriculture or between organized labour and the Department of Labour? To what extent are the choices that are made in these departments conditioned by the presence of such vocal, powerful, and vitally affected interests?[47]

Today we are able to answer some of these questions[48] and, though we are inclined to argue that agencies are generally the dominant partners in agency-group relations, we know that those relations are important, intimate, and mutually supportive.[49] We also have increasing evidence that many groups have been initiated, or at least substantially encouraged, by government bodies. This tendency was first formally recorded by H.H. Hannam in 1953 when he described how Clifford Clark encouraged his efforts to establish the Canadian Federation of Agriculture,[50] but it has been remarked since in fields as diverse as family planning and fishing, economic development and construction.[51]

None of this proves that government agencies and their related interest groups have been busily promoting one another in order to compete in the more complex policy environment created by changes in cabinet structure. But it is consistent with such an interpretation. So is the proliferation of interest groups which has been remarked upon in recent years and the tendency for interest-group politics to be played in a more public fashion than used to be the case. It is enough to encourage us to play with the idea that Canada has developed her own kind of pluralism; bureaucratic pluralism, a process born of the atrophication of party policy-making and competition between agencies over jurisdiction and resources. Although we cannot develop the theme of bureaucratic pluralism here,[52] we should note that it has many of the properties of interest group liberalism but in a form exacerbated by the application of parliamentary cabinet government and of administrative secrecy.

CANADA AND THE SPECIAL-INTEREST STATE

Does all of this make Canada a special-interest state? Even if the analysis just presented is totally correct – and we reiterate that it is speculative – there is no conclusive evidence that this country's policy communication system is so arranged that interests are identified and drawn into communication with government solely through their specialized contact with functionally oriented arms of government rather than through their geographic or spatial affiliations. The developments we have referred to are suggestive, however, as are the various forays into a Canadian form of corporatism that have occurred in recent years.[53] On balance, Canada is not a special-interest state, but in this country, as in many industrialized countries, the mechanisms of special-interest communications are increasingly pre-eminent in public debate.

D.V. Smiley seems to concur in this view. In a short but provocative essay on 'Territorialism and Canadian Political Institutions' which appeared in 1977, he argues that:

> Canada cannot effectively be governed unless Ottawa is the focus of significant popular identifications and the political arena in which the interests of powerful groups are resolved. Yet territorialism is the dominant circumstance of our political life. The institutional imperative then is to so modify our political structures as to secure the more effective channelling of territorially-demarcated attitudes and interests through the central government rather than the provinces alone.[54]

So far the federal government has failed to create territorially responsive institutions at the federal level, and the country has not responded to 'such developments as the increasingly narrow specialization of occupational and other interests and the improvements in transportation and communication' by creating politically salient associations on national axes. The forces of federalism have failed to co-opt the forces of regionalism. The pull of territorialism, represented by the provincial governments, has remained unexpectedly prominent.

Why does regionalism prevail in this way? Perhaps because specialization and special interest cannot dominate unless a national consensus pervades the political community. That is, no community can on an extended basis delegate public policy-making to functionally defined policy communities unless there is general understanding and agreement about the basic meaning and direction of the community. To do otherwise is to indulge in the excesses of pluralism that

Lowi denounces. Canada, as our constitutional debates persistently demonstrate, lacks that consensus, for cultural and economic reasons that are tied to the country's geography as well as her history.

One of the more significant and interesting of these constraints on consensus is the fact that the dominant economic mode of certain parts of the country is quite different from that which prevails elsewhere. Thus, as we have noted, the market economy, though identifiable in many parts of Canada, is predominant in the Atlantic region, including eastern Quebec. The market economy, as Galbraith demonstrates, does not possess the kind of differentiation that makes the special interest state desirable, or even possible. Most importantly, it lacks a technostructure. This region, then, is not amenable to the special interest state. As long as such a fundamental divergence of economic structure persists in the country and as long as the traditional economy retains some political strength, it is unlikely that a consensus will emerge that will inaugurate the special-interest state. Thus the tension between space and function, between party and administration, to which we referred earlier is strong enough to impede the full flourishing of the special-interest state in Canada.

Another more elusive, but more important, impediment is the fact that the domination of a functional approach to policy communication lacks the legitimacy of the party system with its roots in representative government. As long as cabinet members retain a sufficient sense of their constituency ties to remember that fact and as long as career officials pay homage to it, special-interest communications cannot consistently dominate policy-making.

These constraints, however, are a thin bulwark against the growing pressure of specialization. Nationally and internationally fundamental economic forces push Canada towards the planning system. Auto-pacts, revisions in the General Agreement on Tariffs and Trade, growing demands for a 'national industrial strategy': all these signal the decline of the market economy and with it the political system that is rooted in localism. The prospects for development that have recently made their presence felt in Atlantic Canada have set off tremors – increasing evidence of planning system firms in the fishery, for example – that hint that the dominant characteristics of the region's economy may soon change. If the Atlantic region, the last bulwark of traditional party politics, does experience such a change, it might not be long before the political and administrative effects make themselves felt in the creation of compatible systems of policy communication. The special-interest state could then become a reality in Canada.

Perhaps it is necessary and desirable that Canada become a special-interest state. Failure to do so may be a fundamental factor in the present malaise which keeps this country, like others, from overcoming the economic problems that have prevailed for most of the last decade. However necessary and desirable such changes may be from an economic perspective, though, the special-interest state will never be truly satisfactory in Canada, or elsewhere, unless it comes to terms with the spatial orientation of the country's parliamentary institutions. This is a problem of political legitimacy which, if it is not resolved, will bring to pass the brooding, concluding sentence of *The Canadian Public Service*:

> A responsive bureaucracy, operating in a context where other components of the political system show no disposition to change, may well turn on its head the master-to-servant relationship which has been the essence of responsible government and the liberal democratic state.

1 Fritz Morstein Marx, *The Administrative State* (Chicago: University of Chicago Press, 1957), p. 2

2 As for example Friedrich A. Hayek, *The Road to Serfdom* (Chicago: University of Chicago Press, 1944)

3 See W.A.W. Neilson and J.C. MacPherson, *The Legislative Process in Canada* (Toronto: Butterworth, 1978) for a recent discussion of these problems in the Canadian context.

4 See Stephen Clarkson, 'Policy and Participation: The Dilemmas of Democratization of the Liberal's Policy Making Process,' paper, CPSA 1971, mimeo

5 Roger Williams, *Politics and Technology* (London: Macmillan, 1971), p. 12

6 Quoted in A.P. Pross, 'The Development of a Forest Policy: A Study of the Ontario Department of Lands and Forests,' unpublished PHD thesis, University of Toronto, 1967), pp. 172-3

7 Ibid., quoting M.G. Lofquist to F.H. Keefer, 9 Feb. 1926, Ferguson Papers, Ontario Archives. On the other hand a letter from the deputy minister of Lands and Forests, W.C. Cain, to several provincial MLA's illustrates both the effects of centralization and the efforts that were made to preserve the illusion

of local influence: 'We are considering now making certain additions to our Provincial Forests and creating an occasional new one, and inasmuch as a part of a suggested Provincial Forest lies within your constituency I am writing to you in order that you may understand it and take whatever credit is necessary for the addition if and when the occasion arises.' Cain to W.L. Miller, MPP Bruce Mines, 9 Jan. 1939, Ontario Department of Lands and Forests, Central Files, #119191 – Provincial Forests.

8 R.S. Lambert with A.P. Pross, *Renewing Nature's Wealth: A Centennial History of the Public Management of Lands, Forests and Wildlife in Ontario, 1763-1967* (Toronto: Copp Clark, 1967), p. 370

9 Ibid., p. 371

10 Ibid., p. 373

11 Herbert Kaufman, *The Forest Ranger: A Study in Administrative Behavior* (Baltimore: Johns Hopkins Press, 1960)

12 J.K. Galbraith, *The New Industrial State* (New York: Mentor, 1971), p. 293

13 Ibid., p. 300

14 Ibid., p. 301

15 Ibid., p. 304

16 R.M. Dawson and N. Ward, *The Government of Canada*, 5th ed. (Toronto: University of Toronto Press, 1970), p. 473

17 *Politics and Technology*, pp. 28-9, from *The Times* 27 May 1968

18 *The Administrative State*, p. 2

19 *Morality and Administration in Democratic Government* (New York: Greenwood, 1969), p. 158

20 A. Paul Pross, 'Pressure Groups: Adaptive Instruments of Political Communication,' in Pross, ed, *Pressure Group Behaviour in Canadian Politics* (Toronto: McGraw-Hill, 1975), pp. 1-27

21 See S.E. Finer, *Anonymous Empire* (London: Pall Mall, 1966), p. 30.

22 See J.J. Richardson and A.G. Jordan, *Governing under Pressure* (Oxford: Martin Robertson, 1979), p. 54, and Randall B. Ripley and Grace A. Franklin, *Congress, the Bureaucracy and Public Policy* (Homewood, Ill.: Dorsey, 1976).

23 A. Paul Pross, *Duality and Public Policy: A Conceptual Framework for Analyzing the Policy System of Atlantic Canada* (Halifax: Dalhousie Institute of Public Affairs, 1980), chap. 5

24 Theodore J. Lowi, *The End of Liberalism* (New York: Norton, 1979)

25 *Governing under Pressure*, p. 195

26 John E. Sinclair, *Interest Groups in America* (Morristown, NJ: General Leaning Press, 1975), p. 35

27 Or, as Lowi characterizes interest-group liberalism: 'Privileges in the form of money or license or underwriting are granted to established interests, largely in

order to keep them established, and largely done in the name of maintaining public order and avoiding disequilibrium. The state grows, but the opportunities for sponsorship and privilege grow proportionately. Power goes up, but in the form of personal plunder rather than public choice. It would not be accurate to evaluate this model as 'socialism for the rich and capitalism for the poor,' because many thousands of low-income persons and groups have profited from the system. The more accurate characterization might be socialism for the organized, capitalism for the unorganized.' *The End of Liberalism*, pp. 278-9

28 See E.E. Schattschneider, 'The Scope and Bias of the Pressure System,' in Randal B. Ripley, ed., *Public Policies and Their Politics* (New York: Norton, 1966), pp. 14-26.

29 Sir George Murray, 'Report on the Organization of the Public Service of Canada,' House of Commons, *Sessional Papers*, 1912, no. 57a, p. 7, quoted in J.E. Hodgetts, *The Canadian Public Service* (Toronto: University of Toronto Press, 1973), p. 51

30 See Hodgetts, *The Canadian Public Service*, chap. 11

31 W.L.M. King to T.A. Low, 1 Sept. 1923, King Papers, Public Archives of Canada, vol. 89, no. 75739. Quoted in part in O. Mary Hill, *Canada's Salesman to the World* (Montreal: McGill-Queen's, 1977), p. 166

32 'The Bureaucratic Elite and Policy Formation,' in W.D.K. Kernaghan, ed., *Bureaucracy in Canadian Government* (Toronto: Methuen, 1969), p. 86

33 'The Civil Service and Policy Formation,' *Canadian Journal of Economics and Political Science*, vol. 23, no. 4 (1957), p. 468

34 Ibid., p. 469

35 As evidenced by the publication in 1965 of John Porter's study of Canadian elites, *The Vertical Mosaic* (Toronto: University of Toronto Press, 1965)

36 J.E. Hodgetts, 'Challenge and Response: A Retrospective View of the Public Service of Canada,' *Canadian Public Administration*, vol. 7, no. 4 (1964), pp. 409-21. More recent research, such as that at present being carried out by Professor's William Coleman and Henry Jacek at McMaster University suggests that the process has a very long history in this country.

37 J.E. Hodgetts, William McCloskey, Reginald Whitaker, and V. Seymour Wilson, *The Biography of an Institution* (Montreal: McGill-Queen's University Press, 1972), p. 473

38 Nelson Polsby, 'Preface,' in L.J. Sharpe, ed., *Decentralist Trends in Western Democracies* (London: Sage, 1979), p. 5

39 *The Forest Ranger*

40 See William MacLeod, *Water Management in the Canadian North* (Ottawa: Canadian Arctic Resources Committee, 1977)

41 See Pross, *Duality and Public Policy*, chap. VI.

42 In *The New Industrial State*

43 Canada, Royal Commission on Government Organization, *Report* (Ottawa, 1962), vol. V – 24-4-52

44 Mitchell Sharp, 'Decision-Making in the Federal Cabinet,' *Canadian Public Administration*, vol. 19, no. 1 (1976), p. 3

45 Ibid., p. 5

46 Ibid., p. 6

47 'The Civil Service and Policy Formation,' pp. 475-6

48 For example, in David Kwavnick, *Organized Labour and Pressure Politics* (Montreal: McGill-Queen's University Press, 1972)

49 See Pross, 'Pressure Groups: Adaptive Instruments,' and Fred Thompson and W.T. Stanbury, *The Political Economy of Interest Groups in the Legislative Process in Canada* (Montreal: Institute for Research on Public Policy, occasional paper no. 9, 1979).

50 'The Interest Group and Its Activities,' Institute of Public Administration of Canada, *Proceedings of the Fifth Annual Conference* (Toronto, 1953), p. 173

51 See, respectively, Marc Lalonde, Minister of National Health and Welfare, House of Commons, *Debates*, 20 June 1975, p. 6954 (daily ed.); R.D.S. Macdonald, 'Inshore Fishing Interests on the Atlantic Coast: Their Response to Extended Jurisdiction by Canada,' *Marine Policy* (July 1979), pp. 171-89; Richard D. French, *How Ottawa Decides: Planning and Industrial Policy-Making, 1968-1980* (Toronto: Canadian Institute for Economic Policy, 1980), esp. pp. 122-5; and N.J. Lawrie, 'The Canadian Construction Association: An Interest Group and Its Environment' (unpub. PHD dissertation, University of Toronto, 1976), esp. p. 219.

52 A preliminary discussion is found in Pross, *Duality and Public Policy*.

53 See Canada, Department of Finance, *The Way Ahead: A Framework for Discussion* (Ottawa, 1976), and Leo Panitch, 'The Development of Corporatism in Liberal Democracies,' *Comparative Political Studies*, vol. 10, no. 1 (1977), pp. 61-90.

54 In *Canadian Public Policy*, vol. III, no. 4 (1977), p. 456

J.R. MALLORY

Curtailing 'Divine Right': The Control of Delegated Legislation in Canada

'It is all too easy to assume that the means employed to achieve the ends of policy are of little consequence and a mere matter of administrative convenience. This is a criticism which can be directed not only at well intentioned and hard pressed servants of the Crown but also at commentators and academic political scientists who find the policy content or ends of subordinate law fascinating and the propriety of the means used to achieve those ends of little consequence.'[1] These words are too true for comfort. Policy is more interesting than process, and political scientists for a generation have turned away from what was believed to be the empty formalism of the past in search of the underlying reality of the political process.

During most of the long and distinguished career of J.E. Hodgetts, the study of the regulatory process was not a subject which engaged the attention of many students of public administration. Perhaps one of the reasons was that the 'management' orientation was easier to fit into modern social science with its emphasis on looking at the organs of government as behavioural phenomena. As a result, the old 'progressive' value-oriented study of civil service reform – which detailed with uncritical and loving care the long patient struggle to exorcise the devil of patronage from civil service recruitment and administration – was gradually displaced by concern with recruitment, socialization, and even representativeness as elements in bureaucratic behaviour. The old questions were dismissed as too formal and superficial, and were replaced by questions which were thought to be more rigorous and intellectually satisfying. In short the study of public administration was becoming a social science.

The role of legal scholarship, with its concern with legal norms and institutional forms, appeared to have even less that was useful to contribute to the study of the administrative process. While in the United States legal scholarship was largely responsible for major institutional reform, culminating in the Administrative Procedure Act of 1946, such procedural rationalization and reform did not happen in Canada. Even twenty years ago there was little scholarly interest in the problem. The sole book by a Canadian, John Kersell's *Parliamentary Supervision of Delegated Legislation*, was the outcome of post-graduate study at the University of London and was published in England.

Moreover, there was a broad liberal-left consensus in the first post-war decade which was led by the academics, businessmen, and politicians who had worked together in Ottawa during the war and who shared a common vision of a greatly expanded role for the state in enhancing the quality of life for us all. To them parliamentary criticism of 'order-in-council government' seemed like the carping of a few reactionaries, particularly when Arnold Heeney was to point out that less than 5 per cent of the approximately ten thousand orders-in-council passed each year during the war and immediate post-war period could be described as of a legislative character.[2] It must have been disconcerting to find J.A. Corry among those critics when his thoughtful and disturbing 'Arms and the Man' appeared in the *Queen's Quarterly* in 1955. It seemed that he was one of the few old-fashioned liberals left who worried about the survival of such almost-forgotten concepts as the rule of law. At that time concern about the rule of law was largely focused on the pursuit of a Bill of Rights and one has the impression that the strongest advocates in the Canadian Bar Association were tax lawyers rather than conscientious constitutionalists and civil libertarians.[3]

Only in the last few years has there developed a new concern over the use and abuse of government and bureaucratic power. This has led some political scientists to a renewed examination of the ambiguities of responsible government. At the same time the economists, who in the past had found it convenient to abstract the political environment from their models, had begun to turn their attention to the costs of regulation, which in Canada are compounded by the existence in a federal system of a great deal of overlapping jurisdiction. A recent remit by the Federal-Provincial First Ministers' Conference to the Economic Council of Canada has stimulated a considerable number of economists, lawyers, and political scientists in the universities to turn their research interests towards a more intensive study of the regulatory process.[4]

Hoping no doubt to take advantage of the new interest by ministers and researchers in the problem, the Joint Parliamentary Committee on Statutory Instruments has produced its long-awaited report on improvements in the process, and the Commons itself has set up a Task Force on Regulatory Reform. Late in 1979 the Clark government introduced its proposals for parliamentary reform which dealt in part with measures to increase the effectiveness of parliamentary scrutiny over the regulatory process. Meanwhile, in response to the growing desire to increase public participation in the process of regulation a number of regulatory agencies have adopted the practice of public hearings in advance of the promulgation of regulations, while the Treasury Board has enjoined departments to increase and formalize consultative procedures with public interest and affected groups in advance of making substantive regulations.

Over seventy years ago Lawrence Lowell could describe cabinet government as 'autocratic,' but an autocracy controlled by parliamentary criticism, public opinion, and the ultimate sanction of a general election.[5] In fact, nowadays we know that the publicity of which he spoke is limited, the criticism as a result often ineffective, and votes of confidence when a government has a majority are nearly an empty ritual.

The tremendous growth in the demands on the state to intervene to regulate the community in the interests of the health, safety, and convenience of the public and to provide a wide range of public goods has greatly exceeded the capacity of legislatures to specify the terms on which this intervention is to take place. It was both inevitable and sensible that the legislature should confer wide discretionary powers on the executive and its agencies to make the rules under which they were to perform these functions. In a world of complex and rapidly changing technology it is unavoidable that we must depend upon an expert agency to determine from time to time the degree of permissible hazard in substances in common use or the rules for the safe operation of common carriers.

The consequence of parliamentary delegation of power to make rules has meant in fact that executive agencies frequently have very wide discretionary powers to make policy. However, the policy was never discussed publicly and the powers conferred were sometimes breathtakingly wide. Reaction against this after the First World War led in the United Kingdom to the appointment of a Committee on Ministers' Powers, which found that in some cases ministers even had the power to amend existing statutes and levy taxes by executive order.[6] Canadian legislatures have been similarly generous in giving away historic and cherished rights of Parliament to this twentieth-century reincarnation of the 'prerogative.' Before the Second World War there was not even a general requirement in Ottawa that orders-in-council be published or even tabled in Parliament. The immense volume of wartime regulation made it desirable that most regulations dealing with the war be published and tabled, and the practice, once established, was continued after the war.

However useful publication may have been as a means of communication with the public, it was otherwise, as Brooke Claxton pointed out in the Throne Speech debate in 1943, 'an empty form.' He urged that such orders be referred to a committee of the House, which should scrutinize them as to both form and content.[7] Nothing came of this, which was perhaps not surprising in the war years. Claxton himself was soon to attain office, and seems not to have pursued the matter further. In any event scrutiny as to form and to content are very different matters, requiring a different mix of skills, knowledge, and staff support. Scrutiny which goes to the merit (or policy involved) of a regulation is indeed part of the role of Parliament. It is normally exercised during the debate on a bill, but if the bill is of a wide enabling nature that debate may fail to raise important policy issues. To debate the merits of subordinate legislation has the further disadvantage of discussion after the event – of Parliament appearing to go back on what it has already approved. It will be a reprise of what the members expert in the issue have already said.

The other kind of scrutiny goes not to merit but to form. This is more important than it sounds. It touches the question of whether there was legal authority to make the regulation in the first place, and whether it makes unforeseen and abusive use of that power. It is the only public and authoritative forum, except for a time-consuming and expensive resort to the courts, in which such issues can be raised. Like the first form of scrutiny, it suffers from being after the event, but it is far easier in practice to secure the modification of a defective order than to secure a reversal of policy.

The end of the war was a time of considerable public disenchantment with what was seen as excessive government regulation. At that time the Conservative opposition in the House made much of 'order-in-council government.' Prompted by a desire to disarm this criticism, Louis St Laurent introduced a Regulation bill in 1950 which provided for the systematic publication and tabling of all orders and regulations having legislative effect. Under the act, the Privy Council Office was required to scrutinize such regulations to achieve greater clarity and uniformity of form. This scrutiny seems to have been fairly perfunctory. Even less successful was the subsequent provision in the Diefenbaker Bill of Rights which required the Minister of Justice to examine all such orders to ensure their conformity with the Bill of Rights.

Parliamentary scrutiny of regulations had been rejected by St Laurent on the ground that most of them were made by the Governor-in-Council rather than by individual ministers. It is difficult to see how this reply met the point. Even if the Special Committee of Council did scrutinize the enormous bulk of orders on behalf of the cabinet, such an exercise is not the same as public scrutiny by a body distanced from the executive and informed by expert study. There were a few parliamentarians who did not let the issue die, and their efforts were reinforced by a handful of academics. Nevertheless, nothing happened for nearly fifteen years.

In 1964, the Special Commons Committee on Procedure and Organization, in its Fifteenth Report, recommended the establishment of a standing committee on delegated legislation which would report abuses of regulatory power to the House, but whose terms of reference should exclude 'the merits of or the policy behind delegated legislation.' That report was to be the basis of sweeping reforms in House and committee procedure, but scrutiny was apparently too delicate a matter, for in 1968 the House set up another special committee to review it again. This committee was able to report in less than a year.[8] The chairman was Mark MacGuigan, a former professor of law, and the committee heard evidence from a number of academic witnesses.

The committee, as I recall, was trying to think through the obvious questions. Would a scrutiny committee, under our system of responsible government, be given enough independence to do its job? Should it look at merit, or just form, and was it possible to disentangle the two in the case – for example – of an unusually wide and unforeseen use of delegated power? Would the committee have expert staff, and if so of what kind? I remember it being argued that such a staff job would be something of a blind alley for a competent lawyer, and that better staffing could be arranged by the simple loan of people from the Department of Justice. How such poachers, with career ambitions to return to higher things in the department, would make good gamekeepers was never explained.

In its report the MacGuigan committee recommended that there should be a small committee of the House to which all regulations should stand permanently referred, and that its impartiality should be demonstrated by some rotation among the parties in the chairmanship. The committee should have 'adequate staff,' and its scrutiny should be based on six criteria, which were: whether regulations were within the terms of the enabling statute; made unusual or unexpected use of the power conferred; trespassed unduly on individual rights and liberties; were in compliance with the Regulations Act with regard to publication, tabling, etc.; purported to come into force before transmission to the Clerk of the Privy Council or unjustly failed to provide that they should not come into force until published; and that for any special reason their form or purport required elucidation. The committee should have the power itself to refer regulations to another standing committee (in order to secure a review of 'merit'). A regulation could be contested in the House by a resolution asking the government for reconsideration, unless there already existed procedures (under a few statutes) for affirmative or negative resolutions.

To this report the government responded on 16 July 1970. The Leader of the House announced that a new Statutory Instruments Act would be introduced to replace the Regulations Act; a cabinet directive would be issued to tighten internal procedures and Standing Orders would be amended to provide for a scrutiny committee. To this committee, he said, 'All regulations with the single exception of regulations the disclosure of which would be injurious to international relations, national defence, security or federal-provincial relations, will stand permanently referred.'[9]

On 25 January 1971, the second reading of the Statutory Instruments Bill was moved by the Minister of Justice. The bill, along with the tightened internal procedures imposed by cabinet directive, was 'an attempt to restore a measure of Parliamentary control over the executive and to redress the balance in the relationship between the individual and the state.'[10] While the government could not accept all of the committee's recommendations, it accepted the obligation to protect the public from the 'improper and unusual' exercise of power which had been delegated by Parliament. The bill reiterated the obligation on the Clerk of the Privy Council and the Minister of Justice to scrutinize instruments in advance, perhaps to indicate that these responsibilities would be carried out in a less perfunctory manner.

The Minister resisted attempts by the opposition to insert some means by which an offending order could be amended or revoked, since this was the responsibility of the executive, which in turn was accountable to Parliament. An alert scrutiny committee would greatly strengthen the hand of the minister and deputy minister of Justice in policing regulating departments and agencies. Earlier in the debate he had observed, 'I am sure the only reason the Bill is in its present form is the fact that some of my colleagues and some of the departments have not fully appreciated what is in the Bill.'[11] The Minister however was adamant in resisting efforts to narrow the effects of section 27 of the bill, which exempted regulations which in the opinion of the Governor-in-Council should not be disclosed 'in the interests of international relations, national defence or security or federal-provincial relations.' Apart from the wideness and vagueness of the exemption, the bill departed from the old Regulations Act in making no provision that the fact of exemption would itself be disclosed, so the committee would not know of the existence of such regulations.

In the end the government decided that the most appropriate form of committee would be a Joint Standing Committee on Regulations and Other Statutory Instruments, and Standing Orders were accordingly amended on 14 October 1971. The act came into force by proclamation on 1 January 1972, and the committee was constituted later in that year.

What has the committee accomplished? As it turned out its effectiveness was considerably strengthened by two things. In the first place the committee was able to provide itself with a small but effective staff, and the second was a fortunate choice in the joint chairman on the Senate side, Eugene Forsey. Senator Forsey had long been capable of scourging his academic colleagues in the scholarly journals for inaccuracy, sloppy wording, and carelessness. His phenomenal memory and unmatched knowledge of parliamentary lore together with his enormous capacity for work made him the ideal chairman for the committee. The work of the committee, which consisted of the perusal of an enormous mass of detailed regulations emanating from scores of departments and agencies was not an activity calculated to give much pleasure. It took a great deal of time and it was, generally speaking, politically unrewarding. It was not an activity likely to commend itself to members of the House, already overburdened with committee work of a politically more useful sort. Attendance by MPs tended therefore to be somewhat thin, and early in its life the committee was forced to request that its quorum be reduced to a minimum. It now stands at seven for formal business such as resolutions and four for receiving evidence, providing that both Houses are represented.

A further handicap to the effectiveness of the committee is that there is widespread ignorance among the public – and even among some MPs – that the committee exists at all. This is partly because it is not concerned with policy, which is what political parties take seriously, but about constitutional values which only rarely arouse public interest. Of course, for all that its terms of reference are designed to confine its mandate to a consideration of 'form' rather than 'merit,' it cannot avoid being confronted by second-order policy issues when it comes across unforeseen and unexpected uses of loosely defined regulatory powers. There will need to be improvements in the machinery of scrutiny if this ambiguity is to be cleared up.

In practice, what the committee has done is engage in a series of battles with departments and agencies which persist in drafting regulations which are sloppy, lacking in apparent statutory authority, or are in other ways defective. It is not unusual for an agency to state that it is armed with an opinion from the Department of Justice that it is acting legally, and then invoke a long constitutional tradition by refusing to disclose this opinion to the committee. One gets the impression that the Department of Justice itself has been one of the least co-operative agencies involved. So much for Mr Turner's confident assurance that the two would work in harmony.

One of the expectations at the time when the new scrutiny machinery was put in place was that the reports of the committee would highlight particularly offensive orders and thus lead to the attendant publicity of a debate in one House or the other. In fact, the reports of the committee are rarely debated at all in the Commons, but somewhat more often in the Senate. Why has this happened? As far as the House is concerned, part of the answer lies in the limited opportunities which exist under Standing Orders. Both Question Time and Private Members' Time are used to focus on current political and policy issues, and have not been used to deal with regulations. The best hope, which I recall being considered at the hearings of the MacGuigan committee, was that such matters could be raised on an Allotted Day. This hope was vain. There may well be too many Allotted Days, and it sometimes appears that opposition parties have great difficulty in finding something to do with them. Invariably, however, they are used for current major policy issues as seen by the party leaders and caucuses, and never to deal with statutory instruments.

An improvement in the opportunities to consider statutory instruments would have been provided by the parliamentary reform package which the Clark government tabled in the House on 23 November 1979, but that government fell before these proposals could be given serious consideration even in committee. The Conservatives, having been out of office for nearly twenty years, were still thinking of parliamentary reform in the light of their experience on the other side of the House. A number of their proposals appeared to widen the opportunities for private members, and several of them would have greatly increased opportunities for the House to deal with regulations.[12]

Among these proposals was a provision that the government be required to table a response to all committee reports within twenty-one sitting days. In addition a motion to concur in a committee's report could be moved by any member and taken either under private members' business or on an Allotted Day or (a pious hope) on government time. Standing Orders were to be revised to allow both affirmative and negative resolutions on delegated legislation. This proposal was not spelled out, and to be effective it would have needed something like an amendment to the Statutory Instruments Act imposing the requirement that certain orders would come into effect only after an affirmative resolution, or that they could be negated in the same manner. Needless to say, governments would not be likely to permit their orders to be put at risk in this way, but the attendant publicity might be a useful deterrent. One last proposal would have been particularly useful. It provided that the regulation clauses of bills which are being considered in committee be simultaneously referred to the Standing Committee on Statutory Instruments for its observations.

One of the most disheartening parts of the Statutory Instruments Committee's work (which remains unavoidable) is that it is dealing with regulations under existing legislation. The problem as often as not is with the enabling statute rather than the regulation itself, since the power delegated may be both wide and ill-defined. Everyone knows that it is extremely difficult to get an act of Parliament amended. The main reason for this is that the parliamentary timetable is so heavily loaded that any House Leader is hard put to find time for anything but major legislation and a limited number of routine and uncontroversial bills. As a result even a minor amendment to an old act will sometimes take years to achieve. Meanwhile, regulations which offend the criteria of the committee will continue to come out.

It is very much easier to catch a defect in a bill before it is passed, and the process of screening bills while they are in the legislative mill – a practice suggested as far back as the MacGuigan committee – has much to commend it. On this proposal there are grounds for hope. On 20 November 1980, the Commons resolved to refer three clauses of the Canada Post Corporation Bill – already at the committee stage – to the Standing Joint Committee on Regulations and Other Statutory Instruments.[13] Of all the government agencies, one of the most difficult that the committee had had to deal with had been the Post Office. Some of this conflict lingered in the parliamentary memory, which is perhaps why the new Post Office bill was the first to be singled out. Let us hope that it is not the last.

On 17 July 1980, the joint committee presented a lengthy report to both Houses recommending clarification and improvement of procedures covering all aspects of the regulatory process, under a reference initially laid on it in the Thirtieth Parliament, and reiterated during the Thirty-first, 'to conduct a comprehensive study of the means by which Parliament can better oversee the government regulatory process.'[14] The report began by recalling the words of the British Committee on Ministers' Powers of 1932 that the delegation of wide powers by Parliament to the executive 'should not lead to a lessening of the fairness, participation and procedural safeguards in law making which now attend the passing of statutes, but not the making of subordinate legislation by Parliament's delegates ... Delegated law making is far too widespread a practice to be without democratic participation, procedural safeguards and parliamentary accountability.'

Clearly the committee had the sense that at last its own concern with procedure could be linked to more recent public and governmental interest in the regulatory process. They noted that the growing interest in 'regulatory reform' seemed to be mainly concerned with the impact of regulation on the public sector and with the costs of regulation generally on the economy. The encouragement of such research by the Economic Council of Canada and such private groups as the Institute for Research on Public Policy had stimulated mission-oriented research by a number of scholars in law and the social sciences. This was bound to create a more receptive atmosphere for the committee's recommendations. As they point out, 'Your Committee welcomes the scrutiny of the worth, effectiveness and cost of government regulation and sees it as complementary to its own work which concerns subordinate legislation only, the protection of the rights and liberties of the subject and the reassertion of parliamentary sovereignty.'

The report goes on with flowing rhetoric to emphasize the theme of liberty. 'What future can there be,' it asks, 'for individual liberty, for the rights of minorities and for democratic and participatory traditions if the highest end of government is its own ease, the exercise of power without responsibility?' Notwithstanding the exigencies of the parliamentary timetable government must be contained by 'the stern restraint of the rule of law, and the control of arbitrary if well meaning acts' through greater parliamentary vigilance. This could be secured by a Standing Joint Committee on Regulatory Review (which would replace the present committee) which would have the duty of directing Parliament's attention to grants of subordinate law-making power through the examination of bills after second reading. Meanwhile the deficiencies of past statutes could be rectified by 'amending Bills introduced in the Senate upon the recommendation of the Regulatory Review Committee and subject to all-party agreement.' Hard-won liberties which have been secured over centuries of conflict require constant vigilance to preserve. 'That is why parliamentary scrutiny committees on delegated legislation have traditionally concerned themselves with the means of effecting policies as set down and not with the policy ends themselves.'

Nevertheless, policy scrutiny of subordinate legislation is of equal importance. Parliamentary scrutiny itself is hardly sufficient, since it is liable to be after the event or cursory because of the stern demands of parliamentary time. Under present arrangements committee scrutiny of merits of subordinate legislation is unlikely to be effective partly because of the frequent changes in committee personnel and partly because of inadequate committee staff. Were these defects remedied it would be desirable to amend Standing Orders to enable such scrutiny either on a standing committee's own motion or on reference from the Regulatory Review Committee. There were dangers in this which must be kept in mind. 'Committees conducting such reviews would need to guard against the danger of their scrutiny of policy being too much influenced by their expert staff who might be simply endeavoring to have their own personal judgments substituted for those of servants of the Crown to whom Parliament had originally delegated subordinate law making authority.'

Under existing procedures the initial prior scrutiny of draft regulations is by the department or agency's own legal advisers. It may well be that as a consequence of this many objectionable, offensive, or *ultra vires* regulations are weeded out, but it is difficult for a legal adviser to prevent a department from such a course if the department is in a determined mood. Furthermore, 'the effectiveness of the internal scrutiny of the Legal Advisers is severely hampered because both they and the departmental legal officers are bound by the very traditions of drafting and received legal opinions of the Department of Justice which your Committee has found to be among the chief causes of objectionable provisions in regulations.' Since the committee's efforts to rectify matters are often unsuccessful for this reason, it follows that a stronger measure of parliamentary control involving procedures for annulment is necessary so that all regulations should be subject to being disallowed by a resolution of either House, unless the regulation is already subject to parliamentary affirmation. While it should be noted that such a resolution, if moved, is likely to be defeated when a government has a majority, they suggest an ancillary procedure which might help matters. What they recommend is, that if such a resolution is moved, it must be debated and voted on within a fixed number of days.

Clearly the committee has now learned to anticipate a wide variety of ruses which governments can use to escape the scrutiny of Parliament. They note that many regulations are made to give effect to policies not embodied in any statute and which Parliament has never considered or even had the opportunity to consider because of the 'Canadian habit of using statutes and Votes in Appropriation Acts merely as vehicles for the conferring of powers on the executive.' There should be a new Subordinate Legislation Act which not only provides for disallowance procedures but also for a restoration of the tabling and laying of subordinate legislation which had been discontinued by the repeal of the Regulations Act.

Hard on the release of the joint committee's report a House of Commons 'task force' issued a discussion paper on regulatory reform in August 1980. This document raised questions rather than provided answers and dealt with the following matters: the need for greater consultation when regulatory action is contemplated; the question of funding and/or support for public interest groups wishing to intervene in such consultations; the role of Parliament in scrutinizing the form and merit of regulations and the need for a Freedom of Information Act to improve public access to regulations. The committee, which reported in December 1980, held twenty-seven meetings between 22 July and 6 October and 'received briefs from a variety of public and private corporations as well as interested individuals.'[15] Evidently one of the major concerns of the task force was in the participatory aspects of the regulatory process.

The Joint Committee on Statutory Instruments had also set much store on the development of prior notification and consultative procedures, such as those now contained in the United States Administrative Procedure Act. They said, 'More effective than any scheme of parliamentary scrutiny of the policy of a proposed subordinate law that can now be devised is an obligation to make the proposed law public, to state the reasons for its making and to consider representations from the public, whether individuals or groups.' They noted that both the Canadian Transport Commission and the Canadian Radio-Television and Telecommunications Commission have developed the habit of holding hearings to assist them in their rule-making functions. Similarly the Economic Council of Canada had recommended a sixty-day 'notice and comment' procedure for regulations which have significant implications in terms of cost or income distribution and are susceptible to cost-benefit analysis.[16] The joint committee would go further. 'The important objective is to allow the reasons for and the policy of all subordinate legislation to be subject to the light of public scrutiny.' As things stand, there is a complete lack of 'any avowal of the policy being effected by subordinate legislation and any opportunity to comment on or contribute to it.' They note with approval that the Treasury Board has now included requirements for 'Socio-economic Impact Analysis covering regulations relating to health, safety or fairness,' a policy in effect since 1 August 1976.[17]

The creation of consultative machinery of this kind no doubt reflects two dominant concerns. There is in the first place the growing concern of the public with the environmental impact of a wide range of economic activities, from simple pollution to the effects of the urgent search for new energy sources. The second flows from the growing scepticism about the growth of the regulatory process, impelling governments to demonstrate the need for control, 'rather than leaving industry to show that their activities were not damaging to the environment.'[18] It does, however, add an important element of discipline to the regulatory process, since the regulated industry must compete in many cases in international markets. Undoubtedly there are interesting prospects of informed debate in the continuing tension between environmental issues and the development of industrial strategy in both the Clean Air Act (1971) and the Environmental Contaminants Act (1975). In resolving these issues there are three sides that now have an opportunity to come together, either under the consultative procedure prescribed for the promulgation of emission standards under the Clean Air Act or in consultative procedures outlined in the Environmental Contaminants Act. The three actors involved – the regulatory agency itself, the industry, and informed environmental groups – are expected to lead to optimal solutions to complex public policy issues in these fields. It can also be argued that the same sort of anxious consideration is equally valid if the issue is deregulation.[19]

In all this one should note that Parliament and public – except at a secondary level – are not involved. The business of the public and its representatives is to prescribe objectives. They are in no position to make judgments on the effectiveness of scientific standards or on how many jobs will be affected. These in the end have to be argued out by the people with the expert knowledge and access to data which probably only they understand. The broad decisions to make substantive changes in policy result from changing public perception and the exercise of will by Parliament. In that process, as we all know, opinion will be moved by the pressure of the vested interests involved, the sense of mission of the administrators in the bureaucracy, and the steady pressure of 'public interest' pressure groups.

Nevertheless, the more procedural concerns of such dedicated parliamentarians as the Joint Committee on Statutory Instruments are of equal importance in the continued successful operation of a civilized constitutional order. There must be some way of imposing effective control on the means as well as the ends of the policy process. Here, far too often, the ultimate control of the courts (long, expensive, and delayed) can have only marginal effect. What is needed is continuous oversight of the process. The danger is not so much that bureaucrats are ruthless and power-hungry; essentially they are overworked and dedicated men. But it is necessary to curb the narrow zeal of the specialist with the wider sensitivity of the politician who is the guardian not only of what the public will tolerate but of constitutional values themselves. Great economic vested interests have their own specialized and attentive public audience, and so do such groups as environmentalists and Canadian economic nationalists. There does not seem to be an attentive public for the issues as seen by such bodies as the Statutory Instruments Committee.

That may be why the reaction to the report of the committee has been so muted. Had the report appeared as a restricted document, it would surely have been leaked and made much of by the press. As it was the press hardly noticed it, and it has attracted little attention in the journals devoted to public policy and administration. While both the Economic Council of Canada and the Institute for Research on Public Policy have published a number of working papers and special studies, these are largely focused on the economics of the 'deregulation debate.' There does seem, nevertheless, to be a shifting of focus which will bring the subject closer to the mainstream of the study of public administration and perhaps some diminution in the now overwhelming interest in the economic, financial, and accounting aspects of control. Part of the problem is no doubt the fact that the joint committee and those who follow it are prone to use the outmoded rhetoric of legalistic constitutionalism which finds no echo in the hearts of those brought up on Keynes, Herbert Simon, and Gabriel Almond. Those who yearn to fine-tune either the economy or the political system do not find such simple-minded fundamentalism congenial.

So the Statutory Instruments Committee labours bravely on in almost total obscurity. It needs to be said again that, while its Commons members make a valuable contribution in spite of extraordinary demands on their time, the most valuable element in the committee is its Senate component. The senators not only have more time at their disposal, but are likely to be on the committee for longer periods of time and thus are more familiar with its work. Furthermore senators are likely to be more dispassionate and less partisan in their work on the committee.

However, the Senate in its present form does not seem to be a body which has inspired respect and affection beyond the confines of the chamber itself. It is commonly, and wrongly, thought to be made up of elderly folk engaged in no apparent activity who would be thought to be totally misguided if they sought to interfere with the will of the elected House of Commons. They are also perceived as a sinister interest doggedly whittling away at tax reform and justifying their numerous corporate directorships by assiduously protecting the interests of big business. The presence of rainmakers and other party backroom types among their number has not added lustre to their image. Nevertheless the general run of senators consists of experienced public men and women, many of them politicians of long experience and wide knowledge. Most of them work at their jobs and some of them work very hard. The trouble is that not many people know it.

Clearly the now numerous architects of constitutional reform in Canada perceive the Senate as the one institution which can be reformed without public outcry in its defence. Particularly at fault are those who believe that greater provincial participation in the organs of central government – intra-state federalism in a new guise – can be achieved by such a radical restructuring of the Senate that all of whatever virtue it had in the past will be lost forever. Perhaps the bluntest recommendation of all was in the Pépin-Robarts report, which asserted 'The Senate should be abolished and replaced by a new second chamber of the Canadian Parliament called the Council of the Federation.'[20] This council would be made up exclusively of 'Delegations representing the provincial governments and therefore acting under instruction' and its authority would cover executive and legislative actions of the federal government which affect provincial interests or jurisdiction. Whatever the merits of this proposal as a palliative to the ills of the Canadian federal system, there can be no doubt that it would completely destroy the role of the Senate as a revising and scrutinizing second chamber. The federal government's proposals of 1978 – the badly-drafted and unlamented bill C-60 – would at least have retained a rechristened Senate as a second legislative chamber, but probably at the cost of making it a more heavily political chamber with its activities refocused away from many of its most useful and least partisan present activities. The Quebec Liberal party's beige paper of 1980, like Pépin-Robarts, sought to create 'a special intergovernmental institution' rather than a legislative chamber.

This is not the place to debate the merits of these various proposals, none of which has a high probability of being realized. What so many of them have in common is the idea that the Senate can be dispensed with at no cost to the working of the constitutional system, and without political cost, since the Senate has few friends and no public support.

Some of these reformers recognize that abolishing the Senate would leave a yawning gap in the present capacity of Parliament as a whole to exercise adequate scrutiny of the executive. Pépin-Robarts, for example, recommended the addition of about sixty seats, filled on a basis of proportional representation, to the Commons.[21] This, it was thought, would enlarge the opportunities for committee work, since these new members would not have constituency responsibilities. The main role of the new members, however, would be 'to contribute to Canadian unity by reducing the sense of alienation and powerlessness which many Canadians feel towards their central institutions.' If that is the purpose, then it does not seem likely that the parties would use these precious seats for the sort of members who would be submerged in the largely invisible and politically unrewarding work of committees.

It has been an added misfortune that the joint committee's report came out at a time when what might have been its attentive public was fully absorbed in yet another stage of the wider debate on major constitutional reform in Canada. This had been compounded by the fact that recently the major actors in these discussions have all too often written off the Senate as a revising and scrutinizing chamber of the classic sort. Since the participation of the Senate in the review and scrutiny of regulations has so far been a key element in achieving what progress there has been this may be a decisive factor in the future of the process. Consequently a much greater burden will fall on the already hard-pressed House of Commons. Whatever amelioration comes from predictable (and necessary) reforms on the procedure of the House in the way of better staffed committees and the like will probably be insufficient. The reforms demanded by the joint committee are in most cases not likely to have a strong appeal to a majority government, whose priorities are likely to be different.

The truth of the matter is that both politics – as perceived by politicians and filtered through the media – and scholarship tend to be victims of fashion. If the fashion is a mixture of constitutional reform and grappling with intractable issues of economic policy (as these days it is bound to be) then politicians will bend all of their resources to these matters and allow other issues to wither from lack of nourishment.

A somewhat similar and insidious emphasis will find itself expressed in the world of scholarship. New systems of analysis, plus the pull exerted by granting agencies and market-conscious publishers, will draw almost the entire social science research community in the direction of 'national goals.' Scholars, after all, do not wish to languish in obscurity or to be thought to be out of the main stream of fashion. Consequently, the study of regulation as an important phenomenon in the relationship between administration and the norms of constitutional government is not a field likely to attract the young and eager scholar, and even the mature scholar will be drawn into what seem to be more urgent problems.

1 Joint Parliamentary Committee on Regulations and Other Statutory Instruments, Thirty-Second Parliament, *Fourth Report*, in Senate *Debates*, 17 July 1980, p. 759

2 'Cabinet Government in Canada: Some Recent Developments in the Machinery of the Central Executive,' *Canadian Journal of Economics and Political Science*, vol. XII, no. 2 (August, 1946), p. 287

3 Cf. the attitude of the Canadian Bar Association in the immediate post-war years. See Walter Surma Tarnopolsky, *The Canadian Bill of Rights* (sec. ed.) (Toronto: McClelland and Stewart, 1975), p. 5

4 Economic Council of Canada, *Responsible Regulation: An Interim Report* (Ottawa, 1979)

5 *The Government of England*, vol. I (New York: Macmillan, 1914), pp. 65-6

6 *Report of the Committee on Ministers' Powers*, Cmd. 4060 (1932). An authoritative discussion of the whole issue is John Willis, *Parliamentary Powers of the English Government Departments* (Cambridge: Harvard University Press, 1933). A more recent comparative study is John E. Kersell, *Parliamentary Supervision of Delegated Legislation* (London: Stevens, 1960).

7 House of Commons, *Debates* (1943), p. 296

8 House of Commons, *Votes and Proceedings*, 22 October 1969, pp. 1411-96

9 House of Commons, *Debates*, 16 June 1970, p. 8156

10 Ibid., 25 January 1971, p. 2734

11 Ibid, 8 March 1971, p. 4065

12 The Baker package of reform proposals was conveniently summarized in *Parliamentary Government*, vol. I, no. 2 (January 1980), together with commentaries on the principal proposals.

13 Senate, *Debates*, 24 November 1980, p. 1374. Earlier, in the House, Hon. Perrin Beatty had asked the Government House Leader 'whether, in keeping with the recommendations made in the report of the Standing Joint Committee on Regulations and other Statutory Instruments, tabled in the House in July, the regulation-enabling clauses of the bill will be sent to the Joint Committee on Regulations and other Statutory Instruments?' At that stage Mr Pinard agreed to consult with the Postmaster-General. House of Commons, *Debates*, 6 November 1980, p. 4521

14 The text of the report is printed as an appendix to Senate, *Debates*, 17 July 1980, pp. 757ff.

15 *Canadian Parliamentary Review*, vol. III, no. 4 (winter 1980-81), p. 26

16 *Responsible Regulation: an Interim Report.*

17 The requirement to prepare, publish in the *Canada Gazette* at least sixty days in advance, and to respond to comments from interested groups is contained in the *Administrative Policy Manual* (revised December 1979), chap. 490.

18 Raymond Robinson, 'Socio-Economic Impact Analysis: Bureaucratic Exercise or Essential Tool?' *Insight* (Journal of the Air Pollution Control Association), vol. XXIX, no. 10 (October 1979), p. 1026

19 Ibid., p. 1027

20 The Task Force on Canadian Unity, *A Future Together* (Ottawa, 1979), p. 128

21 Ibid., p. 106. For a consideration of some of the difficulties inherent in these proposals see John C. Courtney, 'Reflections on Reforming the Canadian Electoral System,' *Canadian Public Administration*, vol. XXIII, no. 3 (fall 1980), p. 427, and J.R. Mallory, 'Parliament in the Eighties,' in R. Kenneth Carty and W. Peter Ward, eds., *Entering the Eighties: Canada in Crisis* (Toronto: Oxford University Press, 1980), p. 120.

O.P. DWIVEDI

On Holding Public Servants Accountable

One of the most important challenges produced by the modern administrative state is the issue of accountability for what and to whom. The administrative state emerged, in the past, as an instrument to cure social ills and to promote common endeavours; as a result, public confidence grew to the extent that it was commonly believed that the state could accomplish all objectives, given sufficient resources. Public servants, as strategic actors in the administrative state were entrusted with such roles as crusading reformers, policy formulators, social change agents, crisis managers, program managers, humanitarian employers, interest brokers, public relations experts, regulators of the economy, and spokesmen for their own organizations. Through the performance of these several and various roles, they acquired enormous power.

However, this exercise of power by such officials created a public feeling that the administrative state, having become too powerful, was in need of restraint. It had grown too big, had become unwieldy, and it had shown tendencies of becoming an 'administration *of* the public' rather than an 'administration *for* the public.'[1] This attitude towards the agents of the administrative state in Canada has grown so much that the state is currently perceived as being beyond control, witness the declaration of the Auditor General of Canada in 1976 that financial management and control in the federal government was ineffective, a declaration which resulted in a thorough investigation of financial management and accountability in the federal public service.

THE BACKGROUND

Of the various commissions of inquiry appointed by the Canadian federal government to examine and report upon the many facets of public service, none left a more far-reaching imprint on governmental operations than the Royal Commission on Government Organization (Glassco commission). It preached a new philosophy of management in the public service. It issued a battle-cry – 'let the managers manage' – and recommended a significant shift in the balance of power among federal institutions. The Glassco commission advocated a massive devolution of authority from the two central agencies (Treasury Board and Civil Service Commission) to various departments, agencies, and commissions. Among the various elements of management, the commission's views on personnel management were sharply critical:

> The charges laid at the doorstep of the personnel management system, and largely confirmed by our investigation, can be bluntly stated: there is a waste of human resources, because of the failure to give orderly consideration to the best methods of providing and utilizing people and the consequent frustration of many individual careers; the procedures are costly and time consuming; personnel management in departments is generally misdirected, mainly because accountability for the effective use of personnel is fragmented or virtually non-existent.[2]

From the Glassco viewpoint, the existing system resulted in confusion and resentment mainly because 'efficient performance cannot be secured where intervention in the supervisory process by a non-managerial body displaces the exercise of necessary authority by departmental management.' Thus, the commission concluded that, once all departments and agencies were given the authority for management of human resources which was essential to good management itself, any anomaly relating to effective performance of the public service 'would be removed at a stroke.'

Winds of change created by the Glassco commission were enthusiastically effected by John J. Carson when, in September 1965, he assumed the chairmanship of the Civil Service Commission. Under his leadership, the CSC embarked on a deliberate program of delegation of authority to departments in the area of recruitment, selection, and promotion. The CSC also began preparing for the days when it would be legally emasculated under the enabling legislation. The advocates of the concept, 'let the managers manage,' and those who wanted to see the Treasury Board, a statutory committee of the cabinet, responsible for personnel and administration policies as well as program and expenditures management found Mr Carson a sympathetic person for their cause.

While the CSC was undergoing major organizational changes, the Treasury Board secretariat was growing, both in size and influence, to undertake the major tasks and responsibilities recommended for it by the Glassco commission. The major recommendations were two: 1 corporate responsibility for managerial decisions (in both the financial and personnel sectors); 2 the Treasury Board would have its own minister and a separate identity as a fully fledged department of government. In essence, the Treasury Board emerged as 'general manager' of the public service. However, complicated administrative manoeuvres had to be undertaken to place with the board the powers required for its new role as the management arm of the cabinet.[3]

Between 1963 and 1966, when the internal realignment of powers and responsibilities in the federal bureaucracy was being effected, the Pearson government appointed a Preparatory Committee on Collective Bargaining which recommended in 1965 in favour of collective bargaining in the public service and suggested that the Treasury Board should be the locus of managerial responsibility for negotiating with employees associations and unions.[4] Thus, the board not only became an overseer of public service programs but also assumed the role of employer on behalf of the government of Canada.

The Treasury Board was proclaimed a separate department on 1 October 1966 under the Government Organization Act, 1966. The secretariat of the Treasury Board, which had previously been a division of the Department of Finance, was transferred to the new portfolio. The newly established, but powerful, department was to be responsible for ensuring effective expenditure management, personnel management, and the development of management improvement practices throughout the public service. Out of these three mandates, it was the expenditure management (done under the Program Branch) which became the focal point of the Treasury Board's relation with all departments and agencies on matters of program priority, content, manpower allocation, and allocation of funds to programs. Effectiveness and efficiency of particular programs were to be judged through expenditures.

Not much room was left for any problem which may have developed later whereby departments and agencies might find themselves hamstrung by a myriad of policy and procedural directives issued constantly by the Treasury Board. To some, the board became too powerful, too privileged, and too prone to substitute its own judgments, its own values, and its own priorities for those of other departments and even for those of the government itself. However, it does have a significant managerial clout, which gives it the popular view of being amorphous, inaccessible, and powerful. There is no doubt that the agency which is authorized to control purse-strings is bound to influence other resources such as personnel and materials.

The source of this authority was the Financial Administration Act of 1966-67 which rendered unto the Treasury Board the following responsibilities for managing the federal public service: (*a*) to determine the manpower requirements of the public service; (*b*) to determine requirements for the training and development; (*c*) to provide for the classification of positions and employees; (*d*) to determine and regulate the pay, hours of work, and leaves; (*e*) to provide for awards to employees for outstanding performance; (*f*) to establish standards of discipline in the public service; (*g*) to establish standards governing physical working conditions, health, and safety of employees; (*h*) to determine and regulate expenses relating to travel; and (*i*) to provide for terms and conditions of employment for effective personnel management in the public service.[5] As can be surmised, the managerial leadership in personnel matters came to rest with the Treasury Board.

Amendments to the Financial Administration Act were accompanied by passage of the Public Service Employment Act, 1967. This legislation defined the jurisdiction of the Public Service Commission, as the emasculated Civil Service Commission was henceforth to be known. Anything not expressly vested in the Commission under this legislation was assumed to be reserved for the Treasury Board. The legislation confirmed the independence of the Public Service Commission; and it empowered the Commission to make appointments based on merit. However, the Commission's selection standards relating to education, knowledge, experience, language, age, residence, or other matters were required to be consistent with the classification standards prescribed by the Treasury Board.[6]

To sum up, overdependence on the rule book created an environment of caution and safety which seems to have frustrated program initiative throughout the government service. Although the control measures adopted by the three watchdogs (Civil Service Commission, Comptroller of Treasury, and Treasury Board) did protect the public service from the spoils systems in the public service, this preoccupation encouraged a bureaucratic environment which inhibited the development and achievement of program objectives and proper assignment of responsibility and authority in the public service. 'It took a long and expensive session on the psychoanalyst's couch, namely the Royal Commission on Government Organization,' thus remarked John Carson, 'to point out the need for the public service to come into the second half of the twentieth century.'[7]

THE COMMISSION ON ACCOUNTABILITY

While the Glassco recommendations along with other principles of management such as PPBS and MBO were being implemented, the country was shocked by the annual report of the Auditor General, who indicted the federal government in a devastating attack on the quality of financial management and warned that the government and indeed Parliament might have lost, or was in the process of losing, control over the public purse. This claim by the public watchdog generated an immediate public demand that the Trudeau government do something. And the government almost immediately did announce the appointment of a Royal Commission on Financial Management and Accountability, chaired by Allen Lambert, a banker, with three other commissioners, Robert Despres, J.E. Hodgetts, and O.G. Stoner.

The Lambert commission was appointed on 26 November 1976, with a mandate 'to examine and report on the management system required in the interrelated areas of: (i) financial management and control, (ii) accountability of deputy minister and heads of Crown agencies relative to the administration of their operations, and (iii) the evaluation of the administrative performance of deputy ministers and heads of crown agencies, and the interdepartmental structure, organization and process applicable thereto.'[8]

The commission's terms of reference included specific instructions to examine how financial management policy should be developed, promulgated, and applied, and to recommend procedures to ensure that necessary changes were identified and current policy regulations and guidelines were adhered to. To expedite this task, the terms of reference also required the commission to examine the organization necessary in central agencies, government departments, and Crown agencies to achieve the foregoing. And, in a dramatic departure from previous royal commissions, the Lambert commission was instructed to examine the institution of Parliament but only from the viewpoint of financial accountability. The terms of reference directed the commission to examine 'systems and procedures to ensure effective accountability to government and, *where appropriate to Parliament*, of the administration of government departments and agencies.'[9] Finally, the mandate contained the question-begging (rhetorical) stipulation that the commissioners ensure that their recommendations form a mutually compatible management system appropriate to the requirements of government.

The focus of the commission was directed to the study and evaluation of financial management practices within departments and Crown agencies and the process of evaluating the administrative performance of deputy ministers and heads of Crown agencies and holding them accountable for the discharge of certain administrative duties. The commission decided to restrict the meaning of accountability in this context mainly to financial accountability, although great emphasis was placed on the evaluation of senior public servants for program results.

In Part I of its report, the commission outlined 'a framework for a mutually compatible management system.' The commission's theory of management is logically integrated and its basic ideas are consistent with one another. However, the suggested management system approach developed by the commission begs critical assessment (as is provided later in the paper). Part II deals with the principle of ministerial responsibility, the organization and functions of central agencies, and the expenditure-planning function in government. Parts III and IV deal with organization, financial management, and accountability in departments and Crown agencies. Major emphasis is placed on the duties and responsibilities of deputy ministers and Crown agency heads. Finally, Part V, entitled 'Accountability to Parliament: Closing the Loop,' contains a short treatment of the main problems which House of Commons committees encounter in their efforts to hold the government accountable through the review of the estimates and public accounts.

The commission emphasizes that any proposal for reform must respect the dictates of responsible government operating within the framework of the parliamentary system. The government must be held responsible to Parliament and the government in turn must necessarily exact an accounting from the public service. As the commission explains:

Such a system of management must unequivocally reinforce the capacity of Parliament to fulfil its historic and crucial role of calling Ministers collectively and individually to account for the conduct of the nation's affair. This must be matched by an increased capacity on the part of Ministers collectively and individually to hold departments and agencies fully accountable for the efficient and effective discharge of their responsibilities.[10]

It will be difficult to avoid centralization with such recommendations. Nevertheless, a return to the pre-Glassco period would not work since, in the judgment of the commission, the size, diversity, and complexity of government had long since passed the point where any highly centralized organization could possibly implement the great number of policies and programs that had been developed to achieve the multiple objectives of the governmental system. Accordingly individual departments and agencies must be delegated authority with responsibility to achieve specific objectives and be provided with the necessary human and financial resources. On the other side of this model were the functions of central control agencies which included working with ministers in clarifying the roles and goals of operating departments and agencies, 'providing strong leadership and direction' with respect to how objectives should be achieved, and assuming over-all jurisdiction related to administrative policy and sound management practices.

This central direction is essential in rendering operational units accountable to the government for their performance as stewards of the public purse. This linkage is of fundamental significance because it determines the extent to which the government can account to Parliament. As the commission made clear: 'Delegation of authority without accountability is an abdication of responsibility on the part of those conferring it, whether Government or Parliament.'[11] The commission developed a model of financial accountability which began with the setting of priorities by government, the translation of these priorities into programs with specific goals, the allocation of resources through the budgetary process subject to central standards and guidelines, the delegation of authority with responsibility to managers to execute programs, the appraisal and measurement of program results, culminating in accountability to Parliament. In this model the cabinet is the control centre linking Parliament to the inward operation of the public service. To quote the report:

> We see accountability as the activating, but fragile element permeating a complex network connecting the Government upward to Parliament and downward and outward to a geographically dispersed bureaucracy grouped in a bewildering array of departments, corporations, boards, and commissions. Accountability moves through this network like the current in a circuit but always in some sort of relation to the control centre, the Cabinet.[12]

The style of management proposed by the Lambert commission does not differ in substance much from that of the Glassco commission. Both commissions proposed that the government should set priorities, undertake financial planning, and allocate resources, but program execution should be left to managers subject only to general guidelines. However, for the Lambert commission, the absence of a proper link to Parliament in the chain of accountability, was most crucial. Thus, its recommendation for the style of management can be aptly summed up from one paragraph of the report:

> Having determined its priorities, established a fiscal plan and allocated resources for carrying out the policies and programs formulated to give effect to its priorities, the Ministry [Cabinet] must assign to departments and agencies responsibility for implementing its plans. While it may establish certain guidelines and controls and reserve certain rights as to direction, it should be up to the individual departments and agencies to manage their affairs in a way that will best achieve the objectives assigned to them with the resources available. What is crucial to this system of management is that the centre should hold the constituent parts to account fully for the manner in which they have discharged the responsibilities assigned to them. Parliament, in turn, should hold the Government equally accountable for the management of the nation's affairs.[13]

ACCOUNTABLE MANAGEMENT

The Lambert commission found several fundamental weaknesses in the existing financial management of the federal government. None of the departments or agencies appears to be held effectively accountable; expenditures contained in the estimates were proposed by departments in ignorance of projected revenues (contained in the budget) and without being related to priorities; and there was weak parliamentary review of expenditure planning. The lack of discipline and co-ordination in financial planning, the commission felt, had 'led to incremental budgeting, crisis planning, poorly conceived ad hoc solutions to problems, and excessive flexibility in program management.'[14] The commission suggested that the federal government prepare a five-year fiscal plan which should be presented to the House of Commons well before the submission of the annual estimates and the budget. Through this instrument, Parliament would be able to examine 'the totality of government spending, its past results, present impact, and future direction.'[15] With suitable changes in the preparation of the estimates and the budget, the House of Commons would have adequate information. Currently, the ability of members of Parliament to exert a degree of influence over expenditures was limited because Parliament never got to see the revenues and expenditures side by side or as a whole. But the suggested fiscal plan could remedy the situation. Also, each department or agency, through its senior officers, could be made individually responsible to specific parliamentary committees for the effectiveness-evaluation of their programs. This method of direct accountability imposed on permanent heads would enable the House of Commons to exact a fair view of not only the negative aspects of the departments' affairs (as presented by the Auditor General's report) but also of their accomplishments. This would also strengthen the personal commitment and loyalty of senior managers to their departmental goals and objectives.

The commission proposed that the Treasury Board be renamed the Board of Management and headed by a senior minister designated as the president and assisted by a junior minister designated the vice-president. The existing Treasury Board Secretariat would be renamed the Personnel Management Secretariat with its deputy designated as the secretary for Personnel Management. This secretariat would assume all current personnel functions of the Treasury Board plus the staffing function now performed by the Public Service Commission.

The Comptroller General's office, including the Program Branch of the Treasury Board, would be renamed the Financial Management Secretariat and its deputy head designated as the Comptroller General. This revamped Board of Management would be the central agency clearly assigned the task of ensuring the effective management of financial and human resources within departments and agencies. The board would provide sufficient central direction and managerial leadership to ensure that departments and agencies would then be held accountable for their performance.

On 31 March 1981, the President of the Treasury Board, Donald Johnston, tabled a progress report concerning improvement in government management and implementation of the Lambert commission recommendations. This report, called *Accountable Management*,[16] is an astonishing document in that it shows, in no uncertain terms, the political will and support of the cabinet to bring a broad range of reforms in government management and better financial accountability. It describes the government's response to unprecedented demands placed on government services in recent decades. It discusses government action in relation to the Lambert commission's recommendations and proposals under the following categories: concept of a fiscal plan, policy and expenditure management system, accountability to Parliament, accountability within government, accountable financial management, accountable personnel management, and a continuing strategy for reforms. The report concludes with a statement from the president of the Treasury Board:

> I remain convinced that no issue is of greater importance in government than financial and human resources management reform. Indeed, I am privileged to have received a mandate from the Prime Minister to co-ordinate the Government's response ... We must continue, with discipline and dedication, to improve management and reduce waste, never losing sight of the fact that government is only the trustee of public funds and that the public must receive value for money.[17]

Thus, the federal government gave its firm commitment to consider and implement the Lambert commission's recommendations, and the president of the Treasury Board was given the mandate to carry out the complex process of enforcement. A brief outline of the main features of the report follows.

The Fiscal Plan. One of the 'two pivotal and interdependent proposals' suggested by the Lambert commission was the preparation of a fiscal plan which could provide Parliament and the public with an opportunity to consider the government's total fiscal plans and its underlying priorities. The fiscal plan was ushered in in October 1980 at the time of presenting the budget to Parliament. An 'envelope system' has been introduced which allocates resources to envelopes that are confirmed first by cabinet. The spending departments and agencies are then grouped into policy committees (e.g., social development policy, economic development policy, foreign and defence policy, and government operations) of cabinet where they must find the necessary trade-offs and make the hard choices in order to fund their programs within a predetermined ceiling on the amount of money available. Thus, the level of spending is first determined by the fiscal strategy of the government as a whole and then departmental expenditure plans are based on the money made available to them through their policy committees. In the past each department received a percentage increase over the amount spent during the previous year. Also introduced is the concept of multi-year projections of the government's anticipated revenues and of its expenditures for specified functions of government.

Policy and Expenditure Management System. The second pivotal recommendation of the Lambert proposals dealt with the way Parliament should hold the government accountable and thereby exercise effective control over the public purse. Towards this, *Accountable Management* proposes, in addition to the multi-year fiscal plan, the establishment by each department of a strategic overview to assist ministers to relate departmental plans to government policy priorities and the over-all expenditure framework. The system also increases ministerial direction and control over policy and planning process in the department. This enables the cabinet to impose limits on public spending and to ensure that sound management by hundreds of departments and agencies provides 'full value for expenditure of the taxpayer's dollar.'[18]

Accountability to Parliament. In order to provide more useful information to Parliament, the Treasury Board has initiated a 'Reporting to Parliament' project, through which Parliament will receive financial and program information which will be divided into three parts: (*a*) a government expenditure plan, which provides an overview of total government expenditure plans and various analyses to encourage a comprehensive understanding of aggregate government expenditures, and also includes expenditure plans for each envelope, multi-year expenditure plans, and supplementary analyses on a government-wide basis; (*b*) appropriations, also known as 'Blue Book,' the estimates in which will contain information on each ministry and program as well as on supply needs; (*c*) program expenditure plans, which are being developed now, to consist of program review of each department concentrating on objectives and effectiveness, analyses of financial requirements and expected performance to justify expenditures requested, and supplementary information on person-years. This approach is a bold step in clarifying responsibilities so as to provide information to Parliament so that it can exact an accounting from the cabinet as a whole and from individual departments and agencies.

Accountability within the Public Service. The Treasury Board believes that, unless departments and agencies are held accountable for achieving their stated goals with minimum direction from central agencies, sound management and strict accountability cannot be achieved. Towards this, each department and agency is *required* to establish clear, annual objectives for all managers, to develop shorter-term operational work programs to facilitate planning and monitoring of managerial efforts, and to conduct program evaluations. Also, departments are required to adopt the internal audit system recommended by the Treasury Board which appraises all departmental operations with a view of determining the efficiency, economy, and effectiveness of internal management policies, practices, and controls. To reach such goals, departments are to be organized in 'responsibility centres directly related to programs, activities and sub-activities that can be identified with particular resources and, wherever possible, with specific measurable outputs associated with the deployment of resources.'[19] Consistent with this approach, departmental heads have been given essential discretion to tailor organizational structures to the needs of their departments.

It is recognized, however, that such detailed accountability from managers cannot be 'exacted' if they have not been given authority over such important matters as personnel. The Lambert commission had recommended that jurisdiction over all important personnel matters in the public service would be vested in the proposed Secretariat for Personnel Management of the Board of Management, with the exception of the protection of the merit principle, the hearing of appeals on staffing decisions, and certain investigations which would remain under the authority of the Public Service Commission. The recommendation for concentrating personnel management authority in one place would make good economic sense in the large business corporation; however, this reasoning cannot be appropriately applied to the public service where other important factors must be considered. The most important of these is the integrity of the merit principle, which Parliament has sought to protect by vesting responsibility for staffing in the public service in a politically independent agency, the Public Service Commission. An important political value to be considered in staffing the public service is that it should be representative of Canada's two languages. Political interests and values do and should pervade the decision-making process in government and take precedence over purely economic considerations. The implication here is that, if necessary, some degree of 'inefficiency' could be suffered in the public service if certain political values are to be upheld. As the Public Service Commissioner, John Edwards, emphasized:

> This decision [Parliament has decreed that staffing shall be carried out within a merit system] means that staffing goes beyond the straight prerogative of management and must serve other values and interests, such as the need to have a Public Service that is representative of Canadian society, the need to ensure that employees and those seeking employment are treated visibly with equity and so on. Thus our tradition has been to create a staffing activity that is a blend of management function and other broader considerations.[20]

It should be remembered that, immediately after the establishment of the Lambert commission, the federal government decided to appoint a Special Committee on the Review of Personnel Management and the Merit Principle in the Public Service, chaired by Guy R. D'Avignon, which submitted its report in October 1979. During its tenure, the committee met with the Royal Commission on Financial Management and Accountability, and both decided to restrict their jurisdictions. The D'Avignon committee, taking lead from the Lambert commission, declared that the current state of personnel management was a result of the failure of successive governments to provide a philosophy of management. It recognized the authority vested in the Treasury Board to function more fully as the corporate manager. It listed the following basic problems of personnel management in the federal government:

> 1 absence of a corporate management, hence of leadership; absence of any philosophy of management, a public service organization without a head;
> 2 excessive and inflexible regulations; slavish adherence to universally applied regulation in the name of merit at the expense of efficiency and effectiveness;
> 3 arising from (1) managers and supervisors who are poorly equipped to manage, no requirement that they undergo even minimally essential training, and low priority accorded training;
> 4 no accountability for effective personnel management.[21]

The committee made 179 recommendations (compared to 165 made by the Lambert commission). The major elements of the committee's extensive list of recommendations were: (*a*) the essence of effective management is the commitment of management, starting at the top, and a clear line of accountability from the junior management level through to the top level; (*b*) while the merit principle remains the cornerstone of staffing, the system itself has brought the principle into disrepute; therefore, certain supplementary principles should be enshrined in law, such as sensitivity and responsiveness, equality of opportunity, efficiency, effectiveness, and equity; (*c*) in order to provide a bold, unified corporate policy direction of the personnel function, the Board of Management (as recommended by the Lambert commission) should have a vice president as well as a Secretary for Personnel Management; consequently, the role of the Public Service Commission would be restricted to mostly audit and appeal functions; and (*d*) public servants should be given greater freedom to participate actively in the political process, with the exception of the senior management group.

These recommendations were fully examined by the federal government, and its response, contained in *Accountable Management*, was as follows. A new category of senior officers, called the management category, would be established with the objectives of increasing managers' sense of identity, providing a common and unified approach to their salary structure, and maximizing the optimal use and deployment of managerial resources in departments and elsewhere.[22] This approach would usher in a new era in personnel policy at the federal level because, so far, the entire position-classification system has been based on a job-oriented (appointment to a position) system rather than on the British system of rank-oriented (appointment to a level/class/career) classification.[23] The major defect of the job-oriented system is that a person cannot be moved between similar positions, which are at the same salary and responsibility levels, without creating a fresh vacancy and going through the normal process of appointment approved by the Public Service Commission. This resulted in such difficulties as (*a*) departmental heads being unable to transfer able officers within their department for one position to another, (*b*) delays in filling positions because each such move had been considered a fresh appointment, and (*c*) inability of central agencies to move persons from one department to another. These difficulties were also recognized by the United States federal government when, in 1978, it created a senior executive service.[24] The Coombs commission of Australia had already made a similar recommendation in 1976 for establishment of a senior executive category.[25] The Canadian plan aimed to minimize the barriers to flexible deployment of senior personnel, such as inter-position transfer within departments, and so to maximize program efficiency and effectiveness. The concept 'offers more managerial authority and flexibility to act in return for greater accountability for results achieved.'[26]

In regard to training and development, the federal government gave its affirmation to provide training to employees so that the public might continue to enjoy the quality and professional service that it deserved. For this, departments were now required to prepare an over-all training plan, allocate resources from its funds, and provide regular evaluation of the effectiveness of such programs undertaken by their employees. Finally, the government introduced a policy on performance review and employee appraisal which would make managers accountable for planning and developing their management team. The government hoped that these managers belonging to the newly established management category would be able to achieve program objectives; those performing well would be rewarded, poor performers would be disciplined.

These initiatives were far-reaching. The federal public service will need time to absorb these changes. It is too early to make any assessment of these reforms; but they do indicate the seriousness and ongoing commitment on the part of the government to improve management effectiveness and to be accountable to the public through Parliament.

MINISTERIAL RESPONSIBILITY

Central to accountability in our parliamentary system of government is the concept of ministerial responsibility. It has been under attack in recent times. The concept, as developed in Britain, has been a firm parliamentary tradition in Canada. The doctrine implies, as noted by A.V. Dicey, 'the legal responsibility of every minister for every act of the Crown in which he takes part.'[27] It means that a minister is accountable to Parliament for anything he or his department does or for anything he has powers to do, whether he personally does it or not. Of course, the legal accountability, as meant by Dicey, relates to those actions where there is a legal remedy because the minister has acted beyond his powers. Dicey was not talking about the political responsibility of ministers for acts which, while legal, are politically unacceptable (as, for example, in the Crichel Down case mentioned below). Herbert Morrison explained that 'if a mistake is made in a Government Department, the Minister is responsible even if he knew nothing about it until, for example, a letter of complaint is received from an M.P., or there is criticism in the press, or a question is put down for answer in the House; even if he has no real personal responsibility whatever, the Minister is still held responsible.'[28] Such a blanket obligation on the part of a political executive has been necessary to protect the integrity and the traditional anonymity of public servants. The only exception to the rule is the case where a public servant acts deliberately outside or contrary to the policy of his department.

Ambiguity in the doctrine, if any, was clarified in the wake of the Crichel Down case of Britain which laid down the following principles governing the formal position of the minister vis-à-vis his public servants.[29] A minister must be personally responsible (*a*) where a public servant carries out an express order, and (*b*) where a public servant acts properly in accordance with the policy laid down by the minister, or as per laws administered by that department. However, where a public servant has taken action of which the minister disapproves and of which he had no prior knowledge and the conduct of the official is reprehensible, then that action relieves the minister of the responsibility. In the Crichel Down case, when the Minister of Agriculture, Sir Thomas Dugdale, resigned his office (not because he had been personally responsible for what had happened), he greatly added by doing so to the honour of public office and thus strengthened the constitutional doctrine. He said in the House of Commons: 'I, as Minister, must accept full responsibility to Parliament for any mistakes and inefficiency of officials in my department, just as, when my officials bring off any successes on my behalf, I take full credit for them.'[30] Such an exemplary instance is a rare phenomenon.

We find that, while in England the statutes generally confer powers on the minister to act, in Canada the statutes commonly provide for a decision by the 'Governor General in Council' – that is, the cabinet. The necessity of obtaining collegial decisions, thereby making the whole cabinet responsible for detailed problems of management, has injected a curious element into the doctrine, whereby in Canada ministers are considered collectively responsible for all government policies and programs. However, individual responsibility seems to have turned into a convention whereby a minister is responsible for any scandalous behaviour or for any admitted personal error *but not for every act* of his public service subordinates. The Lockheed affair and the McDonald royal commission examining the improper activities of the Royal Canadian Mounted Police are but some illustrations of the practice. That is why an instance like the resignation of Sir Thomas Dugdale would perhaps not happen in Canada.

The classical theory of individual responsibility for every and any act of public servants has clearly given way to the newly emerging convention that ministers' responsibility is limited merely to their obligation (collectively or individually) to provide Parliament with information and the answers sought, and to be held personally accountable for action in their departments if it was done on their initiative or in accordance with their stated policy. On this convention of 'limited' ministerial responsibility, the Royal Commission on Australian Government Administration commented:

> while ministers continue to be held accountable to Parliament in the sense of being obliged to answer to it when Parliament so demands, and to indicate corrective action if that is called for, they themselves are not held culpable – and in consequence bound to resign or suffer dismissal – unless the action which stands condemned was theirs, or taken on their direction, or was action with which they ought obviously to have been concerned.[31]

In 1977, a committee of Canadian senior public servants, reporting on the concept of the ombudsman, further strengthened the above view by stating that a minister 'cannot be acquainted with, or personally criticized for, every detail of administration in his department ... Thus, the degree of ministerial responsibility seems to diminish ... as one moves out of the realm of broad policy and into the domain of administrative action that occurs in a specific and limited context.'[32]

On the concept of ministerial responsibility, the Lambert commission commented:

> While we have no wish to dispute the principle of ministerial responsibility, there can be little doubt that today the degree to which a minister really has the effective management and direction of his department is open to question ... The twin assumptions that Parliament has clout as well as the information to exact a relevant accounting, and that the departments can be managed and directed by ministers, do not hold as they once did.[33]

The commission stops short of questioning the appropriateness of the parliamentary system of government. The commission did ask, in its *Progress Report*, 'In the present-day context, can the minister alone continue to be held accountable to Parliament for every aspect of the administrative performance of the department or crown agency?'[34] Obviously, the controversy over the relevance of the doctrine of ministerial responsibility in the management of public service has further deepened. The Lambert commission did not accept the emerging belief that ministerial responsibility was now defunct, although it did admit that the convention was greatly strained under current conditions.[35] During its investigation, the Lambert commission found that senior civil servants, as well as ministers who appeared before it, 'spoke disparagingly of the "myth" of ministerial responsibility, even though they were the first to decry any recommendations which seemed to fly in the face of that myth.'[36] The myth, of course, can be lightly dismissed or can be subjected to various interpretations, both by the performers – ministers and civil servants – and by the parliamentarians and the public. One thing is clear: since no minister can possibly supervise all the administrative acts of even a very small department, it is unrealistic to expect a minister to be accountable for every act of his civil servants. The consequences are unduly hard on ministers and unduly light on the civil servant.

It was with this view in mind the Lambert commission suggested that deputy ministers should appear before the Public Accounts Committee to answer for detailed operations. According to the commission, 'the assignment of responsibility to the deputy does not impair the principle of ministerial responsibility, but reinforces it by replacing myth with reality.'[37] The federal government appears to have tilted towards this position, as can be surmised from *Accountable Management*, and also from a reported statement by the President of the Treasury Board that 'while the minister retains the ultimate responsibility and accountability, the new procedures and data would expose officials (or 'managers') in a regular, thorough way for both criticism and approval.'[38] This emerging view of 'limited' ministerial responsibility has a serious implication for the role of public servants, especially in regard to the concept of civil service anonymity.

ACCOUNTABLE PUBLIC SERVANTS

There are various kinds of accountabilities one could consider for public servants. Some of these are: political, managerial (or administrative), and personal. Political accountability, simply stated, relates to elected politicians who are cabinet ministers and are accountable for their actions, jointly or individually, to Parliament and the electorate. Management accountability, as pointed out by G.F. Osbaldeston, former secretary of the Treasury Board, consists of three kinds.[39] The first relates to accountability for regularity where proper behaviour in the administration of resources is assessed and where no departure from established rules and standards is tolerated. This accountability is enforced by the two central agencies, the Public Service Commission and the Treasury Board secretariat. The second kind of accountability applies to the exercise of judgment relating to program management and objective achievement. This is clearly embedded in the line management where each program manager, and from him to the very top (the minister), is responsible for the decision taken. This accountability is one of the two difficult kinds which is posing a great challenge to accountability experts/consultants. It is at this level – senior management – that the most critical managerial decisions are taken (or neglected). And it is at this level that the resources – financial, human, and material – are committed. No amount of procedural rectitude or 'regularity' accountability imposed by the Treasury Board or the Public Service Commission could achieve program and personal accountability if there is some problem at the program management and implementation level. Finally, there is the output-oriented accountability, a concept easier to apply in the business world than in the government sector.

Personal accountability relates to the ethical conduct of public servants.[40] Ethical problems among public employees range from the apparently very small and insignificant infractions to those having serious bearing upon the nature and the very survival of the government. There are three kinds of unethical conduct: (*a*) activities which are contrary to the legal norms of the country and therefore punishable under the law; (*b*) those which are contrary to the basic principles of morality/ethics held (though not necessarily practised) by that society; and (*c*) those which are undertaken because of the latent, manifest, or perceived pressures felt by a person under the obligations of loyalty, ties of kinship, affection, politics, religion, or sheer need of money.[41] At the same time, one should realize that everywhere, to a greater or lesser degree, public employees are put under strain by the pressures exerted by politicians, influential citizens, and friends and relatives who seek special and speedy favours.

Such conditions may force some government employees to buckle under the pressure or because of temptation act in a manner which is contrary to established laws and regulations. There may be circumstances where program managers and employees may be asked by their superiors (both politicians and appointed officials) to perform certain acts but are careful to place the responsibility at their doorsteps. Rules of conduct, however elaborate, cannot create honesty, nor can they prevent deliberate dishonest or unethical behaviour.[42] Rather, these provide a substitute for taking the right course of action whenever an employee finds difficulty in sorting out personal ethical dilemmas. A good helping tool to increase personal accountability in the public service would be to make the employee a partner in the program management by delegating some responsibility and by forcing him to accept obligations which go along with such delegation. This would increase his sense of participation in the program.

The federal government accepted the Lambert commission's recommendation that deputy heads should be held *personally* accountable to Parliament for their assigned and delegated responsibilities. Their work would be monitored and reviewed by the Treasury Board, and they in turn would monitor and review the managerial performance of their subordinates. But this could result in a plethora of managerial performance evaluations and program evaluations. Under the new system, deputy heads would be facing severe scrutiny as they would have to satisfy three masters: their minister, the Treasury Board (and other central agencies which have delegated authority to implement their programs), and Parliament. Being accountable to three entities may just as well become being answerable to none!

THE ACCOUNTABILITY DILEMMA

We have seen that one of the most important problems of the administered society is that of holding those officials who exercise power and authority accountable to the public. In the past, ministers were in control of their departments and they were held responsible to their respective legislatures. With the advent of the administrative state, they were unable to exercise that control. In theory, they continued to be answerable for the actions of their administrators, who remained protected by the doctrine of civil service anonymity. Thus, the doctrine of ministerial responsibility has become an unworkable principle; and a vacuum has emerged in the governance of the state.

In view of strong public concern over this accountability gap, efforts are being made to close the loop by requiring ministers as well as public servants to be accountable for their actions. Notwithstanding the recommendations of the Lambert commission to secure greater accountability in the parliamentary system of government, the basic dilemma, as identified by J.E. Hodgetts, remains: 'Who is accountable? For what? To whom? How?'[43] These questions require more elaborate considerations than are possible in this essay, but three related issues could be briefly discussed.

Accountability Chain. In the past, the Glassco commission envisaged that the primary responsibility for efficient use of resources would rest with individual departments and agencies and that the proposed changes for decentralization of the role of central agencies would facilitate that process. However, the goal was not met, partially because of normal bureaucratic inertia and positive resistance inherent in the institutional patterns of authority, and partially because the decentralized authority was not supplemented by a clear-cut line of accountability. The Lambert commission's emphasis on making the permanent head accountable for all departmental actions will not work. Effectiveness and final outcome of any public program does not depend solely upon how capable a departmental head is. It also depends upon the prevailing administrative ethos, including a regime of public service standards, sense of dedication and feeling of recognition for work performance, commitment and positive participation of public service unions/associations towards the realization of program objectives, and the feeling among employees that incompetence will not be tolerated. Clearly a greater sense of accountability is needed with several components; accountability to self (an inner consciousness to protect the public interest fairly), being responsive and responsible to senior officers and cabinet ministers, and finally to Parliament. At the same time, the chain/loop will not be complete unless the people hold the parliamentarians accountable for governing the nation. For this, the people have to participate fully in the democratic process.

Moulding the Public Sector in the Image of the Private Sector. The two commissions on government organization and accountability, Glassco and Lambert, shared at least one fundamental weakness: the commissioners perceived the management and accountability problems of the public service from the perspective of the private sector. Instead of seeking to understand how public administration differs in nature from management in the private sector, both commissions seemed to proceed from the premise that business practices are superior and can easily be applied to the needs of government.[44] The commissioners apparently believe that a practice which works well in the private sector should work equally well in the public service. D.C. Rowat explained this weakness in his evaluation of the Glassco commission report: 'The most telling criticism, I think, is that the Commission approached its task with a general bias in favour of free enterprise and business management ... This assumption that business methods are best often blinded it to the essential differences between public and private administration.'[45] Both commissions were almost totally oblivious to the fact that political considerations pervade the entire decision-making process in government and they did not think out the political implications of their recommendations. These commissions failed to appreciate, it seems, that economy and efficiency are by no means the only criteria by which the quality and effectiveness of public administration should be measured. It should be made absolutely clear to those who seek further reforms of government management that the dream of making the public sector behave in the mould of the private industry is impracticable. Not all government departments can act as if they were divisions of a large corporation, or their survival would largely depend upon their ability to create 'profit.' Time and again, the recommendations of various commissions of inquiry have failed to create a business-like environment in the public sector. A businessman, by nature, is suspicious of governmental machinery; hence, his approach is always going to be biased. Government is not a conglomerate; such an assumption will lead to confusion.

Obligations of Public Servants. Earlier, the issue of administrative ethos was raised. Currently, it seems that some public servants do not feel obliged or morally committed to serve the public beyond the call of their negotiated duties. While in the past loyalty and dedication motivated them to excel in serving the state (and thereby serving the community), nowadays securing better and bigger compensation and benefits seems to have become a norm. Of course, the unionism which no doubt raised the financial status of public servants and contributed by negotiations to a better work environment has also brought legalism in the system. Public servants appear to be more concerned with their legal rights and benefits compared to their moral obligations to serve the nation. One of the greatest challenges to modern public service is how to rededicate itself to serve the community and to uphold the public good. Towards this, a training program on the obligations of holding office of public responsibility should be considered which should help in instilling 'standards of objectivity, effectiveness, impartiality, integrity and probity in the conduct of public affairs within the context of maintaining a professional public service dedicated to achieving a high standard of efficiency and competence.'[46] The ethical dimension of public sector management, especially the exercise of discretionary power, needs to be linked with the issue of accountability.

Accountability, then, as a viable instrument of control, can be operative to the extent that (*a*) public servants understand and accept their assigned responsibility (both legal and moral) for the results expected of them; (*b*) public servants have authority commensurate with their responsibility; (*c*) acceptable measures of performance evaluation are utilized; (*d*) results of such evaluations are communicated both to the seniors and to the person concerned; and (*e*) appropriate, equitable, and timely measures are enforced in response to results achieved and the manner in which they are achieved.

In conclusion, recent developments in the public service of Canada have raised at least three major questions:

1 Has the doctrine of ministerial responsibility become an unworkable principle?

2 What would be the consequence on the tradition of civil service anonymity of requiring public servants to appear before parliamentary committees and to account for the policies and programs?

3 Is the concept of management accountability as practised in the private sector being ushered into the federal public service of Canada as the answer for all ills facing the modern administrative state?

This is a revised version of a paper presented at the Conference on International Developments on Public Administration, Sydney, Australia, 20-21 July 1981. Some portions have also appeared in the *Indian Journal of Public Administration*, vol. 26, no. 3 (July-September 1980), pp. 757-77.

1 See Gerald Caiden, 'Symposium on "Public Policy and Administrative Reform": Introduction,' *Policy Studies Journal*, vol. 9, no. 8 (1980-81), p. 1136

2 Royal Commission on Government Organization, vol. 1, *Management of the Public Service* (Ottawa, 1962), p. 255

3 For details, see J.E. Hodgetts, *The Canadian Public Service: A Physiology of Government, 1867-1970* (Toronto: University of Toronto Press, 1973), pp. 257-62.

4 For a review of the background and the recommendations of the preparatory committee, see O.P. Dwivedi, 'Recent Developments in Staff Relationships in the Public Service of Canada,' *Public Administration* (Sydney), vol. 24 (December 1965), pp. 359-67.
5 Financial Administration Act, RSC 1970, section 7 (1)
6 Public Service Employment Act, 1967, section 12(1)
7 John J. Carson, 'The Role of the Public Service as a Force in Our Environment,' address to the National Planning Conference of the Community Planning Association of Canada, Ottawa, 9 October 1967, p. 11
8 Royal Commission on Financial Management and Accountability (Lambert commission), *Final Report* (Ottawa, March 1979), p. vi
9 Ibid., p. vii (emphasis added)
10 Ibid., p. 31
11 Ibid., p. 32
12 Ibid., p. 9
13 Ibid., p. 64
14 Ibid., p. 71
15 Ibid., p. 79
16 Treasury Board, *Accountable Management* (a progress report on reforms in the management of the Government of Canada and implementation of the recommendations of the Royal Commission on Financial Management and Accountability) (Ottawa, March 1981).
17 Ibid., p. iv
18 Ibid., p. iv
19 Ibid., p. 13
20 DREE seminar on the Canadian System of Government, notes for speech, Ottawa, 27 June 1979, p. 7
21 Special Committee on the Review of Personnel Management and the Merit Principle, *Report* (Ottawa, 1979), p. 5
22 *Accountable Management*, p. 20
23 For a fuller description of both systems, and their applicability in Canada, see J.E. Hodgetts and O.P. Dwivedi, *Provincial Governments as Employers: A Survey of Public Personnel Administration in Canada's Provinces* (Montreal: McGill-Queen's University Press, 1974), pp. 121-5.
24 For an evaluation of the SES, see Bernard Rosen, 'Uncertainty in the Senior Executive Service,' *Public Administration Review*, vol. 41, no. 2 (March/April 1981), pp. 203-7.
25 Royal Commission on Australian Government Administration, *Report* (Canberra, 1976), p. 272
26 *Accountable Management*, p. 22

27 *Law of the Constitution* (London, 1893, 10th ed.), p. 303

28 *Government and Parliament* (London, 1959), p. 321

29 Geoffrey Marshall and G.C. Moodie, *Some Problems of the Constitution* (London, 1959), pp. 67-87

30 Quoted in John Freeman, 'The Public Administrator and the Public in U.K.,' *Indian Journal of Public Administration*, vol. XII, no. 1 (1967), p. 13

31 P. 60

32 *Report of the Committee on the Concept of the Ombudsman* (Ottawa, 1977), pp. 16-17

33 *Final Report*, p. 373

34 *Progress Report* (Ottawa, 1977), p. 33

35 *Final Report*, pp. 371-4

36 J.E. Hodgetts, 'Government and People: The Quest for Accountability,' a paper presented at the Annual Conference of Canadian Political Science Association, Halifax, 27 May 1981, pp. 4-5

37 *Final Report*, p. 57

38 Statement of Donald J. Johnston, President of the Treasury Board, reported by Douglas Fisher, in 'A Chance to Open Up the Bureaucracy,' *Executive* (May 1981), p. 105

39 In a speech to the International Personnel Management Association, 19 November 1976, p. 17

40 See W.D.K. Kernaghan, *Ethical Conduct: Guidelines for Government Employees* (Toronto, 1974); and O.P. Dwivedi, 'A Code of Conduct for Civil Servants,' *Dalhousie Review* (1964-5), pp. 452-58.

41 See O.P. Dwivedi, *Public Service Ethics* (Brussels: International Institute of Administrative Sciences, 1978), p. 3.

42 *Report of the Committee on Conduct in Local Government* (Lord Redcliffe-Maud Committee), vol. I (London, 1974), p. 6

43 'Government Responsiveness to the Public Interest: Has Progress Been Made?,' *Canadian Public Administration*, vol. 24, no. 2 (summer 1981), p. 229

44 See J.R. Nethercote, 'The Lambert Commentaries' (Ottawa, 1979), mimeograph, pp. 70-2. The author expresses gratitude to Nethercote for comments on an earlier draft of this essay.

45 'Canada's Royal Commission on Government Organization,' *Public Administration* (London), vol. 41, no. 2 (summer 1963), p. 199

46 O.P. Dwivedi and Ernest A. Engelbert, 'Education and Training for Values and Ethics in the Public Service: An International Perspective,' *Public Personnel Management Journal*, vol. 10, no. 1 (1981), p. 144

DONALD C. ROWAT

The Right of Public Access to Official Documents

In a democratic society ... knowledge should not be ... monopolized by the bureaucracy. J.E. HODGETTS

Essential to the rule of law in a democracy is control over the executive side of government. And essential to this control is public access to official documents. The legislature, the courts, and the public cannot control the executive unless they know what it is doing. In a democracy, the people have a right to know how they are being governed.

Yet the vast majority of democratic countries still adhere to the general principle that administrative information must be kept secret unless the executive gives permission for its release. This principle of 'discretionary secrecy' means that the executive has the discretion to keep secret whatever documents and information it wishes, and is free to do so to cover up mistakes or to protect its own partisan interests. It also means that the public are not sure of getting the information they need to control the executive or to make intelligent judgments on public issues. They have no right to see or use the vast store of documents and data which have been paid for with their taxes.

Recently several democratic countries have reached the conclusion that this principle is wrong and ought to be the reverse: all administrative information must be open to the public except that which needs to be kept secret as defined by law. These countries have therefore adopted laws which establish the principle of governmental openness and provide a right of public access to all administrative documents and information, except for specific matters that are narrowly defined. Such laws involve a radical shift in the balance between governmental secrecy and openness. Hence, if Canada desires to move towards greater governmental openness, it has much to learn from the experience with these laws and the proposals for similar laws in other countries.

The country having the longest experience with the principle of openness is Sweden. Its law providing public access to official documents dates back to 1766. Other countries have adopted a similar law, but in much more recent times. Those which adopted one long enough ago to have had some experience with its actual working are: Finland (1951), the United States (1966, revised 1974), Denmark (1970), and Norway (1970). Also, in 1973 Austria provided a limited right of public access to official information by creating for its federal administration an enforceable 'duty to inform.' Countries other than Canada in which laws on public access have been adopted or proposed recently are: France (1978), the Netherlands (1978), the United Kingdom, Australia, New Zealand, Switzerland, West Germany and Japan. Because considerable literature is available on the nature of these laws, this essay will discuss only the lessons that may be learned from the experience so far with them, recent developments in Canada, and the problem of cabinet secrecy.

LESSONS FROM EXPERIENCE ELSEWHERE

In view of the rapid spread of the idea, it seems clear that a law prescribing the right of public access to official documents is a reform whose time has come, as part of the world's gradual development of a better form of democracy and more effective legal controls over administrations. Experience with the older laws in Scandinavia and the United States has demonstrated that it is quite possible to implement such a right without the wheels of government grinding to a halt. This experience has also demonstrated that the full establishment of the principle of public access will require a radical change in law, practices, and attitudes. Although practices and attitudes may not be changed sufficiently by the mere passing of a law, this is a necessary condition for the change. A new law which clearly declares a reversal of the principle of secrecy has great symbolic and dramatic value in altering both public and official attitudes. But, as shown by the failure of the first American law of 1946, and the limited success of the law of 1966 until its amendment in 1974, such a law will not succeed unless it contains strong provisions for its enforcement. Public officials are too used to the old tradition of discretionary secrecy under which they arbitrarily withhold information for their own convenience or for fear of disapproval by their superiors. They will not change their ways unless required by law to do so.

Experience with the older laws also shows that a strong and successful law must have five main features. First, it must unequivocally declare that the general principle in government administration is to be public access to documents and that secrecy is the exception. Second, it must facilitate full and easy public access, for instance by not limiting requests to specific documents (as in Denmark and Norway), or to citizens with a personal interest in a case, and by requiring public registers of all documents and low fees for searches and copies, with the fees waived if the request is for a public purpose. Third, it must list narrowly and specifically the types of documents that may be kept secret. Thus it must specify that they may be kept secret only if their release would harm a public interest; how long they may be kept secret; it must permit earlier release if this would not be harmful; and it must require non-secret parts of documents to be released. Fourth, it must contain strong provisions for the enforcement of access, such as a limited time for replying to a request or appeal and requiring reasons for a refusal, as well as penalties for non-compliance. And fifth, it must provide an easy appeal to an independent authority, including a final appeal to a court, with the costs recoverable even when the appellant loses if the court judges the appeal to be in the public interest.

Moreover, if there is to be full provision for openness, the scope of the law should be broad. Unless separate laws are passed for the purpose, it should contain provisions for access to personal files, and for their correction and control, for open meetings of governmental bodies, and for extending its scope to cover all levels of government. Finally, because so many other laws contain provisions for secrecy, either the new law must override them, or they must be suitably amended to confrom with it. Preferably it should have the force of a constitutional law, as in Sweden.

A lesson from experience with the recent or proposed adoption of access laws is that, in a parliamentary system where the executive controls the introduction of legislation, the government will resist sponsoring a strong law because this will limit its own powers and because it finds the present system of discretionary secrecy so much to its own advantage. All of the governments that have sponsored access laws in recent years have produced weaker versions than the laws of Sweden or the United States. Governments in parliamentary systems are likely to resort to the spurious argument that a right of appeal to the courts will interfere with ministerial responsibility to Parliament. Yet such a right increases rather than interferes with ministerial responsibility because it prevents the ministers from permanently hiding information for personal or partisan advantage. And from a broader point of view, a strong access law forces them to release more information about all of the activities for which they are responsible, thus giving Parliament, and through it the public, a better basis for controlling the government.

RECENT DEVELOPMENTS IN CANADA'S PROVINCES

Canada, too, has participated in the trend among the Western democracies towards adopting public access laws. One of the advantages of a federal system is that a single state (or province) can experiment with a new governmental institution, and if it is successful it can then be copied by other states and may be adopted in suitably adjusted form at the federal level. Thus, the Ombudsman was introduced at the state level in all decentralized federations, and has also been adopted at the federal level in Australia. Similarly, laws on public access were introduced first at the provincial level in Canada. This is not surprising because provincial governments, not being responsible for foreign affairs, defence, or national security, have less reason for secrecy than has the federal government. Two of the provinces, Nova Scotia and New Brunswick, have passed an access law, and in the most populous provinces, Ontario and Quebec, official commissions have recently recommended such a law.[1] The governments of Quebec and Newfoundland introduced access bills in 1981, and other provinces are likely to pass a law on the subject within the next few years.

When Nova Scotia proclaimed its Freedom of Information Act in November 1977, it became the first province, and the first jurisdiction in the Commonwealth, to establish a public right of access to government documents. A noteworthy feature of this act is that it also incorporates a right to personal privacy regarding government-held information. It provides the right to inspect, correct, and limit distribution of information contained in personal files. Such information may not be disclosed, even to another arm of government, without the consent of the person concerned. The act further provides that any agency of government must disclose the existence of all data banks where such information is kept, and it prohibits the selling or renting of a person's name or address for mailing without permission.

Another unusual feature of the act is that it gives a list of types of information that must be made available, as well as a list of exempt categories to which the public may not have access. In a case of conflict between the two lists, however, the secrecy list takes priority. Also, most of the secrecy exemptions are couched in broad language, such as information that 'might' (rather than 'would') influence particular negotiations, or 'would be likely to' (rather than 'would') disclose a particular type of information. For these reasons, the first reading of the bill produced an outcry from some citizens' groups, who feared that information which had been made available in the past might now be withheld. The legislature therefore passed an amendment providing that the act would not restrict access to material that had been available 'by custom or practice' in the past.[2]

The act does, however, contain some strong provisions. For instance, a written request for information must be answered within fifteen working days. If only part of the information requested is exempt from disclosure, the remainder must be disclosed. If a written request for information is denied, the applicant must be advised in writing of the reasons and of the appeal procedure.

The most controversial aspect of the act is the mechanism for appeals. An appeal must first go to the deputy head of the department, with a further appeal to the minister. If the minister upholds the denial, an appeal may be taken to the legislature, where it must be presented by a member. The theory behind this procedure is that it is supposed to preserve ministerial responsibility to the legislature, while an appeal to the courts is said to interfere with ministerial responsibility. But it is obvious that the minister will be inclined to uphold the decision of his own deputy, and indeed will very likely have influenced the decision in the first place, so that in a sense the minister is a judge in his own case. Furthermore, if the government is supported by a majority in the legislature, an appeal to that body is not very likely to overturn the minister's decision. This appeal procedure vitiates one of the main objects of the right to force the production of documents: to prevent a minister from withholding information for personal or party advantage, or to protect his officials rather than the public interest. Nova Scotia's new Conservative government therefore introduced a revised act in 1981 providing for an appeal to the courts.

New Brunswick's Right to Information Act was approved by the provincial legislature in June 1978, but not proclaimed until January 1980. It contains the main principles of the American law, but the exemptions are too broad. An unusual feature of this act is that it requires a request for information to go to the appropriate minister. An appeal from his decision may go to either the ombudsman or a judge of the Supreme Court. Where the appeal goes to the ombudsman, he will, in accordance with the usual powers of an ombudsman, make a recommendation to the minister, who must again review the case and make another decision. If still dissatisfied, the applicant can then appeal to a judge of the Supreme Court who has power to order the minister to grant the request for information.

It can be seen that this procedure has the essence of the Scandinavian one, which allows appeals to go to either the ombudsman or the courts. However, it does not make use of the ombudsman's normal functions to avoid a large number of appeals going to the ministers and to the courts. The ombudsman normally receives complaints against officials and makes recommendations to them, their superiors, or the minister *before* the minister becomes concerned. Often a case is settled without the minister having to become involved. The requirement that a written request for information must go to a minister is severely limiting, and is likely to overload the minister. Moreover, an ombudsman's recommendation for release is not likely to persuade the minister to reverse his own decision, and only applicants willing to risk high court costs will appeal to a Supreme Court judge, where they have hope of getting a favourable final determination. If the requirement that a request must go to a minister were removed, the burden on ministers would be lifted, the ombudsman would revert to his normal role in handling complaints, and his chances of persuading the minister to reverse a decision of one of his officials would be greatly increased.

THE FEDERAL GOVERNMENT

A federal access law may be in effect soon after this book is published. In December 1975 a parliamentary committee tabled a report approving in principle the concept of such a law. This report was approved by the House of Commons in February 1976, and in June 1977 the former Liberal government committed itself to introducing some kind of bill on the subject by issuing a Green Paper, *Legislation on Public Access to Government Documents*,[3] which presented arguments for alternative provisions in such a bill.

The tenor of the discussion in the Green Paper, however, indicated that the government was likely to introduce a weak law. Thus, the document favoured a broadly worded list of exemptions and opposed a right of appeal to the courts, even though such a right is an integral part of the laws in Scandinavia and the United States. For this reason, the Green Paper has been strongly criticized, particularly by the Canadian Bar Association and by a research study prepared for it by Professor Murray Rankin.[4]

In December 1977 the Green Paper was referred for study to a parliamentary committee, and in June 1978 the committee reported in favour of a stronger law.[5] It proposed strong enforcement provisions comparable to those in the American law, and it disagreed with the broad wording of the Green Paper's exemptions and its preference for ministers making final decisions on appeals. Thus it opposed the prefacing of exemptions by the word 'might.' The Green Paper had suggested an exemption for documents the disclosure of which 'might be injurious.' The committee felt that this test was too broad and recommended that the wording should instead be 'could be reasonably expected to be.' It also proposed a more restrictive wording for each of the exemptions, in ten areas: national defence, international relations, federal-provincial relations, cabinet documents, policy advice, law enforcement, personal privacy, legal opinions, commercial or financial information, and statutory exemptions. And it recommended that departments be given the power to release a document even if it falls within an exempt category.

On the question of appeals, it proposed a combination of two of the alternatives discussed in the Green Paper: an information commissioner and appeal to the courts. The information commissioner would have only an advisory power, like an ombudsman; but if the commissioner's recommendation that a document should be released was not accepted by a department or minister, an appeal could be made to the courts for a final decision. The advantage of having an information commissioner as an intermediate step is that he would settle most cases before they went to court, thus saving time and money. In support of a final appeal to the courts, the committee agreed with Professor Rankin's contention that:

no constitutional, legal, or practical impediment stands in the way of judicial involvement in the adjudication of freedom of information questions, and that the argument that ministerial responsibility precludes it is a time-worn dogma that collapses upon an examination of English and Canadian constitutional precedents. His study concludes that to hand the final decision on disclosure of information to the unreviewable discretion of a Minister 'who is hardly a disinterested party' would make a sham of any system of access to Government documents.[6]

The government later announced that it planned to introduce an access bill in Parliament, but it had not done so by the time of its defeat in May 1979. Earlier, however, it had sponsored the passage of the Canadian Human Rights Act in 1977, which went into effect in March 1978. Part IV of this act controls the use of personal information held by the federal government and gives citizens the right to inspect their personal files and to file a correction or counter-statement to any information on file. A file may be withheld from a citizen if its subject matter concerns any one of a long list of exemptions, but there is provision for appeal to a privacy commissioner who, like an ombudsman, can make a recommendation. Also, in April 1978 the government introduced a bill, based on a report by a committee of senior officials,[7] to create a general ombudsman plan like the ones now installed in all provinces except Prince Edward Island. Under this bill, the privacy commissioner would have become an assistant ombudsman. However, the bill had not been approved by the time of the government's defeat.

The succeeding minority Conservative government, headed by Joe Clark, refused to sponsor a similar bill, but it did introduce a fairly strong bill on freedom of information, on 24 October 1979 (Bill C-15). Though the exemptions in the bill were too broad, it did provide for appeals to an ombudsman-like information commissioner and ultimately to the Federal Court. It appeared to be acceptable in principle to all political parties, but had not passed by the time of the government's defeat in December 1979 and its replacement by the Liberal government after the election of February 1980. In July 1980 the new Trudeau government introduced the Access to Information Act and the Privacy Act (Bill C-43), which was a revision of the previous Conservative bill, but also incorporated, as Schedule II, a bill to replace Part IV of the Human Rights Act.[8] Schedule II extends the right of personal access to personal files to any files containing personal information, brings the exemptions into line with those in the public access part of the act, provides a parallel two-tier system of appeals to the privacy commissioner and the Federal Court, and removes the privacy commissioner from membership in the Human Rights Commission. In an effort to gain opposition agreement to the quick passage of Bill C-43, Secretary of State Fox later proposed several minor amendments, but these did not alter the basics of the bill. By the end of 1981, Parliament had not yet passed the bill, and Mr Fox appeared to have changed his mind about its speedy approval.

The Access to Information Act is so similar to Bill C-15 that it has most of the same virtues and defects. Some of the revisions are improvements but others weaken it so much that it may fairly be viewed as a watered-down version of the Conservative bill.

Most press discussion of the Access act has been directed at the surprising conversion by the Liberal government to the view that there should be an ultimate appeal to the courts. The Access act has adopted the main provisions of Bill C-15 for a two-step system of appeals, first to an information commissioner and then to the Federal Court. This unexpected development, combined with the government's claim that it had also improved the Conservatives' bill, so mesmerized the proponents of a strong bill that their initial reaction, before reading the fine print, was to praise it unduly. Some proponents still have not read the fine print.

It is true that Bill C-15 and the Access act contain two of the essential principles of an effective act: a general declaration in favour of openness and the establishment of a public right of access by provision for appealing refusals of access to an independent authority. But a basic criticism of both is that they contain a long list of broad exemptions that do not give the information commissioner and the Federal Court effective grounds for recommending or ordering the release of requested records. Thus, most of the exemptions are for a whole class of records and contain no balancing, or harm, test – no requirement that the government must balance the potential harm from releasing a record against the public interest in its disclosure. In such cases, all the government needs to do to justify withholding a record is demonstrate that it falls within the class of records listed in the exemption, and the court has no other grounds for ordering release even if the release would clearly do no harm.

Worse still, some of the exemptions go against the whole spirit of a freedom of information act by absolutely prohibiting certain types of records from being released, thus turning these exemptions into an extension of the Official Secrets Act.[9] As a result, some types of information that were formerly released by custom may in future have to be kept secret. Such mandatory exemptions in the new bill include: information required to be withheld by other statutes or obtained in confidence from another government; personal information; financial, commercial, or technical information supplied to the government in confidence by third parties; and memoranda to the cabinet, cabinet discussion papers, and other cabinet documents (which must be withheld for twenty years unless released by authority of the prime minister).

In these areas, secrecy will now be fortified by law, and access to records, even when this would be warranted for a public purpose and would do no harm, will be prohibited. For instance, the mandatory exemption for personal information is very broad and contains no harm test, in contrast to the American law, which prohibits public access to personal records only where this would cause an 'unwarranted' invasion of privacy. One result is that there will be no right of access to personal files for necessary research on social problems. The privacy part of Bill C-43 provides that the head of an institution at his discretion may grant and control access for research and statistical purposes. But the bill provides no *right* of access for such purposes and hence no grounds for appeal by a requesting researcher. His access to personal records may be refused unfairly at an official's whim, even though he is willing to sign an undertaking not to release information that identifies individuals.

More serious is the prohibition against the release of information supplied confidentially by third parties.[10] Under this exemption, which did not appear in Bill C-15 and was added to the Access act, business firms would have complete control over the release of information they provide to the government merely by treating it as confidential. Yet the government cannot regulate business adequately or accountably unless the public has access to certain types of business information regardless of the wishes of the business being regulated. This obvious pandering to business interests should not have been added to the act. Mr Fox has since proposed an amendment allowing the release of business information in the public interest.

Exemptions in the act that are of a permissive nature, whereby an official may withhold the information but is not required to do so, include: federal-provincial and international affairs; the defence of Canada; the prevention of subversive activities; law enforcement and the investigation of crime; the economic interests of Canada; audits, testing procedures, and tests if the results are 'likely to be misleading'; information subject to the solicitor-client privilege or that would threaten the safety of an individual; deliberations or advice by or for a government institution; and plans for government negotiations, administration, or personnel management. Some of these exemptions, such as federal-provincial affairs, the results of tests, and governmental deliberations, advice or plans, are not at all necessary, since any information on them that ought to be kept secret could easily be withheld under some of the other broad exemptions, such as those for cabinet documents.

The sweeping mandatory exemptions for cabinet and related documents, and the broad permissive one for deliberations, advice, or plans, are particularly disturbing because they will result in the withholding of many policy documents that ought to be made available for full public discussion of proposed measures, and so that Parliament and the public will know the basis on which the government has made its decisions. These exemptions will thus limit the accountability of the government to Parliament. It is hard to imagine a significant government record or document that could not be kept secret under them, especially since they are class exemptions, so that the government only has to show that a record belongs to one of the exempted classes, not that its release would be harmful. These exemptions should be narrowed and should contain a harm test. Moreover, the act should require policy documents and the reports of task forces and consultants to be prepared in such a way that background information and the discussion of policy options are separated from any actual recommendations to the cabinet and are released to the public, as a necessary basis for the public discussion of policy issues.

There are also other ways in which the act has been made restrictive. Though it is obvious that the sensitivity of secret records declines rapidly with the passage of time, most of the exemptions do not have a time limit on the withholding of information, and the one provided for cabinet records and governmental deliberations, advice, or plans (20 years) is far too long. Also, requesters are limited to citizens or landed immigrants, whereas the Swedish and American laws are made available to anyone. Canadians have even succeeded in getting access to documents under the American act about Canadian affairs that they could not get from the Canadian government. The Canadian law should be made reciprocal. Anyway, foreigners can circumvent the restriction simply by getting a Canadian to make the request for them.[11] Moreover, the fees charged to requesters and the costs of appeal to the Federal Court are too restrictive, and too much is left to be filled in by regulations under the act. The government institutions to be covered by the act are spelled out in a backwards way by listing in an appendix those that are to be covered, leaving those not covered – and why – to remain a mystery, rather than simply saying that all are to be covered, with perhaps a few made exempt if necessary for specified reasons.

The act also has other deficiencies. The time allowed for replying to a request or deciding on an appeal is too long, and the government's powers to refuse to state if a record exists and to omit secret records from the official index of government records are too broad. 'Secret law' (internal guidelines for making decisions affecting the rights of individuals) is not required to be made publicly available, and the procedures for classifying secret documents are not spelled out.[12] Also, ministers' papers are not covered by the act nor defined as 'public' along the lines of the American Presidential Records Act of 1978,[13] and there are no provisions preventing the destruction of records, providing penalties for non-compliance by officials, or requiring a comprehensive annual report to Parliament on the working of the act.

In the light of these criticisms it is obvious that the federal Access Act is far from having all of the characteristics of a strong bill that were derived from our study of foreign experience. Nevertheless, the act does constitute an important step in the direction of greater openness. With some key amendments, notably to reduce the number and scope of the exemptions, to change the mandatory exemptions to permissive ones, and to add a harm test where there is only a class test, it could be turned into a strong law. Such amendments are not likely to be made, however, because the government naturally likes the convenience of confidential deliberations, wishes to protect itself from politically embarrassing disclosures, and is supported by a bureaucracy that, as Professor Hodgetts has pointed out, enjoys basking in the power of its near-monopoly of knowledge. Indeed, the likelihood under our cabinet system of the federal or provincial governments sponsoring a really strong law is very slim unless public opinion becomes strong enough to force their hands. Yet, the public's right of access to government records is such a basic right for a democracy that it ought to be enshrined in the constitution, as it is in

Sweden. A strong statement of this right should be contained in the new Bill of Rights, which in turn should be enforceable upon all levels of government, so that ordinary laws containing unnecessary provisions for secrecy could not be made to override it.

BEYOND AN ACCESS LAW[14]

Even if the Access Act were to be strengthened, this would not be enough to meet our need for greater openness in government. The reason is that the apex of power in our system of government – the cabinet – conducts its affairs in secret. This results in serious limitations not only on the government's accountability to Parliament, but also on its ability to make publicly acceptable policy, because the public are frozen out of its deliberations. Our cabinet system is seriously deficient in its ability to provide for public participation in policy-making, because all major legislative measures are decided in secret by the government before they are presented to Parliament, which only dots the 'i's and crosses the 't's. A government will rarely alter the main features of a bill once it is presented to Parliament, and affected groups have little prospect of significantly changing a measure at this stage. New techniques for public participation in policy-making are needed to overcome this disability.

Not only the cabinet's decisions on proposed laws but also orders-in-council, ministerial regulations, and decisions affecting individual persons or corporations are made in secret. Indeed, the cabinet's practice of secrecy has permeated the whole administrative system to such a degree that most independent regulatory bodies make their rules and decisions in secret. One of the great advantages of such bodies is that they can be freed from the influence of cabinet secrecy without altering the cabinet system of government. We should immediately avail ourselves of this advantage by requiring that their deliberations be open to the public.

If we are to overcome the crippling effect of governmental secrecy on public participation in the affairs of government, much needs to be done on all these fronts. We need to invent, or explore experience elsewhere for, new techniques for public participation in all three areas of executive decision-making – decisions on proposed legislation, on regulations, and on individual cases.

Regarding proposed legislation, the federal and provincial cabinets, as a result of their secret deliberations, suffer from a lack of communication with the public and especially affected interest groups.

Hence, they have inadequate opportunities to garner proposals for legislative measures from relevant groups in society and must rely on the bureaucracy for such proposals. Nor do they have an adequate way of gauging the public's reaction to proposed measures or of receiving proposals to improve these measures. There may literally be no public opinion on an issue or proposed measure because the public have inadequate knowledge about it and have had no opportunity to discuss it. This is in sharp contrast to the situation in the United States, where under the congressional system all bills are introduced by individual members of Congress and are studied and discussed publicly by congressional committees and interest groups – sometimes for years – before they reach the floor of one of the houses in the form of a legislative measure. Even then, they must undergo a long period of congressional consideration, and frequently major amendments, before they are finally approved.

Under the cabinet system a traditional method of trying to meet the disability of insufficient public discussion of policy problems has been the use of royal commissions to hold public hearings, stir up public interest in an issue, receive proposals from interested groups, and make recommendations. Another method has been the publishing of a white paper as a statement of government policy in order to get a public reaction before a bill is drafted. A more recent technique has been the release of a green paper on an issue in order to present alternative proposals and receive views from the public *before* the government becomes committed to a particular policy.

Another device that ought to be adopted is the release of draft bills on important measures before final bills are presented to Parliament, so that the public and affected groups will have time to study and react to them, and make proposals for major amendments. The cabinet would thus have an opportunity to accept proposed amendments that would improve the bills and make them more acceptable, since it is unlikely to accept major amendments after bills are introduced. This device is already used in several parliamentary countries in Western Europe, notably Switzerland and Sweden.[15]

In making regulations, the cabinet, departments, and regulatory bodies should likewise release draft orders and regulations for public discussion, possible objection, and proposed amendment before their adoption. A similar procedure should be followed for decision-making in individual cases. Where administrative decisions will affect individuals or corporations, provision should be made for a public hearing to receive the views of interested parties, especially those whose interests will be directly affected. A few departments and several regulatory bodies, notably the Canadian Radio-Television and Telecommunications Commission, the Canadian Transport Commission, and the National Energy Board, are already following these procedures, and they are used generally by departments and regulatory commissions in the United States.[16] Although one could not expect the secret precincts of the cabinet and its ministries to be invaded immediately in this way, there is no reason why such practices should not be demanded at once of most regulatory bodies. If they work well there, they should then be adopted by ministers and their departments, and finally by the cabinet in making important orders-in-council. Only by such devices as these will the pernicious way in which cabinet secrecy prevents public participation in decision-making be overcome.

The epigraph is taken from 'Public Power and Ivory Power,' in T. Lloyd and J. McLeod, eds., *Agenda 70* (Toronto, 1968), p. 270.

The essay is a revision and expansion of the second half of my 'Laws on Access to Official Documents,' *Indian Journal of Public Administration*, vol. XXV, no. 4 (Oct./Dec. 1979), pp. 987-1015. Information on developments elsewhere may be found there, and also in the book I edited, *Administrative Secrecy in Developed Countries* (London: Macmillan; and New York: Columbia University Press, 1979), and in my study for the Ontario Commission on Freedom of Information and Individual Privacy, *Public Access to Government Documents* (Toronto, 1978).

1 *Information et liberté* (Québec, 1981); *Public Government for Private People: The Report of the Commission on Freedom of Information and Individual Privacy*, vol. I (Toronto, 1980). On New Brunswick, see B.G. Smith and J. McCamus, 'The New Brunswick Right to Information Act,' in J. McCamus, ed., *Freedom of Information: Canadian Perspectives* (Toronto: Butterworth, 1981).
2 See Tom Riley, 'Freedom of Information: The N.S. Law,' *Civil Service Review*, vol. 50, no. 30 (September 1977), p. 29.
3 Issued by Honourable John Roberts, Secretary of State (Ottawa, 1977)
4 T. Murray Rankin, *Freedom of Information in Canada: Will the Doors Stay Shut?* (Ottawa: Canadian Bar Association, 1977), p. 155

5 Joint Committee on Regulations and Other Statutory Instruments, *Minutes of Proceedings and Evidence*, issue no. 34 (27 June 1978), pp. 3-12

6 Ibid., p. 9

7 Committee on the Concept of the Ombudsman, *Report* (Ottawa, 1977)

8 For information on bills C-15 and C-43 see my edited volume, *The Right to Know: Essays on Governmental Publicity and Public Access to Information* (Ottawa: Department of Political Science, Carleton University, 3rd ed. 1981). It contains a reproduction of the two bills, the cabinet discussion papers released with Bill C-43, essays commenting on the bills, a summary of the Ontario commission's recommendations, a bibliography of recent materials, and also my comparative article from the *Indian Journal of Public Administration* (Oct./Dec. 1979) and my briefs to the committees of the House of Commons that considered bills C-15 and C-43.

9 For a strong statement of this criticism, see Heather Mitchell, 'Freedom of Information and Official Secrets,' *Canadian Forum* (February 1981), pp. 18-19.

10 See ibid., p. 19; also Access, A Canadian Committee on the Right to Public Information, *Submission on C-43, Access to Information Bill* (Ottawa, October 1980), p. 18.

11 Mr Fox proposed a minor amendment allowing access by foreigners under conditions to be laid down by regulation.

12 See my 'Canada's Security Classification System and a Freedom of Information Act,' in McCamus, ed., *Freedom of Information*.

13 See Richard J. Bazillion, 'An Appraisal of Bill C-43,' *CAUT Bulletin* (December 1980), p. 11

14 This section is based on my 'Can Lid Be Lifted on Ottawa's Secrecy?' *Globe and Mail* (9 April 1981), p. 7.

15 On the use of this device in Sweden see Heather Mitchell, *Access to Information and Policy Making: A Comparative Study*, Research Publication 16 (Toronto: Ontario Commission on Freedom of Information and Individual Privacy, 1980), chap. II on Sweden.

16 See David J. Mullan, *Rule-Making Hearings: A General Statute for Ontario?* Research Publication 9 (Toronto: Ontario Commission on Freedom of Information and Individual Privacy, 1979).

J.W. GROVE

Administering the Unadministrable? The Case of Atomic Energy

The beginning of the nuclear age can be dated more precisely than any other era in human history, indeed with almost ludicrous precision. It began at 3:20 Chicago time in the afternoon of 2 December 1942. At that moment the world's first nuclear reactor, then called only an 'atomic pile,' went critical, generating less than a watt of power before it was shut down because of mounting levels of heat and escaping radioactivity (the pile had no shielding and no cooling system). This was a scientific achievement of the first importance, for it demonstrated the practicability of a self-sustaining and controlled nuclear chain reaction. The immediate aim of the experiment, however, was neither purely scientific nor peaceful, for what was sought was not controlled energy but uncontrolled energy. The 'Fermi experiment' was part of what was believed by the Allies to be a race with Nazi Germany to produce an atomic bomb. It was not until three years later, with the ending of the war in Japan, that attention could be turned to the problems of administering the atom for peace.

Administering the Atom for Peace is the title Professor Hodgetts chose for a book he published in 1964. Its origins lay in a meeting organized by the International Political Science Association for its Fifth World Congress in Paris in September 1961, and UNESCO was a co-sponsor of the project. At that meeting, lasting several days, a group of social scientists, scientists, and administrators came together to discuss the administration of nuclear energy for peaceful purposes. Reports were prepared as a background for our discussions by people from six countries: Canada, France, Italy, Japan, Britain, and the United States. Professor Hodgetts was the *rapporteur-général*, as well as the author of one of the reports, and he was given a free hand by the sponsors to write up the proceedings in any way he chose. Very sensibly, he decided against simply annotating a collection of conference papers and summarizing the discussions, and produced instead an original work that is still worth careful study.

Since I had the good fortune to participate in the conception of the book, I thought an appropriate tribute to him on the occasion of his official retirement would be to 'revisit' some of the issues that were then raised, and, in particular, those issues which at the time we all tended to underplay or failed to foresee with sufficient clarity. We were perhaps too confident then of the capacity of well-tried forms of executive bureaucratic control to cope with what was to become a rapidly expanding, aggressive, and potentially extremely hazardous industrial technology. We under-rated the extent to which committed technical experts could disagree on matters of public health and safety. We underestimated the extent to which public opposition to nuclear energy on environmental and safety grounds would spread throughout the world. And we failed to foresee not only the seriousness of the problem of warlike nuclear proliferation that would result from the export of peaceful nuclear technology, but also the potential problem of nuclear terrorism using stolen or 'diverted' radioactive materials. The big question that Professor Hodgetts asked at the beginning of his book was: 'Have engineers and scientists created problems that are beyond the administrative reach of the social engineer?'[1] We still do not know the answer to that question. What we do know is that nuclear energy poses one of the greatest challenges of any that the administrative state must face and try to overcome in the last years of the twentieth century.

In this essay, I shall look briefly at some of the dimensions of this challenge: at the problems of nuclear safety, nuclear waste management, nuclear proliferation (that is, the potential spread of the capacity, through 'peaceful' nuclear power production, to produce weapons of war), and at the possibilities of nuclear terrorism. These are very large subjects, and it is impossible in so short a compass to treat them at all fully. Moreover, the details of the many administrative challenges they pose must remain largely implicit; but I shall in the conclusion indicate, summarily at least, what I see as constituting the agenda.

NUCLEAR POWER AS AN 'ESSENTIAL MISSION'

As Albert Wohlstetter and his colleagues say in their important monograph, *Moving toward Life in a Nuclear Armed Crowd*,[2] 'the nuclear industry has ... suffered from a chronic state of premature commitment.' This has deep historical roots. The vast 'Manhattan District' that produced the first atomic weapons was also the first great scientific and technological 'mission' in history. The mission was unequivocal: to produce an atomic bomb, and to produce it in the shortest possible time at whatever the cost. To give effect to this mission it became necessary to break the traditional research-development cycle.[3] Normally, development occurs as an aftermath of research, sometimes long after; but the Manhattan Project required that all types of research and development be conducted simultaneously. Thus, industrial plants were already under construction before many of the engineering problems were solved, and applied research was being done before all the problems in theoretical physics and chemistry had been worked out. In a sense one can say that a whole vast complex of research laboratories, engineering facilities, and production plants costing billions of dollars at today's prices was already in place before it was finally known that the mission would succeed or that its 'product' would even be needed (the war might be over).

Much of this sense of urgency spilled over into peaceful nuclear programs. This was due in part, of course, to the fact that the first 'peaceful' nuclear nations were also committed to a weapons program. But even in Canada, which had no intention of manufacturing nuclear weapons, there was something of the same sense of mission, a conviction that nuclear power on a big scale must be high on the list of priorities for post-war policy. All nuclear power programs therefore tended to be 'crash' programs. It was taken as axiomatic that there was a mission to be accomplished and that problems would have to be solved as the mission proceeded; some of them, such as the problems of the safe movement, storage, and final disposal of radioactive wastes, the secure sealing of obsolescent reactors, and environmental pollution, at some undefined time in the future. In 1976, Sir Brian Flowers, a member of the governing board of the United Kingdom Atomic Energy Authority and Chairman of the Royal Commission on Environmental Pollution, gave the following warning: 'Let us not develop a reliance on nuclear power before we can do it in an acceptable manner. That doesn't mean stop. It means for heaven's sake stop to think.'[4]

Many people today, throughout the world, would argue that this sage advice came thirty years too late.

NUCLEAR SAFETY

On 26 March 1979, *Time* magazine reviewed what it described as 'an atom-powered thriller,' the movie, 'The China Syndrome,' and followed this with an assessment of the possibility of such an event actually occurring.[5] Said *Time*: 'A plant could suffer a meltdown ... [but] the very fact that such an accident is possible has dictated safeguards that make the probability of its occurring infinitesimal.' It is one of life's little ironies that two days later (at 4 a.m. on 28 March) an accident of almost precisely the kind foretold in 'The China Syndrome' (which included the possibility but not the actual occurrence of a meltdown) took place at the nuclear power plant operated by the Metropolitan Edison Company, a subsidiary of the General Public Utilities Corporation, at Three Mile Island in Middletown, Pennsylvania. There was no meltdown and no death, and for the next many months only 'acceptable' quantities of radioactive substances were discharged into the river and vented into the atmosphere. What was left, however, was an inoperable reactor and a radioactive mess which recent estimates hold may cost as much as $1½ billion at 1980 prices to clean up. This is far more than the reactor (also at 1980 prices) cost to build, and executives of the utility company were reported in late 1980 as saying that without massive support from governments the company would have to declare bankruptcy. The reactor cannot be sealed safely in perpetuity in its present state, so the clean-up must proceed whether or not the reactor is ever recommissioned. In fact, two years after the accident, the clean-up had come to a virtual standstill.[6] Radioactive water was still leaking into the containment building, adding to the 8½-feet deep pool at the rate of about one inch a month. Until this water is removed, nothing else can be done, and it must be neutralized before it can be discharged into the Susquehanna River. The company now states that it is unlikely that the removal of the partly melted reactor core (the last stage of the clean-up) can be completed before 1985 at the earliest. In fact, nobody knows the exact extent of the damage inside the reactor vessel itself because it is as yet impossible to enter it. In spite of ardent efforts (including a public relations campaign) by the utility and its various holding companies to minimize the affair, this was an accident of quite appalling proportions when set against a whole series of other 'incidents' that had occurred, and are still occurring, in nuclear plants around the world; an accident thus far second only to the still somewhat mysterious explosion at a Soviet nuclear site in the Urals in the late 1950s[7] and possibly, though this is less certain, to the accident that occurred in a nuclear plant near Bratislava, in Czechoslovakia on 24 February 1977.

The immediate repercussions of Three Mile Island were world-wide; among many others: the dismantling and complete rebuilding of two reactors in Sweden on orders from the Swedish government; the ordering by the province of Ontario of modifications to reactor boilers made by Babcock and Wilcox (Canada), a subsidiary of the multinational corporation that designed the boilers for Three Mile Island; a resounding outcry from anti-nuclear forces everywhere; and the sabotage by an anti-nuclear group (possibly aided and abetted by Israeli agents) of a French reactor intended for export to Iraq. Public confidence in the future of nuclear energy was severely shaken. The legacy was not merely a set of technical problems to be solved by scientists and engineers in the United States alone, but a plethora of political and administrative problems relating to the rebuilding of world-wide public confidence, the adequacy of regulation and inspection (in which Three Mile Island was found notably deficient), and the operation of mechanisms of public accountability in all free countries with a nuclear power capability.

The threats to health and safety that may accompany the production of nuclear power are frequently said to be no more severe, or even less severe, than other comparable man-made hazards, in part at least because, while the latter arise routinely from the deliberate discharge of noxious wastes into the environment, often in an unregulated fashion, in the case of nuclear energy such emissions are either altogether forbidden or are closely controlled. But this is a somewhat specious argument since in the nuclear industry the problem really centres on the possibility of accidental or enforced emissions of very large doses of highly toxic materials when something goes wrong. For example, a nuclear physicist, one of the members of the commission that was set up by President Carter to enquire into the Three Mile Island accident, has publicly stated that the typical commercial nuclear power plant contains, at any given time, among other toxic substances, an amount of cesium-137 and strontium-90 roughly equivalent to what would be released by the detonation of a 25-megaton atomic bomb. It is the recognition of such facts that has historically justified the imposition by public authorities – in principle at least – of more stringent types of controls than are imposed in any other area of public regulation. There are, of course, wide differences of opinion among experts about the potential gravity of these hazards as well as about the possibility of their occurring, and it is not always easy for the administrator to disentangle genuine scientific and professional grounds for differing assessments from biases generated either by the interests the experts serve or by their strong personal and intellectual commitments. In these matters, no less than in other areas of life, there are often no 'plain facts.'

The hazards that may arise from some accident in the process of production of nuclear power or at the waste disposal stage of the nuclear cycle may be caused by human error or carelessness, by factors beyond human control (accidents nobody can foresee, or 'acts of God,' or 'natural causes') or by 'contrived accident,' that is, by deliberate sabotage. The first of these can be reduced by rigorous training and vigilant supervision at every stage of the construction-to-operation process but can never be entirely eliminated. This is an area, also, one suspects, in which familiarity may breed boredom and a relaxation of vigilance. When a reactor, for example, is operating smoothly there is little for the technicians to do except 'watch the dials.' At the construction stage there may be temptations, and even economic pressures, to cut corners. As all the world knows, Three Mile Island began with a sticking valve, but there is some evidence that that type of valve was badly designed in the first place (i.e., it was likely to stick), and, in any event, what ensued was exacerbated by human incapacities in face of a traumatic situation. And small errors can have large consequences, as we learnt in September 1980, when the dropping of a workman's wrench led, through a chain of events, to the explosion of a Titan missile in its silo; when some corroded bolts in a British reactor were found, in 1969, to pose a serious risk (if the bolts had fallen into the reactor it might not have been possible to shut it down); when at the beginning of 1981, pieces of metal, possibly from a welder's helmet, and two pieces of a 15-foot-long chain were found in the cooling system of one of the reactors at the Bruce Point Generating Station owned and operated by Ontario Hydro; and when, in 1975, technicians on a routine search for airleaks beneath the control room of the nuclear plant at Browns Ferry, using the apparently approved technique of a naked candle flame, filled a hole they had found with polyurethane foam which the candle then ignited causing a fire that they were unable to extinguish (by the time the rapidly-spreading fire was put out seven hours later, the radiation monitors had been put out of action, the reactors had with difficulty been shut down, and seven of the plant's twelve safety systems had failed).

As to factors beyond human control (natural causes) nothing, by definition, can be done; but this does not explain, for example, the extraordinary tempting of fate that is involved in locating nuclear plants in earthquake zones. A nuclear plant of the Three Mile Island type under construction by a large American-based multinational in the Philippines is placed not only in one of the world's more risky earthquake zones – as indeed are some plants in other parts of the world including the United States – but near four active volcanoes, and in an area that was hit by a tidal wave in 1971. As to the third factor, terrorist or deliberate sabotage, I shall say more later.

NUCLEAR WASTE

Most of the world's radioactive waste, in sheer bulk, comes from the manufacture of nuclear weapons; but for technical reasons (principally the shorter fuel 'burn-up' time required for the production of weapon-grade plutonium) it is less concentrated than the waste from nuclear power production and is therefore, quantity for quantity, less dangerous. In addition, there is naturally radioactive waste from the mining of uranium ore and from the refining process ('tailings') at the so-called front end of the nuclear fuel cycle, and waste produced during the operation of the reactor system itself, such as irradiated coolant and all other material and equipment that must be replaced because it has been irradiated by contact. Some wastes are liquid, others solid; some are 'low-level' in radioactive content, others 'intermediate,' and some (chiefly the spent fuel) are 'high-level' wastes. All are radioactive to some degree; those that cannot, after a relatively short period, be vented safely into the atmosphere or discharged into a convenient body of water require prolonged storage, and the rest need permanent disposal because of the very long half-lives of their radioactive components.

Until recently, little serious attention was paid to the problem of waste disposal. There are various reasons for this. In the early years, as I remarked earlier, there was an undue optimism among scientists and administrators about waste disposal. It was thought that the issue could be safely left until it became pressing, when it would be comparatively easy to solve, simply as a technical problem. The use of spent fuel reprocessing techniques would in any case greatly reduce its extent. In the long run, fusion power would virtually eliminate it.

In the meantime, the development of breeder reactors (fuelled by plutonium made by the reactor itself) and their substitution for 'conventional' reactors using uranium as a fuel would ease the problem still further. It was also the case that work on waste disposal held little attraction for most of the industry's scientists and technologists (there were other more challenging and interesting problems) and those who did work on it were accorded little recognition. All this is reflected in the relatively small sums spent on developing disposal technology (between 1968 and 1977 in the United States for example, federal expenditures amounted to less than $75 million a year). Lastly, there was little public recognition of the issue, though occasionally 'solutions' such as the French proposal, in 1960, to dump their nuclear wastes into the Mediterranean provoked an international outcry.

Lately, however, the need for a lasting solution, perhaps even involving a massive international co-operative effort, has been recognized. Reprocessing and the breeder reactor have alike become suspect because of their potential contribution to the proliferation of nuclear weapons. Fusion power still lies far in the future. Meanwhile the stockpiles of waste, especially of those countries (like the United States and Canada) that do not routinely reprocess spent fuel, are becoming less and less manageable as the available 'on site' storage facilities are filled. Public concern has grown over the existence of large stocks of waste in, or in close proximity to, heavily populated areas, and about the transport of waste to more remote sites. Waste, it is said, has become the Achilles heel of the nuclear industry. When, for example, in Britain in 1975, it was announced that negotiations were under way to import a large quantity of Japanese spent nuclear fuel for reprocessing, there was a storm of protest against what the London *Daily Mirror* described as 'A plan to make Britain the world's nuclear dustbin.'

It is now abundantly clear that waste disposal is no longer, if indeed it ever was, simply a technical problem. It is a political and administrative problem. There is public apprehension about safety and health, fired by an accumulation of incidents involving leaks in temporary storage tanks, evidence of leaching into water supplies, revelations of dumpings of refinery wastes into abandoned quarries and ravines, and even the past use of radioactive rubble as building fill. Ironically, public feeling is acting to repress rather than to hasten the adoption of firm policies for waste management. Administrators increasingly find themselves in a no-win situation as politicians become too sensitive about public reactions to take positive decisions (in the United States, for example, several states have simply enacted laws banning permanent waste disposal sites within their borders). This poses one of the severest challenges of any that administrators in this arena of public policy have had to face.

The recent (1980) report of the International Fuel Cycle Evaluation (in which 66 nations took part) saw no insurmountable technological barriers to the safe and economic storage in perpetuity of high-level wastes. Indeed, the technical problems appear to be virtually solved, the currently most favoured method among experts being the vitrification of the waste, encapsulation in multi-walled metal containers, and deep burial in geologically stable rock formations.[8] The major outstanding problem lies in the choice of suitable sites, which involves not only careful technical study of the site characteristics but also, not unimportantly, overcoming the resistance of environmental groups (one hopes, by reasoned reassurance) that are opposed to the particular sites selected. But the IFCE report has argued that the major health and environmental hazards in nuclear power are not in the reactor waste but at the front end of the nuclear power cycle, that is, in the natural radioactivity from the tailings from uranium mining and refining operations. This means that the radiological impact of waste management is mainly correlated with uranium demand, which is of course large for the once-through cycles and least for the fast-breeder cycle. Thus, if once-through cycles (as in existing American light-water and the Canadian CANDU programs) are to be retained, 'front-end waste' becomes the major long-term problem. Effective removal of the chief radioactive hazards during the actual milling stage is in principle possible, but it is difficult and costly, given the quantity of potential waste material to be processed. Optimists in the American nuclear industry argue that, even by the end of the present century, the total accumulated 'peaceful' high-level waste (from the United States reactors alone, of course) could still be fitted into an 80-foot cube. But since that cube would remain dangerously radioactive for a period into the future that is longer than the whole of the human past since Neanderthal Man (about 100,000 years), and since, moreover, the waste is *not* 'fitted into a cube' but is highly dispersed, this is not a reassuring argument.

NUCLEAR PROLIFERATION

As Professor Hodgetts said at the beginning of his book, the peaceful applications of nuclear energy are inseparably linked to efforts to achieve international control of its military uses. The most fundamental of the reasons why this is so is that the 'conventional' nuclear power reactor, of whatever type, including CANDU, also produces as a by-product a quantity of plutonium that can, in principle, be diverted to the manufacture of weapons. However, 'commercial grade' or power-reactor plutonium contains contaminants which have a high rate of spontaneous fission and thus could trigger a premature chain reaction, making the yield of a weapon unpredictable; so that its use is less attractive to dedicated weapons producers than regular 'weapons-grade' plutonium produced directly from uranium metal. In this respect, the greatest danger for international security in the longer term seems to lie in the development of the fast-breeder reactor, which is capable of producing more (in some types, twice as much) plutonium than it consumes; and to extract enough 'pure' plutonium for a bomb from a breeder's fuel is relatively simple and inexpensive. On the other hand, one of the advantages of the fast breeder (apart from its greater efficiency) is that by, so to speak, 'feeding on itself' it greatly reduces, though it does not eliminate, the problem of radioactive wastes.[9] It is also an alternative source of nuclear power as world supplies of natural uranium dwindle. These factors pose a serious dilemma for the policy-maker. The initial hope expressed in the so-called Acheson-Lilienthal Plan, and based on an early generation of reactors, was that the fuel rods could be left in the reactor long enough to so contaminate the by-product that it would be 'denatured,' that is, rendered unusable for military purposes; but this proved to be physically unrealizable. Though other methods of rendering wastes unusable militarily are being sought, this could not deter a nation that already possesses the means of turning the wastes from its own 'peaceful' reactors to military use if it is determined to do so (that is, a nation that possesses a complete nuclear fuel cycle).

Proponents of the fast-breeder reactor have argued that the 'once-through' or 'throw-away' fuel cycle – uranium-burning reactors and no reprocessing – not only produces a serious waste disposal problem but also provides, in the shape of the temporary storage facilities on each storage site, a potential plutonium mine. Initially, the fuel rods are so 'hot' that they are inaccessible to theft or diversion unless the diverter already possesses a sophisticated reprocessing plant. But the level of radioactivity falls rapidly – by a factor of 300 in the first year, and by a factor of 2000 over the first ten years – so that if the rods have been stored long enough they become quite accessible. That is to say, the argument is that a policy of using 'conventional' reactors without reprocessing – which has been the policy in the United States and Canada – is not a satisfactory non-proliferation policy. Every nation with a nuclear power plant and a spent fuel storage facility, the argument goes, has set up an option to build nuclear weapons; and Walter Marshall, a United Kingdom Atomic Energy Authority official, has estimated that (short of an all-out ban on future reactor construction, and on the assumption that the once-through fuel cycle is maintained) by the year 2000 there will be enough stored plutonium in the world for the manufacture of a quarter of a million bombs. Marshall has argued that adoption of the breeder reactor can actually *reduce* the amount of plutonium in the world by 'fine tuning' the breeders to produce substantially less plutonium than they consume (which can be done) and by then refuelling them with the plutonium extracted by reprocessing from existing stocks of 'conventional' spent fuel. He meets the objection that the production of plutonium through reprocessing is precisely what the non-proliferation opponents of reprocessing wish to avoid, by advocating that it be done in such a way as to leave the plutonium 'contaminated' with about 80 per cent depleted uranium and other highly radioactive products. This material can be incinerated in breeders but could only provide weapon-grade material if it were further reprocessed in a fully shielded plant. The dilemma, however, is that, while this might reduce the risk of nuclear terrorism (see below), it would not deter any nation that was determined on possessing a stock of weapons and had built the necessary reprocessing capacity.

One of the ironies of the Nuclear Non-Proliferation Treaty of 1968 (sponsored by Britain, the Soviet Union, and the United States) lies in Article IV, which commits the parties to 'the fullest possible exchange of (nuclear) equipment, materials and scientific and technological information.' Given the intimate connection between the peaceful and warlike uses of nuclear energy, this in effect encourages what the Treaty otherwise seeks to prohibit, namely the spread (even if clandestinely and contrary to other agreements) of the capacity to produce nuclear weapons. The economic case for nuclear power in the Third World (the apparent intention of Article IV) is slight in many of the larger and/or more developed of those countries, and in the smaller and/or less developed it is non-existent, since nuclear power is highly capital-intensive and its commercial viability depends on the availability of sophisticated technological manpower for operation and maintenance, high demand and continuous utilization, national transmission ('grid') systems, and a wide social distribution of up-to-date electrical appliances.

The desire to possess nuclear power on the part of the governments of Third World nations is often said to be determined more by national prestige (like the desire for a national airline – even if it can only afford to fly two or three 'hand-me-down' aircraft) and by aspirations to join the nuclear club and resentment at dependent status, than by economic interest; though it has been strongly argued by some (for example, by Ebinger) that in an era of ever-dwindling fossil fuel resources the nuclear 'have-nots' are fully justified in their resistance to attempts to limit the club to a handful of powers and that any future policy of international control must accept the sovereign equality of all nations.[10] Moreover, the 'have-nots' may justifiably fear for their own security from nuclear attacks (e.g., Iraq vis-à-vis Israel). The policies of the Western governments in face of these aspirations have been characterized, with some justice, as schizophrenic: on the one hand, a hunger for business, and the use of nuclear technology and materials exports as an instrument of foreign policy,[11] and on the other hand, a constant fear of the consequences of making this technology more widely available. The pressure to do just that is reinforced by the actions of the multinationals (notoriously hard for the administrative state to control) since the dependent Third World provides a profitable dumping ground for the technology that the multinationals are having difficulty in selling to the West.

In a letter to the *New York Times* in 1979,[12] Philip Stern pointed out that domestic orders for nuclear plants had fallen dramatically since 1973, since which time some 20 American plants had been cancelled and some 200 postponed, and that neither General Electric nor Westinghouse, the two largest nuclear plant producers in the United States, had received a single new domestic order since 1974. 'So now, with massive assistance from the Export-Import Bank, [GE and Westinghouse] are shipping their domestically unsaleable wares overseas, and to a select group of countries: a rogues' gallery of repressive regimes.' He added that the plant under construction in the Philippines would cost three times that country's annual investment in agriculture, that 70 per cent of the population would receive no direct benefits from it because they lived in rural areas that would not be reached by the plant's electricity, and that the reactor, 'like others being exported,' would not meet even the safety standards that apply to facilities in the United States.

In the early years of the nuclear age it was strongly argued (and nowhere more strongly then by nuclear scientists themselves) that the safety of mankind depended on limiting the possession of atomic weapons to a very few countries. Yet at the present time roughly a dozen nations either possess nuclear weapons or are believed to be on the point of possessing the capacity to produce them. The latter include India, Pakistan, South Africa, Argentina, Brazil, Taiwan, Israel, and South Korea, not all of whom have accepted even such international safeguards as currently exist or are signatories to the Non-Proliferation Agreement; and it is estimated that at least forty countries could have joined the nuclear weapons club by the year 2000.

The enormous political and administrative problems posed by the attempt to limit the spread of nuclear weapons, problems that are exacerbated by the fact that much of it takes place in defiance of national and international controls, are implicit in the story of Pakistan's determination to build a bomb in face of (at least officially stated) efforts on the part of the major nuclear powers to prevent it from doing so. In order to pursue that determination, Pakistan has adopted a series of clandestine measures and world-wide 'cover' operations disguising its real intent so as to obtain the necessary resources.

The situation is further complicated by the fact that many *research* reactors are also capable of producing sizeable quantities of fissionable materials that can be used for explosives, and without breaking any agreement. It is almost certain that the so-called 'peaceful device' that was exploded by India beneath the Rajasthan Desert in May 1974 used plutonium from the Canadian-built CIRUS reactor which Canada gave to India, since this reactor, unlike India's power reactors (of which there were four at that time, two Canadian-built and two US-built) was not subject to inspection by the International Atomic Energy Agency. The 'device' which released between 10 and 15 kilotons of energy could have been built with about one year's yield from normal operation of the CIRUS reactor.

As Wohlstetter and his colleagues have argued: 'In this complicated and fateful area of policy, very often actions taken for the best of ends perversely defeat them. If our policies are to cope with the spread of military-nuclear technology rather than encourage it, it is essential that they be more than symbolic and well-intended.' *Moving toward Life in a Nuclear Armed Crowd*, which includes one of the most thorough and comprehensive assessments of the proliferation peril yet undertaken, makes clear that a fundamental change in the international rules is required: 'The evidence is strong that the benefits of nuclear power can be retained along with restraints to lessen its dangers. ... Clearly, new international rules which might be widely accepted will have to take account of the diverse situation of countries with respect to access to fuels, widely differing levels of technology, and different perceptions of dangers to [their] security.' Devising such rules will be a formidable task: 'However, the consequences of the spread of nuclear explosives warrant making a great and sustained effort to eliminate the worst risks.'[13]

What is urgently needed is a greater recognition of the common danger.

NUCLEAR TERRORISM

Until quite recently the prospect of the use of nuclear devices by terrorist groups ('unofficial terror'), let alone by individual political fanatics or by persons seeking merely to extort ransom money for their own ends, seemed to belong in the realms of fantasy fiction (one of the earliest treatments of this theme was the 1950 movie *Seven Days to Noon*, for which the late Paul Dehn, a British writer resident in Holywood, wrote the script). It was originally widely supposed that the intense security surrounding the industry, as well as the high value of fissile material to commercial enterprises dealing in it, would be more than sufficient to prevent it from falling into the wrong hands (and presumably, that 'insiders' would be totally reliable!). While the fuel is in the reactor it is in a highly radioactive environment and is in any case protected, at least in principle, by strict security at the plant. Radioactive waste is not a very attractive place from which to steal fissile material either (at least for small raiding groups) because great care is taken to keep the fissionable concentration as low as possible (if that were not done, there would be a real risk of the waste 'going critical' – which may be what happened in the Soviet Union at the Urals site in the 1950s). Thus, the most vulnerable links in the chain may be while nuclear fuel itself is being manufactured or transported and while spent fuel removed from the reactors is in transit for reprocessing. The latter prospect is usually countered by the argument that spent fuel rods destined for reprocessing are still so radioactive that no terrorists would get far with them before their hair started to fall out. The level of radioactivity, however, as mentioned earlier, drops relatively rapidly, so that old rods possibly constitute some threat. More realistically, perhaps, the greater threat may be said to come from clandestine purchase of uranium or other materials which are then supplied to well-organized terrorist groups under cover and through intermediaries by, or with the tacit approval of, sympathetic state authorities. Standards of security apparently vary widely in rigour from one country to another, and even where they are notionally high, there have been some alarming 'losses' and instances of material unaccounted for. It is extremely difficult to maintain an inventory control that is fail-safe, and some loss is inevitable in the process of fabrication. The most dramatic example of loss, perhaps, of those that have become known (in this case through the US Freedom of Information Act) is the missing 100 to 200 lbs. of uranium (the exact amount seems never to have been determined) from the Nuclear Materials and Equipment Corporation of Apollo, Pennsylvania, in the 1960s. This is the material that is believed to have gone to Israel.[14] Reportedly a number of nonnationals were present in the plant during those years, including an Israeli metallurgist and two technicians from Argentina; and the company is known to have had contracts to supply nuclear services in several countries, of which Israel was one. One of the released documents noted that 'the verification of overseas shipments is largely based on the assumed integrity of the domestic shipper and of the foreign receiver'!

According to a report in *The New York Times Magazine*[15] some sixty nuclear threats were made against American cities and institutions between 1970 and 1980, four of them against New York City alone. So far the threats have been empty, but that against New York City in 1975 (by a person or group demanding $30 million in ransom) included a drawing of a nuclear device which was 'sophisticated, precise and obviously made by someone who had more than a passing acquaintance with physics.' The article goes on to describe in general terms the operations and special equipment of a federal agency called the Nuclear Emergency Search Team, a team of scientists and technicians which has been established to handle all threats that provide evidence that the threat may mean something. Though the unit may be used for other purposes (for example, some of its personnel were assigned to help the Canadian authorities locate the pieces of the Soviet nuclear-powered spacecraft that came down in the north in 1978), its chief objective is to analyse the seriousness of the threat and to locate the device if there is one, and, in the last resort, disarm it. It works in complete secrecy; necessarily, since (as was put to the *New York Times* reporter): 'Any group of terrorists smart enough to build a bomb is going to be smart enough to protect it.' In fact, its existence was not revealed to the US Congress itself for three years, and then only in the course of closed testimony before the House Armed Services Committee. A press release was subsequently issued, but 'reluctantly' and on a Sunday at midnight.

According to the report, three kinds of people have been behind these nuclear extortion attempts: 'psychotics, ideological terrorists, and fortune hunters'; but it is not clear whether this categorization is merely newspaper speculation or is based on facts and inferences known to NEST. In any event, it seems likely that only those in the second category could ever be in a position to back up their threats given the risks and difficulties involved. But this is not an empty class – that is to say, the possibility does exist that a terrorist group could at some time and in some country either possess a home-made bomb, or hijack a nuclear weapon, penetrate a nuclear power plant control room in order to cause a core meltdown, or sabotage a waste storage facility. It must be borne in mind, however, that this is not specifically a nuclear problem. The problem is terrorism itself. The nuclear route is only one of several 'disaster' options that might be open to terrorist forces (radiological weaponry would be another). The lesson is a general one: that the more complex and interdependent a highly technological society becomes, the more vulnerable it is; and therefore, for good or ill, the more 'security' protection it must possess for the defence of its key installations, institutions, and processes.

CONCLUSION: NUCLEAR POWER AND THE ADMINISTRATIVE STATE

The concept 'administrative state' was very largely the invention of a small group of American political scientists, of whom Dwight Waldo is perhaps the foremost representative. But they were anticipated by Max Weber. The 'administrative technicians' (in Waldo's phrase) of the German state, about whom Weber was chiefly writing in his studies of bureaucracy, had no doubt that it was they who should rule. Weber saw the peril in this, and saw clearly that the central issue was to secure that bureaucracy was made accountable and subject to public control (an issue to which Professor Hodgetts has devoted much of his scholarly work). Waldo, reflecting traditional American ideas and values, wrote: 'Bureaucracies have never grown up, so far as we are aware, to "mould the framework of our culture" or to "rebuild the pattern of our lives", but for much more immediate and mundane objectives upon which at least the ruling groups were agreed. Science, has created a whole new realm of discourse.'[16] By 'science' he meant, of course, primarily 'scientific management' – the rise of the 'administrative technician' par excellence; but the term is now capable of much greater extension.

In an important sense, nuclear energy constitutes a paradigm. It is presented as one of the 'technological imperatives' to which we must all submit. Knowledge about nuclear energy and its technological exploitation is highly esoteric knowledge. Moreover, its close connections with life and death, especially in its military potential, mean that it must be surrounded, at least in many of its aspects, by veils of secrecy. Thus the way is clear for 'rule by technicians.'

It was obvious from the start that the esoteric nature of the technology and the secrecy of its military potential must seriously hamper public and parliamentary scrutiny; but what was perhaps less obvious at the time Professor Hodgetts wrote his book was that the executive itself might be kept in the dark by the technocrats in the industry and in the military and by public regulatory agencies. Yet this has happened, and those incidents that are now a matter of public record give cause for some disquiet. In an address to the (British) Science, Technology, and Society Association in February 1979,[17] Mr Wedgewood Benn, a leading Labour party politician, and for twelve years the minister responsible for atomic energy in Britain, gave some examples from his own experience. The Soviet nuclear disaster, though known (he believes) to the United Kingdom Atomic Energy Authority, was not reported to the minister or to the cabinet. Nor was the disappearance in 1968 of the uranium that is supposed to have gone to Israel. In 1970 a government agency contract was signed with Rio Tinto Zinc, a London-based multinational, to buy 7500 tons of uranium from a South African mine, in direct contravention of government policy towards South Africa and (again) without the knowledge of the cabinet. A leak of radioactive material, in 1976, from a waste storage silo at Windscale, Britain's nuclear reprocessing plant, was not brought to

Mr Benn's attention until nearly two months after it was discovered. Though the incident was not considered serious, it was covered up because a public enquiry was then under way concerning a large extension of Windscale's reprocessing facilities and the agency believed that publicity might damage the chances of the plan going through (it appears that even the relevant health and safety authorities were not informed until twelve days after the leak was noticed). One cannot help but agree with Mr Benn that: 'A minister is not just a manager who got there by election. He is a representative of the public in the heart of the government. He is a member of the public at the top ... and to do his job he must know what is going on.'

It is perhaps natural for technocrats to resent public attempts to thwart them, and for bureaucrats to believe that they are the best judges of what is right for the public to know. Natural or not, these are persistent tendencies, and in this particular area of difficult and dangerous public policy it is even more than ever necessary that the lay representatives of the public 'in the heart of the government' should know and be in firm control of what they know.

A second vital issue concerning nuclear energy and the administrative state is the almost total lack of direct public input into the policy-making process. There is a great deal of confrontational politicking, but it is only quite recently that concerned groups have begun to make some inroads into the thinking of the industry and the agencies that administer it. There are public relations campaigns by the industry and regulatory agencies, but these are normally aimed at reassuring the public that there is nothing to worry about, whether it is the matter of the siting of a waste burial site or of a new plant, or of the safety of existing reactor technology. The confrontational politics that marks the nuclear scene is in rather sharp contrast to other areas of environmental protection of safety, health, and welfare where public input to administrators, though often strictly limited, is at least more readily admitted.

There are, thirdly, serious problems about regulation. The tendency in this, as in other highly sensitive areas of public regulation (like air safety), is for more stringent standards to follow, rather than to precede, the occurrence of serious incidents. To some extent this is inevitable, since it is impossible to foresee all contingencies. But the fact is that, for example, virtually all major advances in air safety regulation have followed serious, and sometimes disastrous, accidents involving the loss of many lives. And it is rather remarkable that it took a near disaster like Three Mile Island to force an official admission that there were indeed serious shortcomings in the system of inspection and enforcement of nuclear safety standards in the United States, a contention that serious students of the industry had been urging for many years. In this, the regulatory arena, we should remember, too, the well-known tendency for regulatory agencies to become, if not actually the captives, at least the spokesmen and protectors of the industries they were created to regulate.

In the last resort, however, the most serious challenge to the capacities of the administrative state is that of nuclear proliferation. To this, the big question addressed by Professor Hodgetts must again be posed: 'Have engineers and scientists created problems that are beyond the administrative [and, we must add, the political] reach of the social engineer?' The issue is overriding because it cannot simply be laid at the door of the two (or possibly three) great superpowers; it arises from the general sense of insecurity that is felt by all (notionally sovereign) states in a nuclear world. The possibility of unlimited nuclear proliferation results directly from the spread of 'peaceful' technology and immeasurably increases the prospect of all-out nuclear war. If limited nuclear wars are ever fought they are likely to be few. Sooner rather than later, such a war would escalate, bringing worldwide destruction and destitution. The survivors of an all-out nuclear war will no longer possess a capability for nuclear technology, peaceful or otherwise; and the nuclear age, which began in a makeshift laboratory forty years ago will have come to an end.

1 (New York: Atherton Press; London: Prentice-Hall International, 1964), p. 3

2 Reprinted in abridged form in *Minerva* (autumn-winter 1977). The original monograph was prepared by Pan Heuristics, Los Angeles, CA., December 1975.

3 Hodgetts, *Administering the Atom for Peace*, p. 5

4 Introducing to the press the 6th Report of the Royal Commission on Environmental Pollution, *Nuclear Power and the Environment*, Cmnd. 6618, September 1976

5 Pp. 70, 71

6 *New York Times*, 18 January 1981. A very full and interesting accounting of what happened at Three Mile Island is to be found in two consecutive issues

of the *New Yorker* magazine, 6 April 1981 at p. 49, and 13 April 1981 at p. 46. The author is Daniel Ford.

7 See Zhores Medvedev, *Nuclear Disaster in the Urals* (New York: Random House, Vintage Books ed., 1980). According to Medvedev the explosion occurred in buried nuclear waste. The CIA, whose files on the case are still laundered, even under the Freedom of Information Act, appears to have thought that it was a reactor that exploded. Whatever the cause, there is much evidence that it led to extensive radioactive damage and many casualties.

8 See, for example, Bernard Cohen, 'The Disposal of Radioactive Wastes from Fission Reactors,' *Scientific American*, vol. 236, no. 6 (June 1977).

9 It does not eliminate the problem because materials such as the coolant are themselves irradiated in the course of the reactor's operation.

10 Charles K. Ebinger, *International Politics of Nuclear Energy*, the Washington Papers, no. 57 (Sage Publications, 1978)

11 For example, the sale of 38 tons of nuclear fuel to India, ordered by President Carter in 1980 in face of stiff opposition from Congress, was directly related to the Carter administration's desire to maintain good relations with India following the Soviet invasion of Afghanistan, although it was directly contrary to President Carter's own non-proliferation policy.

12 Sunday, 8 April 1979. Philip Stern is the author of a well-known book about the Oppenheimer case.

13 *Moving toward Life in a Nuclear Armed Crowd*, pp. 389, 538

14 *New York Times*, Sunday, 6 November 1977, p. 3

15 Sunday, 14 December 1980, pp. 36ff

16 *The Administrative State* (New York: Ronald Press Company, 1948), p. 101

17 Reported in *Science, Technology and Human Values*, vol. 4, no. 28 (summer 1979)

D.C. CORBETT

Canadian Examples, Australian Adaptations

Retirement is a time for throwing things away. One has to move out of an office, and that means moving books and papers into crowded spaces at home or else deciding one will never need them again. Those are heroic decisions. Which are the interests that will stay alive, which are the ones that are already dead? If I were Ted Hodgetts, which books and papers could I bear to give up? I had another look at Taylor Cole's *Canadian Bureaucracy*[1] the other day, and decided to keep it. It was a somewhat limited book on the subject; it emphasized personnel selection, and was published in 1949.

Taylor Cole made his contribution to comparative political and administrative studies on a broad front. His knowledge of European, American, and Commonwealth systems put him among the leaders of the field in his time. He was junior co-author with Carl Friedrich of another comparative study, *Responsible Bureaucracy*[2] concerned mainly with the Swiss civil service. What is impressive about his Canadian exercise is its modesty and yet its range. It covers the provinces, some leading statutory authorities such as the CBC and the Bank of Canada, even the provincial teaching services. It gives attention to employee organizations, something few others did at that time. There are good bits in Cole, so it comes as a surprise that Hodgetts does not even give his work a mention in *The Canadian Public Service*, parts of which necessarily cover ground which Cole had covered. The reason is perhaps that Hodgetts invariably goes to primary sources for his material, and has no need to rely on other scholars' work except when he wants to discuss a significant comment or interpretation which one of them has made. Cole is not included.

References to Cole are almost equally and conspicuously absent from other books by Hodgetts in association with various colleagues.[3]

And at the time of our publication of *Canadian Public Administration: A Book of Readings*, in 1960, I shared the prevailing slight regard for the book of our leading predecessor. Now, however, I am of the opinion that Cole was indeed worth discussing, particularly for his very firm view that a mistake was being made in Canada when the powers of the Civil Service Commission were under attack and when it was being proposed by the Gordon commission, as early as 1946, that the Treasury Board become the pre-eminent body in public personnel management. Cole regarded it as dangerous to weaken the Commission. He wrote:

> Most constructive personnel changes in the past have emanated from the Civil Service Commission, Parliamentary investigating commissions [*sic*], or the staff associations – in any case, from sources outside the Treasury Board. At the same time, the Civil Service Commission has gone far in achieving the purpose for which it was originally established as an independent agency, namely to keep out the spoilsman. The problem of patronage is still a sufficient problem, however, to justify opposition to weakening the Commission's position as proposed in the Gordon Report.[4]

Here we come to one of the main issues in Hodgetts' major works. As a contributor to the Glassco commission's labours, Hodgetts, though he does not accept responsibility for all of Glassco's doctrines, was associated with Glassco's forceful reassertion of the Gordon report's thesis: personnel management needed to be closely linked with financial management and therefore personnel powers should be assigned to departmental managers, but under the broad supervision of the Treasury Board, with the Civil Service Commission playing a minor part.

Ten years after Glassco, Hodgetts reflects on the proper role and powers of the Civil Service Commission (Public Service Commission after 1967) in his *The Canadian Public Service* (1973). This time he confirms what was a view only indirectly attributable to him previously: the Treasury Board should have the major role. He saw the Treasury Board's rise to supremacy in the 1960s as the culmination of a hundred-year-long evolution, beginning with order-in-council PC3 of 2 July 1867 and progressing by way of Sir George Murray's *Report* of 1913. Six years later, in the Lambert commission's *Report*, Hodgetts is once again associated with recommendations for transfer of power from the Public Service Commission to a proposed Secretary for Personnel Management under the Treasury Board, which Lambert recommended be renamed Board of Management. The Public Service Commission would still have a role in appeals, but not much would be left of its earlier proud stature, steadily declining since the 1920s. I happen to agree with most of what Cole said and therefore must disagree with the course taken by successive Canadian governments, a course which Hodgetts has evidently approved of and quite probably has influenced.

One is bound to feel uncomfortable when disagreeing with a friend and benefactor who also happens to be the pre-eminent authority on the subject. It is not Cole's rather weakly buttressed arguments which bring me to this uncomfortable conclusion. My reason for risking it is my Australian experience; I acknowledge immediately the tenuousness of its relevance, and that admission adds another reason for discomfort. However, I will take courage from the fact that occasionally administrative principles are transportable, and the study of comparative administration is not without its practical uses, though such claims must be made modestly. Hodgetts uses such words as 'confusion' and 'ambiguity' when describing a personnel management system where authority is divided among Parliament, cabinet ministers, Treasury Board, departmental heads and a semi-independent, quasi-autonomous Civil Service Commission. He acknowledges the historic reason for the division and the Civil Service Commission's semi-independence – the need to fight the spoilsman; but he is obviously not happy about it. 'In recent times,' he wrote, 'the tremendous expansion of staff coupled with the conviction that the merit system is no longer threatened by the dragon of patronage have fostered the view that parliament no longer needs this protective device.'[5] 'Nor is it felt that the negative control mentality induced by a guardian civil service commission is in the best interests of the public service.'[6] Taylor Cole's opposite contention was based on his American and British observations. He catalogues a number of Canadian departments where patronage was rife and then observes: 'The number of these patronage positions, while considerably higher than the percentage in England, has also been appreciably lower than in the federal service of the United States.'[7]

There are two important factors which can make patronage a persistent feature of government in modern industrial societies with elected representative institutions. The first is the tendency for one political party to stay in power most of the time; the second is high unemployment and public service staff cuts. Hodgetts himself was early and forceful in pointing out the danger of one-party rule for Canadian government. In 1955 he wrote, 'A generation of Liberal politicians and a generation of presumably neutral senior permanent officials have worked hand-in-hand to create what is now advertised as the Liberal Programme. One imputes no blame to these senior officials if one argues that they are now as fully committed to the Programme as their political chiefs.'[8] He went on to speculate about what would happen if the party in power should change.

It would take more than an independent Civil Service Commission to prevent this sort of thing happening. In Australia, even with its powerful Public Service Boards, it is arguable that something quite similar happened, for example in Canberra in the Menzies era or in South Australia in the Dunstan decade. The Public Service Boards themselves take on the colouring of their masters, not in the partisan sense but at least in the sense that they understand each other well and share many opinions, commitments, and values. This osmosis, or cultural hegemony, or emergence of a power élite, or whatever you wish to call it, is not quite the same thing as simple patronage. True, it does tend to predetermine the types of people who are selected and rapidly promoted, but it is broad affinity which serves as the test for advancement, not political party membership or personal service to a political patron. Nevertheless, gradual convergence of party and bureaucracy makes crude patronage less conspicuous and easier to hide, though also less useful or necessary to secure compliance with the victorious party's mandate.

It is the next stage which is more worrying: the return to power of a hungry party long in the wilderness. It will normally want to install its own senior advisers in appointed positions. The old mandarins may remain, but in general their influence will have gone. A few will perform humiliating contortions or will be recognized as pure technocrats equally serviceable to any party. At times like these, even a powerful Public Service Commission or Public Service Board is again only a weak obstacle to the victorious party's pressure. If the commission or board sticks stalwartly to the merit principle, there are many other places to which the government's favourites can be appointed besides the positions under the commission's control; and, in any case, a sensible commission will feel itself cross-pressured by a moral obligation to see to it that the new party in power gets full co-operation from the bureaucracy in carrying out its program, even if a few heads have to roll to bring that about. Patronage has a faint but perceptible legitimacy under conditions of long turns in power for one party followed by brief innings for the permanent opposition. Patronage, at all events, does happen at the senior levels under these conditions.

A powerful commission, on the other hand, can do a great deal to ensure that patronage is limited to clearing and refilling the top policy-sensitive positions and transferring those individuals who are clearly seen to be either partisan themselves or compromised by personal association with policies disapproved of by the incoming party. If a commission fails to keep patronage within those limits, then it is a failure indeed. There should be continuity and continued reward for neutral, professional merit in 99 per cent of the public service, and a commission worth its salt can make sure of it. Hodgetts, or anyone else who considers old-fashioned civil service commissions to be an anachronism, might question whether a modern political party's leaders would want to take their spoils among the ranks of the lower-paid and less influential civil servants. Would not such practices be counter-productive politically? Is a strong commission necessary to protect the jobs and prospects of subordinate personnel in positions of no political consequence? My answer is a qualified 'yes, a strong commission is still necessary.'

The qualification is that the second patronage-inducing factor has to be taken into account at this point. Whether the spoilsman will try to get at base-grade, entry-level jobs and middle-level promotions depends on the state of the employment market and on whether the civil service is growing or being cut back. When jobs are scarce, and political hangers-on include several who either have no job or are desperate to get out of dull or dead-end jobs, there will be patronage unless there is a strong system and a strong enforcer to prevent it. Deputy ministers will not ordinarily make the merit principle their first priority; they have other concerns. A Treasury Board, Board of Management, or Secretary for Personnel might make merit their first priority, but one can see no compelling reason why they should. One should be able to count on a conspicuous, proud, statutory body, with quasi-judicial functions and the independence and sense of honour that goes with them, to make the protection of the merit principle its first responsibility, and service to the current government its second-order duty.

For the reasons given above, I am of the opinion that strong, independent personnel agencies are potentially valuable in countries such as Canada and Australia, in spite of the loss of unity in the management of resources which their presence causes. Unity of command is a principle of administration more honoured in the breach than in the observance in democratic systems. Cabinets cannot control everything, which is one of the reasons why, as Hodgetts observed, more and more independent statutory authorities have come into existence. A loss of unity among the central co-ordinating agencies is inevitable when both the Civil Service Commission and the Treasury Board have resource-rationing powers. The result is managerial untidiness, but it may be good government, even representative and responsible government. Parliament's ability to intervene strategically with over-riding legislative power can still prevent competition among the central co-ordinating authorities from getting out of hand. In his 1964 essay, 'Challenge and Response,' Ted Hodgetts wrote about the uneasy duality of a Civil Service Commission's responsibilities.[9] On the one hand it is the creature of Parliament, responsible to Parliament for maintaining the merit principle: it is a statutory authority with autonomous powers. On the other hand, it is also a central co-ordinating agency of the executive branch of government. These two kinds of responsibility become uncomfortable when the cabinet wants the Commission to do things which are contrary to the spirit of the Commission's statutory charter, and the real world is full of such conflicts. Such potential tensions are more common when the Commission's powers are broad, as they were in Canada from 1920 until the 1950s, and in the Australian case where Public Service Boards still retain their role as the executive government's principal adviser on machinery of government matters.

Hodgetts noted the anomalous possibilities lurking in the Commission's dual role, but in 1964 put the question aside as one for further research. Though his later research produced magnificent books of administrative history, including *Biography of an Institution*, and a substantial contribution to the Lambert report, I am still not satisfied that he did full justice to the parliamentary side of the Commission's obligations.

However, as confessed earlier, I raise this question less from knowledge of the Canadian realities than from practical experience of their Australian counterparts, while bearing in mind the distinctive features of the Australian case. Nevertheless, it is heartening to find that R.B. Bryce, on the basis of vast Canadian experience and a full appreciation of the Treasury Board's claims, has commented, 'There is more to be said in favour of the Public Service Commission than is in the (Lambert) Report.'[10] He says this after considering the pro's and con's of transferring 'almost all of the present work of the Public Service Commission to the Board of Management, and more particularly to its Secretary for Personnel Management' and leaving 'the Commission an auditing function – one more difficult in process than the financial audit, in my opinion, when you take into account the subtlety of bureaucratic patronage which is now much more of a problem than political patronage – and an appeal court role. This is a logical and plausible proposal, as one would expect from Professor Hodgetts with his vast knowledge of this field. However, it worries me.' Amen to that.

The danger of bureaucratic patronage is, of course, the point to note. Today, in administering its act, a Public Service Board or Commission may have to guard against pressures for promotion of favourites of senior public servants more than of politicians. Departmental managers can sometimes be most insistent that they are the only fair-minded arbiters of merit, defining merit as 'whatever qualities will enable the department to get its business done.' Someone, of course, has to be concerned with the needs of the service as a whole, taking a view of it as consisting of more than the sum of its departmental parts. A committee of senior departmental heads can help, but will do no better than committees usually do when given a continuing managerial responsibility.

When Hodgetts visited Australia in 1980 he gave lectures and seminars on issues arising out of the Lambert commission's report on accountability, and was much sought after because the question of accountability is as much to the fore in Australian public administration as it is in Canada. On two occasions he was at pains to preface his remarks with a broad disclaimer about the relevance of Canadian ideas in the Australian context, because, as he noted, the institutions of public service management, and some of the conventions which have grown up around these institutions, are so different from their Canadian counterparts. He noted, in particular that the Australian Public Service Boards have no exact Canadian counterpart. They can best be understood, perhaps, by conceiving of a body which combines some of the functions of the Canadian Public Service Commission; some aspects of the Public Service Staff Relations Board; the

Personnel Policy Branch of the Treasury Board Secretariat which looks after classification and pay and is the employer for the purposes of collective bargaining; the Program Branch of the Treasury Board Secretariat which is involved in organizations, establishment control, and manpower ceilings; and those parts of the Privy Council Office which may from time to time assist the government in design or redesign of major parts of the machinery of government. They are not, of course, as influential all the time as this list of comparisons would suggest; depending on how the board is regarded by the government of the day, their influence waxes and wanes; but they can be important administrative power centres, and in the notable case of the New South Wales Public Service Board in the 1950s, 1960s, and early 1970s, it was common for commentators to portray the Board as the head of an integrated, hierarchical, administrative machine of which the departments were subordinate parts. No other Board, in recent times has had quite that status, and it is not uncommon particularly for newly elected governments to reduce the Board's power and to insist on imposing strong, direct ministerial authority over the administration; but reversion to Board ascendancy is also not uncommon.

The Australian Commonwealth government, on the other hand, is somewhat different, in that the Treasury Department usually overshadows the Board's power – but the Treasury's power has to do with departmental growth rates, whereas the Board still has the power to advance or retard the career prospects of individuals, and that gives it a grip on something vital. Whether such potentially powerful Public Service Boards are a 'good thing' is as proper a question in Australia as it has always been in Canada, and students of public administration debate it here just as they have in Canada. Gerald Caiden, for example, maintained that their power, on balance, contributed to the system's efficiency.[11] In my own pre-bureaucratic, academic period, I was doubtful, and wrote, Glassco-like, in favour of letting the departmental managers manage,[12] though recommending that the Board retain a monitoring or post-audit form of control over the use departments made of powers delegated to them by the Board – a sort of two-way bet. Nevertheless, when I look at the Canadian federal public service, I see the Commission as far weaker than, it seems to me, a properly managed public service requires.

One can properly warn students of comparative administration against making simple-minded transfers of ideas. Practices or institutions which work well in one country may not work in another. So far, in this chapter, emphasis has been placed on similarities and differences in the area of public personnel management. Careful students such as Hodgetts need no such warnings; they make the same point themselves. What, then, should one make of the rather frequent occurrence of recommendations in Australia, that this or that Canadian administrative institution be adopted? Should these occurrences be ascribed to lack of caution on the part of the proposer, or are there sometimes good grounds for advocating a transfer of successful practices or institutions from one place to the other? Each instance should be looked at sceptically, but without prejudice.

A short list of examples of institutional borrowing which flowed from Australian interest in Canadian administrative reforms would include at least the following: the cabinet committee structure in the Whitlam (1972-75) government at the national level and the Lewis (1975-76) government in New South Wales; executive training and development programs for state and federal public services closely resembling the Career Assignment Program (1968 onwards) of the Canadian federal civil service; the extension of the functions of the Australian Auditor-General to include efficiency auditing (1979). The interest in the Lambert report on the part of Australian public administrators may present us with still further cases of either imitation or coincidental and simultaneous recognition of similar needs. There are also examples of Australian public administration taking warning from over-optimism in Canada about new techniques such as program budgeting.

If one wished to lengthen the list, and to include not only actual changes but also proposals for Australian reforms along lines previously tried in Canada, among the examples would be the widespread interest by state premiers in the Canadian system of tax sharing, prior to 1970, which they abandoned when they quailed at actually imposing state income taxes and when they were offered by Prime Minister Gorton $15 million increase in their grants instead. The story of this apparent trade-off of principles for profit is told in a number of places, including a book of mine, *Looking at Canada*.[13] It is interesting to note that the Fraser government, since 1975, also espoused taxation of incomes by the states, but has so far been unable to persuade any state government to venture into income taxation. The Canadian example is frequently mentioned, but more often as a warning than as a model for imitation.

Professor Russell Mathews, the leading Australian academic authority on federal finance, frequently points out the relevance of Canadian taxation formulae in his writings,[14] and can be credited with a substantial influence on the thinking of senior officers in the Australian federal and state treasuries. Another example of a Canadian solution proposed for an Australian problem was the adoption of a numerical scoring system to assess the eligibility of intending immigrants. This was adopted in the 1960s in Canada and in the 1970s Australia adopted a modified version.[15] In 1980 the Australian version came under considerable press criticism for what were regarded as discriminatory features favouring Europeans, and the new minister, Mr McPhee, promised to review it and perhaps give it up altogether. These are examples of borrowed public policies and administrative devices to go with them. Leaning more toward administrative technique, and involving little in the way of policy, one could cite the Australian adoption of Mandata, a computerized personnel inventory system closely modelled on the Canadian Data Stream system adopted in the early 1970s and in service by 1973. Australia's Mandata project has had a rough passage: hardly a month goes by without opposition parliamentarians deriding it as wasteful, unwarranted, and unproductive, though its acknowledged difficulties may not in fact be much more than one would prudently have had to expect when introducing an ambitious new manpower data collecting and processing system.

Polonius said to his bored son Laertes: 'Neither a borrower nor a lender be.' If practitioners of public administration were to heed this advice there would be fewer reforms, and perhaps fewer mistakes. In practice, we often borrow either from the examples of our successful peers in nearby, comparable jurisdictions or else from afar, perhaps relying on distance and mystery to enhance the enchantment of the borrowed policy, institution, or practice. With proper caution, public service work can benefit from the 'lateral thinking,' or stimulus to imagination derived from comparative study.

To show Ted Hodgetts in his true colours as a judicious comparative scholar, one can turn to his main writings. On the surface they seem almost exclusively Canadian but that impression may well be deceptive. In his book, *The Canadian Public Service*, for example, in the last chapter Hodgetts advocates the adoption in the Canadian federal public service of policy ministries, small, with satellites of various kinds responsible for the operational end of their programs, contracting out some of the operational work to provincial or local or regional agencies or to the private sector. The fact that this is similar to Swedish ministries is not mentioned, though Hodgetts would be more familiar with this comparison than anyone would need to be in order to make this point.

Why didn't he? It seems possible that he stuck to Canadian precedents (several of which are mentioned in the chapter) for two reasons: one, a conviction that in a book about Canadian government it would be superfluous and perhaps distracting to introduce a comparison from abroad especially in the last chapter, which is already something of a digression from description into prescription. Second, he may have thought that international comparisons weaken rather than strengthen an argument in favour of the adoption of an unfamiliar idea. 'Here is a stranger; heave half a brick at him,' could have been the prejudice to watch out for. Hodgetts might well suspect such an attitude on the part of those of his readers whom it was important to persuade.

Looking for clues to a scholar's thought processes and beliefs is either a nasty trick or a trap for the unwary. Hodgetts must be one of the most broadminded of commentators on public affairs. In print he avoids taking stands on narrow issues which divide his readers along political lines. He saves his expressions of belief for issues which are at a deeper level of concern or beyond the margins of contemporary political debate. He clearly does have convictions and expresses them, and they are the proper stuff for critical analysis, even if they seem to defy easy labels. To see the lengths to which Hodgetts would go in order to avoid scoring political points, it is instructive to re-read his 1957 essay, 'The Civil Service and Policy Formation.' It is chockful of rhetorical questions, where a less cautious or disciplined person would have made statements. Nevertheless, at the end, Hodgetts takes a stand. He is discussing the famous Friedrich-Finer debate over the nature of responsibility. Friedrich, it will be remembered, held that responsibility is an ethical code, a trait of character, and that public servants must be carefully chosen and then relied upon to behave responsibly because of their sense of honour. Finer, on the other hand, held that responsibility is a relationship: one is responsible to someone for something, and public servants are responsible when they are held accountable to a higher authority. Here is what Hodgetts had to say on the question: 'If those who exercise choice within the bureaucracy are to be responsible for their decisions it is not enough that they look only inward ... They must, as Finer emphasised, be responsible to some superior authority outside themselves if we are to have any real protection against bureaucratic excesses.'[16]

Immediately it will be seen that the same theme remains dominant in the Lambert commission's report. Its whole purpose is to strengthen accountability as a relationship of public servants to ministers and ultimately through Parliament to the electorate. Hodgetts, as co-author, commits himself again in this important public statement to a particular set of principles. We could call them liberal-democratic, but they are more than that. He is taking a stand against the Platonic proposition that good men are entitled to rule because of their inherent goodness, and is putting his faith in checks and balances. There is here both scepticism about the virtue of the ordinary person in his role as bureaucrat and faith in constitutional arrangements based on popular support – that is to say, faith in the ordinary person's civic morality to prevent abuse of power, given the constitutional power to do so.

Friedrich may have been élitist in his philosophy – certainly that was often said about him. Nevertheless, some of what he said may need to be considered even by true democrats who might like to dismiss it because of its source. This brings me back, by a roundabout route, to Taylor Cole and the question of comparative administration as an approach to useful knowledge about the machinery of government. Canada has developed a strenuously autochthonous and autonomous tradition of administrative studies, perhaps out of fear of domination by American cultural imperialism. There has been support from British scholars for such insularity: comparative administration never had much of a run in British universities, if one makes an exception of occasional excursions by Professor Robson to have a sceptical look at French administrative law, or by Professor A.H. Hanson to look at Indian planning, or by wayward Englishmen such as Douglas Verney who have made intensive studies of Swedish and other exotic nationalized industries. Comparative administration, it seems, was a province populated by Americans and Europeans. Australian students of public administration have not been notably more eclectic than their Canadian counterparts. Perhaps we should change. Perhaps we should all go back to Taylor Cole, and even more to his mentor Carl Friedrich, and ask ourselves whether the deeper questions of public administration do not reveal themselves when we take an explicitly comparative perspective. Perhaps accountability, the focal issue of Lambert and of Hodgetts' work, is at root an ethical issue, one that can be strengthened by administrative changes except in the context of an underlying consensus about administrative ends, goals, purposes, objectives, values, norms, call them what you will. By comparing political cultures and the ethical context in which administrative systems work we may come to a well-informed understanding of what these systems are and how they work.

This view may seem to sit uncomfortably next to the points made earlier in this paper about the need for strong Public Service Commissions. Why are they needed, if institutional checks and balances are insufficient and only a civic culture of ethical responsibility will suffice to insure accountable public administration? Perhaps the contradiction can be resolved by stressing the role of a Commission as teacher, pastor, standard-setter, or priestly custodian of the holy scriptures. An effective church needs also to be in the world, and a Commission needs to have, and be seen to have, temporal as well as spiritual power. (The metaphor has got out of hand. All work may be worthy in the eyes of the Father, no doubt, but it would be difficult to persuade even a true believer that a Public Service Board's work is not the work of the devil.)

The Canadian administrative state is, ideologically, a product of individualist liberalism. Most of the leading scholarly commentators on the system have also grown up well within that ideological framework. How can one be more specific about these values or beliefs? Probably they were best articulated by nineteenth-century English liberals such as John Stuart Mill and T.H. Green, and the list begins with qualified confidence in reason as a guide to socially desirable reform; commitment to civil liberties, but not to the point of anarchistic abandonment of strength in government sufficient to right those social wrongs which are amenable to correction by a benevolent, non-authoritarian state; faith in the ability and desire of a majority of citizens to uphold a code of social morality which tolerates diversity of customs and condemns cruelty; confidence in the responsiveness of most politicians and public servants to these humane values with only a relatively light regime of checks over their behaviour, such as elections; a Parliament with an opposition of sorts; a press which reports at least some of the scandals; and a court system which occasionally puts up obstacles to the power of officials in the name of constitutional propriety.

Hodgetts would have been confirmed in this creed by such teachers as Professors Alexander Brady, Robert McGregor Dawson, and Vincent Bladen. That such beliefs were not incompatible with moderate democratic socialism was the strong conviction of another leading University of Toronto teacher of that era, Frank Underhill, who had a wide influence, whether or not Hodgetts was a student of his in that house of many mansions.

The small 'l' liberal creed which is under discussion has had a battering at the hands of effective critics. It takes no great insight to point out that the optimistic social meliorism of liberal social scientists took a great deal for granted. The ethical ideas which secure scholars, lawyers, politicians, and publicists could espouse and express might not be held so firmly by persons whose lives were very different. Some exponents of this creed were accused of making the arrogant assumption, unconsciously perhaps, that their values would be accepted by enlightened people of a different culture; imperialism went hand in hand with liberalism in the minds of a few, though the more common view was perhaps an unexamined, even humble, belief that, all races and cultures being equal in the eyes of God or history, what seemed right and true, at a fundamental level, to a person of good conscience reared in one cultural tradition would perhaps also seem right and true to an equally clear-minded person brought up in a different cultural tradition. All value systems were deemed equal; but perhaps that was because they were assumed to conform, underneath their trappings, to the Judeo-Christian, liberal, optimistic, rational values of the Anglo-Saxon educated classes in Victorian and Edwardian times. The creed we are discussing also assumed the ascendency of reason over passion most of the time and in most public relationships, though the more lurid light shed by psychological inquiry might cause others to doubt whether public behaviour could be rationally understood or controlled, and the wars and police state horrors of the twentieth century would cause many to give up their hopes of reason as a social restraint.

In the latter half of the twentieth century there have been at least two other important challenges to these values. The first of these was the increasing sophistication of the bureaucracy and its increasing cultural diversity. Not only were there more public servants with high qualifications, as the 1960s and 1970s went on, but, significantly, these highly educated public servants came from a broad range of disciplines and professional schools, representing a variety of cultures, attitudes, world-views, and implicit or explicit ideologies. A pluralistic, increasingly representative bureaucracy was emerging. Most obvious in the Canadian case was the rise of French-speaking Canadian civil servants to senior positions across the full range of departments in the Canadian federal service, and, as the seventies arrived, these were, increasingly, French-speaking Canadians who were completely loyal to their culture and did not try to alter their egos to suit the preferences of a dominant English-speaking elite. These slow changes towards sophistication, cosmopolitan pluralism, and representativeness, it should be pointed out, began in the Canadian public services before there were corresponding changes in Australia.

In Australia, though higher education became an increasingly common attribute of the upper and middle levels in the national and state public services, it tended to be an education in economics, engineering, technology, or science, and the value systems inculcated by these educational regimes were perhaps less diverse and less humane than in the Canadian case. It could also be argued that a high degree of cultural homogeneity, not to say chauvinism, characterized the Australian educated classes (unless one takes up the issue of Irish Catholic versus Anglo-Saxon Protestant approaches to public morality, as some students have done). True multicultural heterogeneity was still a distant future prospect in the Australian senior public services at the beginning of the 1980s. A representative bureaucracy might be still unattained in Canada; it was not yet in sight in Australia in the late 1960s or early 1970s. As regards women's access to equal career opportunities, again the Canadian federal civil service and the civil service of a province such as Ontario had progressed beyond their counterparts in Australia, and affirmative action programs which were beginning to be an accepted commonplace in Canadian public employment, were apparently still considered strange and dangerous by most Australian governments and statutory authorities.

Another challenge to individualist liberal assumptions in recent times has been the growth of white-collar unionism. White-collar unionism took liberals by surprise. Their expectation was that as any person comes up in the world he or she asserts an increasing degree of individualism. Freedom from want and freedom from fear, supposed to be the hallmarks of secure white-collar occupations such as the civil service, were thought to provide a foundation for individual accountability by public servants untramelled by collectivist cross-pressures or conflicts of interest which might be introduced into the system by the advent of strong public service unionism. The liberal constitutional orthodoxy was therefore somewhat critical and hesitant about this development. Yet, on the other hand, freedom of association is an equally revered principle in the liberal creed, and the need for employees to unite in order to present their case to a powerful employer could not be doubted.

In the Canadian case, the strengthening of public service unions can be seen by recalling certain notable events since 1960. First was the success of the Civil Service Federation in persuading all the major political parties prior to the 1963 election to commit themselves to supporting collective bargaining for civil servants.[17] This was what led to the enactment, in 1967, on the recommendation of the Pearson government, of the Public Service Staff Relations Act. What was notable about the willingness of Parliament to pass this legislation was that it remained willing despite the occurrence of serious postal strikes, which led to considerable outcry in the press and in the constituencies. Either the pressure of the unions, or else the earnest belief in collective bargaining on the part of the government and the Parliament, must account for the passage of this act, since little political advantage was to be gained by it except in a few constituencies such as Ottawa, and the offsetting loss of votes in other areas might have been equal or even greater.

In the more recent past, Canadian public sector industrial relations have continued to loom large. It would be fair to say that from 1917 to 1967 Canadian public personnel legislation and personnel management practices were preoccupied with the rights of individuals. Individual merit had to be fairly assessed and compared when selecting people for appointment or promotion. Individual grievances had to be heard and judged. In the 1950s the Civil Service Commission, as custodian of the merit principle, was still the major personnel agency, and not until the late 1950s and 1960s did an increasing number of personnel management functions come under the control of the Treasury Board to the point where it, rather than the Civil Service Commission, became the dominant public personnel management authority. In 1967 the (federal) Public Service Staff Relations Board was established to administer the new collective bargaining legislation. This further diminished the scope and role of the Public Service Commission (so named in 1967) compared with its predecessor, the Civil Service Commission. It was as though the previous order of things, in which the individual rights of applicants and employees were at the centre of the stage, had been superseded by a new collectivist order in which budgets (the Treasury Board) and collective bargaining (the PSSRB) were central. What would liberal commentators say about this?

As far as Ted Hodgetts is concerned, we have his views as expressed in *The Canadian Public Service*: 'For public servants, the Public Service Staff Relations Act of 1967 provided a fitting centennial achievement, marking the culmination of a long up-hill struggle to attain the most effective methods of permitting them to face an historically authoritarian management team on a more realistic, egalitarian footing.'[18] Hodgetts, on this litmus test, reacted as more of an egalitarian collectivist than an individualist. This was T.H. Green-style liberalism, where equal rights depend on collective action, rather than Benthamite atomistic liberalism, where self-interest, self-help, and an assumed free market automatically solve all social problems. Perhaps this shows that Canadian liberal education was sound in one important sense: it taught one to be receptive to new events and ideas even when they challenge the fundamental values which were its unspoken major premise.

The post-individualist phase in public personnel management is already well advanced in Australia. In Australia, the pre-eminence of the unions in public personnel management predates the emergence of strong public service unions in Canada. Unionism has always been stronger in Australia than in Canada, in almost all occupations, including public sector employment. The compulsory arbitration system dominates industrial relations in Australia, though collective negotiation and non-compulsory resolution of differences also play a major part. This, however, does not mean that a collectivist philosophy already dominates all Australian public service personnel legislation or administration. The relevant statutes, and the practices of the public service boards, are still crowded with mementos of the individualist, liberal ethic. Individual rights of employees are jealously defined and protected. The very legalism of the Australian industrial relations system seems to produce scrupulous safeguards for some of the individual's rights, because industrial law in Australia has inevitably become assimilated into the selectively individualistic, liberal, common-law traditions of the courts.

This is not a paradox. Collectivism and individualism are not always polar concepts; they sometimes march together, as in this instance. Australian public personnel management is in the hands of Public Service boards and of the officers who serve these Boards,

Commonwealth or state as the case may be. These agencies are constantly dealing with unions and union advocates, skilled in Australian industrial law. The substance of their dealings is twofold. One part has to do with individual rights in promotion appeals, classification disputes, and disciplinary sanctions and appeals concerning them. The other part has to do with collective wage claims and negotiations leading towards industrial agreements, or else the hearing of a dispute over wages and conditions before an industrial arbitral tribunal or commission, and the determination by the tribunal of a binding decision or award. Thus, an Australian state public service board member necessarily lives his working life as a practising devotee of the individualist and collectivist liberal creed, struggling with the contradictions among the parts of that complex heritage. So too, a Canadian scholar of public administration inhabits the same cultural-intellectual-ideological space.

As Hodgetts' work illustrates, the liberal scholar reconciles as best he can the values he inherits when, as often happens, they conflict, and he celebrates the happy incidence of harmony among them whenever it occurs. The distance apart in physical space and historical circumstance is great but not overwhelming. One can perhaps best end this tour of two administrative systems with a quotation from J.W. Pickersgill, after he had made a visit to this side of the Pacific:

> I have become gradually aware, during the past twenty years, that Australia has more in common with Canada than any other country. We are the only two federations with British parliamentary government. Our history under the British crown is roughly equal in length. Though both economies were originally based on farming, and still depend on exports from the farm for much of their national incomes, both are highly urbanised – Australia even more than Canada. There are wide disparities in the developed wealth and the potential of the Australian states, though not as great as among rich and poor provinces in Canada. Both countries have problems of federal-provincial or federal-state relations. But all this does not make Australia a mirror image of Canada: the differences are almost as illuminating as the similarities.[19]

1 *The Canadian Bureaucracy: A Study of Canadian Civil Servants and Other Public Employees, 1939-1947* (Durham, NC: Duke University Press, 1949)

2 *Responsible Bureaucracy: A Study of the Swiss Civil Service* (Cambridge, Mass., Harvard University Press, 1932)

3 Two such books were published: J.E. Hodgetts and O.P. Dwivedi, *Provincial Governments as Employers: A Survey of Public Personnel Administration in Canada's Provinces* (Montreal, 1974); and J.E. Hodgetts, William McCloskey, Reginald Whitaker, and V. Seymour Wilson, *The Biography of an Institution: The Civil Service Commission of Canada, 1908-1967* (Montreal, 1972).

4 *The Canadian Bureaucracy*, pp. 276-7

5 *The Canadian Public Service* (Toronto, 1974), p. 264

6 Ibid.

7 *The Canadian Bureaucracy*, p. 23

8 'The Liberal and the Bureaucrat,' *Queen's Quarterly*, vol. LXII (summer 1955), p. 182

9 'Challenge and Response: A Retrospective View of the Public Service of Canada,' *Canadian Public Administration*, vol. 7, no. 4 (winter 1964), p. 414

10 'Reflections on the Lambert Report,' *Canadian Public Administration*, vol. 22, no. 4 (winter 1979), p. 577

11 *The Commonwealth Bureaucracy* (Melbourne: Melbourne University Press, 1967), pp. 208-9

12 Committee of Inquiry into the Public Service of South Australia, *Report* (Adelaide: Government Printer, 1975)

13 (Melbourne: Nelson, 1976), p. 144

14 See, for example, 'The Distribution of Tax Sharing Entitlements among the States' (Canberra: Centre for Research on Federal Financial Relations, Australian National University (reprint series)), esp. pp. 30-1.

15 See Freda Hawkins, *Immigration Policy and Management in Selected Countries* (Ottawa: Information Canada, 1974), esp. p. 37.

16 'The Civil Service and Policy Formation,' *Canadian Journal of Economics and Political Science*, vol. 23 (1957), pp. 467-79, reprinted in Hodgetts and Corbett, eds., *Canadian Public Administration: A Book of Readings* (Toronto: Macmillan, 1970), p. 452

17 See O.P. Dwivedi, 'Recent Developments in Staff Relationships in the Public Service of Canada,' *Public Administration* (Australia), vol. XXIV, no. 4 (December 1965), pp. 359-67; Sir Kenneth Bailey, 'Industrial Relations in the Canadian Public Service,' ibid., vol. XXX, no. 1 (March 1971), pp. 52-66. Both of these articles have an interesting Canadian-Australian comparative dimension.

18 (Toronto: University of Toronto Press, 1973), pp. 334-5

19 *The Financial Post*, Toronto, 26 June 1976. I am grateful to Peter Crabb of Macquarie University and Kenneth Wiltshire of the University of Queensland for bringing this passage to my attention.

R.W. PHIDD

The Administrative State and the Limits of Rationality

EFFICIENCY AND RESPONSIVENESS

The administrative state has been identified by some analysts of public administration as a three-faceted development consisting of 1 / the organizational revolution in society, 2 / the expansion of the functions of modern government, and 3 / the allocation of continuing aspects of public functions to administrative structures.[1] Some have evaluated the administrative state from the perspective of a concern with political theory and the history of ideas. Others have identified the administrative state with big government which requires a large apparatus to carry out its many functions; to this group, the development of the administrative machinery corresponds broadly to the evolution of industrial order. Central to the study of the administrative state has been the perceived necessity of developing technical skills in order to achieve economic and administrative efficiency.

Yet several other analysts have been critical of the relationship between the administrative state and the growth of democratic participatory governments. The combined concern with efficiency and participatory democracy has demonstrated that the administrative state has had to reconcile the inherent tensions between the efficiency objectives of management science with its centralist bias, and the responsive and participatory traditions of political science with its decentralist bias. These concerns have been a central element of the study of public administration. Stated differently, these scholars of public administration have been concerned with the values which motivate strategic actors in the administrative state.

The managers of the administrative state have consistently advocated further specialization of tasks in order to improve the division of responsibilities along lines outlined by the early scientific management school.[2] Notwithstanding the criticisms of this school, by logical positivists among others, the essential thrust of post-war public administration reform was towards more business administration and management principles in government. It was premised on the belief that this would lead to comparable performance between business and government. The cumulative effect of the endorsement of this principle has led many to assert that there has been 'an arrival of management in government.' Thus there are currently managerial and political imperatives in the modern administrative state, which lead to inherent tensions between the efficiency objectives of management science and the responsive participatory tradition of political science. In the words of J.E. Hodgetts:

> In the evolution of our liberal democratic system of government there has always been a tension between the principle of representation and the practical necessity to get ahead with the tasks of governance as expeditiously and efficiently as possible. The mustering of majorities by political parties working through free elections, universal suffrage, and an open market place in ideas is designed to provide a political executive with the popular support it needs to govern and administer – always contingent on its capacity to maintain its hold on the elected legislature.[3]

Management in government is currently seen from the perspective of 'the search for the best use of resources in pursuit of objectives subject to change.'[4] Between the 1930s and the 1970s a number of royal commissions and task forces in the major Western countries endorsed management ideology and advocated the adoption of management techniques throughout government. Some reformers advocated the adoption of these techniques by the system as a whole, while others directed their recommendations only to the higher echelons of the system. Thus by the late 1970s the advocates of managerial reforms had outlined strategies for the government as a whole as well as for the financial and personnel systems.

In Canada, the continuous concern with strengthening efficiency in government was espoused by a number of royal commissions and task forces. In 1962, the Royal Commission on Government Organization (Glassco) recommended changes especially in central management through a more specialized Treasury Board, which was later separated from the Department of Finance, and through greater delegation of authority to departments in the management of specific activities.[5] In 1979, the Royal Commission of Financial Management and Accountability (Lambert), though concerned with financial management and accountability primarily, outlined a framework for a mutually compatible management system with specialized lead roles performed by two central agencies, the Department of Finance to be concerned with the fiscal plan, and a reconstituted Treasury Board (a board of management) to be concerned with financial resources and personnel, both equipped to assist ministers in the job of clearly defining the roles and responsibilities of operating departments.[6] The *Report* of the Special Committee on the Review of Personnel Management and the Merit Principle (D'Avignon)[7] adopted a comprehensive approach to the management of human resources in the public service through the development of a unified corporate policy direction of the personnel function and, accordingly, it recommended the creation of 'a strong central agency of outstanding competence, accountable to the government for all aspects of personnel management, including those management functions now under the PSEA (Public Service Employment Agency).' It further asserted that 'adherence to merit requires a Public Service Commission acting as a strong, independent auditor.'[8]

The three reports clearly demonstrate the extent to which management ideology has permeated at least three facets of government administration. As the Lambert commission emphasized:

> Essentially, our proposals are based on the related convictions that responsibility at the political level for the subject matter of the Fiscal Plan can only be vested in the most senior of Cabinet committees, that on Priorities and Planning under the chairmanship of the Prime Minister; second, that responsibility for establishing the government's fiscal position cannot be divorced from responsibility for setting expenditure limits for departments and agencies; third, that there must be a single focus for the Government's collective management responsibility; and, fourth, that the Fiscal Plan must be based on the best available information about the Government's priorities and objectives and the possibilities that exist for realizing them, both in terms of what the economy can support and of what can be done within government.[9]

The position adopted here is that, while the three reports flirted with decentralization, their overriding concern with the efficiency ethos led primarily to proposals for more centralized management.

Their basic premise may be stated as follows: if government is to improve its performance, then it must be staffed with well-trained personnel; strategic positions must be appropriately distributed, with control systems instituted.

The proliferation of demands on governments introduced interdependent challenges to the scientific, industrial, and welfare state. These led to further recommendations for the integration of public budgeting and public personnel techniques resulting from the fact that the cost of government could not be divorced from the demand for a highly diversified manpower to formulate an increasingly more complex set of societal objectives.[10] The most recent development for improving the Canadian expenditure and personnel management systems in the early 1980s clearly illustrates this point: in fact, the Lambert commission and the D'Avignon committee, cited above, were most influential in instituting the reforms of the early 1980s.

The approach to the study of the administrative state which has been relatively silent during this reform process is that concerned with political theory and the history of ideas mentioned earlier. This dimension must be reinstated if we are to develop a framework for a critical analysis of the issues facing the contemporary administrative state. Such approach would build on the foundation established by J.E. Hodgetts in Canada; it would establish a trend towards a political theory of the administrative state.

THE RIGHTS OF CITIZENS, PUBLIC OFFICIALS, AND THE SOCIAL RESPONSIBILITY OF BUSINESS

Historically, one consequence of the rise of the administrative state and the involvement of government in the economy was the corresponding increase in governmental regulation and the concomitant impingement on individual rights.[11] These issues have not been adequately explored. The expansion of the administrative state led to a demand for specialized public personnel with responsibilities in the area of safeguarding citizen rights; ironically, this led to a further increase in the number of public employees. At least two institutional innovations have been proposed or adopted as a means of bolstering the faltering system of accountability. First, there is the device of the Scandinavian ombudsman who can be likened to the long-standing auditor general, acting as a parliamentary official not as part of the executive, and in several respects independent of the bureaucracy. Second, there is the device drawn from the United Kingdom, a special scrutiny committee of Parliament which maintains a watchful eye on legislation assigning discretionary powers to the bureaucracy and which, under appropriate conditions, brings to the attention of Parliament the cases in which such powers have been abused.[12]

The issue of rights must be discussed from the perspective of the interaction between the capitalist and the administrative states. In western democracies the production and distribution of goods are primarily conducted and allocated through markets. However, increased governmental involvement in the promotion of goods and services has led to an increase in public regulation. Thus, some sectors of society are demanding new programs, and other sectors are demanding less regulation. Yet the essential assumption of governmental support for business was that businessmen were expected to be held accountable to the public.[13] Accordingly, there have been debates over the social responsibilities of business.

The introduction of health, education, welfare, and public employment legislation introduced new issues concerning the rights of citizens as well as of public employees who carry out special responsibilities.[14] In the first instance of citizens' rights, the demand for specialized manpower led to the development of a host of professional groups who are accountable to their peers. In the second instance, the public employees are expected to be accountable to the public service and to the society as a whole. Consequently, there are legal, moral, ethical, and professional considerations which have compounded the problem of accountability in the administrative state – for example, the issue of independence versus control.

The massive governmental involvement in societal activities significantly impinged on individual rights. In addition, since the early 1970s the failure of governments to manage the economy effectively has intensified demands for privatization and deregulation. As a result, the administrative state which evolved simultaneously with industrialization has been under attack from some politicians and the business community. Poor economic performance has been attributed to the increased regulation mentioned above. In Canada, this philosophy has been voiced by the Fraser Institute, which has resuscitated values expressed earlier by Mises and Hayek who had indicated that the administrative state had tendencies to become bureaucratic and dehumanizing. From their perspective, the rise of the administrative state was responsible for the decline in the role of markets which efficiently allocated resources in society.[15]

This issue was a major component of the economic planning debate which took place during the 1930s. In fact, there are important political values which have shaped the debate over economic planning in most Western democracies. The debate suggests that we should examine the roles of citizens, politicians, public officials, and businessmen in planning and executing the tasks of the administrative state.

DIVERGENT INFLUENCES ON THE ADMINISTRATIVE STATE

Whereas the classical models of the administrative state were to be found in France and Germany, the basic model of popular democracy developed on the North American continent.[16] In many ways, the American political tradition is antithetical to the *étatiste* tradition which has been prevalent in France and pre-war Germany. (The two traditions are explored in Morstein Marx's and Dwight Waldo's treatments of the administrative state.[17]) The American tradition accordingly emphasizes the efficient utilization of resources, business civilization, and mass participation; hence the American tradition of public administration embodies both laissez-faire and populist elements.

The Canadian administrative state has been influenced by both the British and American traditions. J.E. Hodgetts has described the evolution of the Canadian administrative state which after the Second World War became increasingly more centralized. However, this trend was partially offset by the growth in populist parties, some of which had historical roots in the Western farm movements, and by the growth of strong provincial governments.[18] Regional ideologies influenced the degree to which the administrative state was centralized or decentralized. Accordingly, the growth in the administrative state was increasingly challenged by parties with populist and leftist tendencies. They in turn have influenced changes in other political parties and in the legislative and executive branches. Yet, as indicated above, the participatory tradition is somewhat contradictory to the management philosophy which emphasizes efficiency in the allocation of resources.

Another feature of the ambivalence in the administrative state comes from the British tradition in which responsible government is sometimes emphasized in contrast to representative government; leaders are expected to be responsible, not necessarily representative. The tensions between the administrative state and democracy emerge from contradictions between the tenets of the administrative state – specialization, professionalization, and economy of resources – and the tenets of democracy – participation, control over leaders, individual realization, and egalitarianism.[19] From the decision-making perspective, democratic theory endorses pluralistic and segmental decisions.[20] This tradition has frequently led to demands for effective controls by political leaders over the bureaucracy or more generally over the administrative state. In contrast, management ideology has generally endorsed centralized planning and decision-making. These approaches were endorsed especially by the central agencies in government.

As the trends towards centralized management developed, mass political parties began to demand increased control over the executive branch. In Canada, where there was no theory and tradition of separation of powers, the central concern was with superimposing parliamentary control over the cabinet and, more generally, over the administrative branch of government. The intensification of the struggle between improving political leadership and improving the skills of the bureaucracy was ultimately reflected in Pierre Elliott Trudeau's famous statement in the early 1970s that the bureaucrats were no longer kings. However, the strategy of prime ministerial control is not necessarily regarded as representative, and there have been attacks against its development as a type of 'presidentialization' of the cabinet system of government in Canada. These critics viewed the cabinet as a decentralized system of management, given the fact that there is a tradition of ministerial and departmental accountability. The Lambert commission attempted to accommodate this viewpoint by advocating a mutually compatible management system, which suggests that complementary roles are performed by selected ministers and departments in public sector management.

Various efforts have been made to impose political control over the administrative state. First, the growth of the cabinet committee system reflects, in part, the desire on the part of prime ministers to control the bureaucracy. This view has been publicly expressed by Mitchell Sharp, a former public servant and cabinet minister.[21] Second, there were proposals for reforming Parliament so that it could better control the executive. Third, a trend towards increased provincial involvement in federal decisions has been evident. These three elements were manifested during the short tenure of the Clark Conservative government in Ottawa in 1979.[22] They were present in the earlier Diefenbaker interlude when the post-war hegemony of the bureaucracy was first challenged. They were further reflected in two themes stressed by the Lambert commission. First, the commission emphasized the need for stronger management controls in government in response to a decline in the use of financial and economic management criteria; to this end, financial reforms were advocated. Second, the commission emphasized the need for parliamentary reform and control of financial matters, and these efforts reinforced a crusade mounted earlier by the Auditor General for more responsible financial management within the Government of Canada. Accordingly, in both the political and administrative realms there were pressures for broadening the system of accountability.

As indicated above, another source of reforms emanated from the growth in the power of the provinces which have improved the quality of their public officials and have increased the size of their bureaucracies. In effect, Canadian citizens are faced with competition from growing bureaucracies at the federal, provincial, and municipal levels of government. This is partially reflected in demands for decentralization of the federal public services. In the constitutional realm it was expressed in terms of stronger representation of regional interests in federal institutions. These issues were discussed at length at the First Ministers Constitutional Conference held in Ottawa in September 1980.[23] As such, they vividly demonstrate some dilemmas of the Canadian administrative state in that, while the British North America Act partially conditions the type of public service which can operate in Canada, it is silent on the issues we have been discussing here.

LIMITATIONS AND DILEMMAS

In our study of the administrative state we should always remember political theory and the history of ideas, dimensions so well emphasized by Dwight Waldo in the United States, Peter Self in Britain, and J.E. Hodgetts in Canada, among others. These analysts have pointed to the need for balancing political and administrative rationality in order to develop a more responsive administrative state. They have also been concerned with the longitudinal implications of the various reform movements mentioned earlier and have recommended the development of normative standards for the administrative state.

The exploitation of natural resources and the satisfaction of public wants have always been elements of central concern to students of the administrative state. In recent years, urbanization and environmental issues have heightened the concern for the management of non-renewable resources, especially with respect to the decline of agricultural land, the degradation of the environment,[24] and the need for the formulation of policies which would provide for safe, wholesome and nutritious food. In addition, the post-1973 escalation in energy and food prices, generally considered 'administered prices,' increased concern over the management of scarce non-renewable resources. This issue is further compounded in the Canadian state by historical forces which, since the First World War, have intensified the concentration of industrial development in the east and created expanding requirements for agricultural development in the west.[25] The expansion of the oil and gas industry, particularly in western Canada, has now further complicated the role of the state in the formulation of energy and food policies. Thus the energy and agricultural policy debates in the early 1980s are illustrative of the challenges with which the modern administrative state must effectively grapple.

The energy and the food policy issues suggest that we incorporate into our analysis the contributions made by different professional groups towards the functioning of the modern administrative state: for example, the role of economists, physicists, and geographers in policy development. Thus there are those who see the solution in greater reliance on the price system; for example, by increases in land prices, demand will be automatically adjusted and other resources substituted. Geographers and environmentalists, however, have always been greater advocates of increased use of legal and administrative regulations as a means of controlling land use.[26] Another perspective is presented by scientists who are more inclined to identify shortages with inadequate distribution of scientific and technological capabilities. Once again, issues of choice and change are central to the debate over the role of the administrative state.

Thus the problems of economic stress, the conservation of scarce resources such as energy, minerals, and food, or more generally these so-called supply management issues have changed the nature of the planning debate and may very well alter the pattern of administrative relationships within the state. By way of illustration, the introduction of increased planning regulations either in the energy and urban development sphere or in the control of rural land use imposes serious encroachments on the rights of individuals – for example, on the freedom of farmers to sell land to their chosen buyers. As the history of the evolution of the administrative state reveals, however, these issues are not new.[27]

The fiscal crisis of the state provides a further example of the dilemmas faced by the administrative state. The current debate over the control of public expenditures vividly illustrates this dilemma. As indicated earlier, some critics of the administrative state have questioned its legitimacy.[28] Within the laissez-faire tradition the state was considered to have a very limited set of responsibilities, a view which twentieth-century developments have drastically reversed. In the light of this view, the ultimate test of the state's legitimate exercise of power is in the citizens' willingness to support public programs through taxation. From this perspective, the current debate over tax expenditures is understandable.

At this point, the representative and the consensual nature of public policies becomes evident, in that we are inevitably confronted with issues which provide a starting point for a possible political theory of the administrative state. The foregoing indicates that the administrative state is not as omnipotent as some critics have suggested: the absence of public participation and support provides a necessary limit.[29] And the presence of external constraints on domestic policies and programs by foreign groups and states provides another example of its relative impotence.[30]

The administrative state is further challenged by the inability of the national governments to deal with the most acute problems facing management in the 1980s, such as shortages in energy and food. These crucial areas present allocative problems which are both global and national. The global aspects are well described in Richard J. Barnett's *The Lean Years: Politics in the Age of Scarcity*.[31] The so-called energy and food crises have really presented new challenges for the administrative state. Thus there are demands for stronger as well as weaker governmental regulations. The Conservative government which took office in 1979 emphasized the need for increased privatization, the importance of markets, and the need for greater reliance on the price system to perform a stronger role in resource allocation. In contrast, the 1980 Liberal National Energy Program, in an attempt to control the influence of multinational corporations, made allowance for the establishment of a series of state enterprises with a lead role to be played by Petro-Canada.[32]

At least two propositions can be formulated with respect to the role of administrative state in the 1980s. First, if the administrative state is considered to be a *sine qua non* for economic growth and for the improved general welfare experienced after the Second World War, then it may very well meet the challenges of the 1980s. Second, if the administrative state is considered to be the cause of the decline in economic growth during the 1970s due to increased governmental intervention, then the obvious solution is to be found a movement towards greater privatization and deregulation – in a return to the good old days of limited governmental interference. Together the two propositions have been a source of growing tensions between levels of governments and between special interests, albeit regional or sectoral. These two propositions have provided focal points for political debate and have led to the realignment of political parties in Western democracies. A logical conclusion for those who support the administrative state may be stated as follows: if the administrative state is to be effective, then it must establish institutions to manage scarce resources; an issue well outlined in Raymond Vernon's *Big Business and the State*.[33] Here the European experiment with state enterprises in controlling the impact of multinational corporations has provided an example of a new approach to managing the administrative state. In Canada, the creation of Petro-Canada occurred when there were strong criticisms of Crown corporations. There is much contemporary controversy between those who see the administrative state as a cause of many problems in society and those who see the administrative state, with certain modifications, as the means of establishing a societal system with greater equity.[34]

The dilemma of the administrative state can now be seen squarely in the context of political ideology when it is recognized that the search for more efficient management cannot be discussed outside of the broader context of the objectives of the state. We are, therefore, confronted with the issue of efficiency for what purpose. The earlier tradition of the administrative state – the European view – had identified the responsibilities of public officials as an indispensable element in assisting citizens in the development of public policies. A more informed public meant greater access to information and improved means of evaluating public programs. Yet the evaluation of public programs requires knowledge derived from a variety of professionals within the respective areas of the bureaucracy as well as outside, whether in medicine, in social welfare policies, or in financial management. There is no institutional mechanism other than the state, defined in its broadest sense, which can facilitate the development of this broadly based system of public knowledge. Herein lies our central dilemma.[35]

Since the 1930s there have been major proposals for creating public agencies independent of the executive branch. These agencies would strengthen the system of public participation by providing knowledge which would assist citizens and parliamentarians in improving their capacity for evaluating public programs. The Lambert commission and the Auditor General have made limited recommendations along these lines. Yet it is most difficult to get a proper perspective on this issue because of the multiplicity of competing value systems which influence governmental decision-making. In this regard, political parties must perform a central role, but they have become increasingly dependent on strategic centres of knowledge. The existence of competing value systems in Western societies is reflected in the fact that the public has periodically shifted its support from political parties with leftist leanings to political parties of the opposite tendency and *vice versa*.

This concern over frequent shifts in electoral support with its corresponding reorganization of the public bureaucracy has led one influential British public official to view such changes as a cause for concern with respect to the erosion of the efficiency principle in government.[36] These changes have been expensive, yet they vividly demonstrate that in popular democracies the efficiency objective espoused by management science ideology cannot be religiously supported. Thus decisions affecting public spending which ultimately convey the authoritative allocation of values must reflect the will of the public, or perhaps publics. Stated differently, the efficiency goal must be couched in terms which accommodate either the majority or a combination of the special interests which operate within the political system. Democracies are constantly in search of methods which appropriately reflect the public interest (used in this instance to mean the accommodation of a variety of special interests). Thus the operation of the administrative state is affected by the inherent tension between the efficiency objectives of management science and the responsive participatory demands of democracy. We are therefore constantly in search of methods for retaining a democratic system of government in an increasingly administered Canadian society. These issues have been discussed under the general theme of the nature and scope of the administrative state.[37] What can the political science or political economy tradition offer with respect to improved understanding of the administrative state?

A possible solution to the dilemma can be found in Arthur Okun's penetrating analysis entitled *Equality and Efficiency: The Big Tradeoff*. He argues that both efficiency and economic equality can be increased by attacking some inequalities of opportunity, such as racial and sexual discrimination in jobs and access to capital. Changes are required in these areas to resolve the double standards of a capitalist democracy which on the one hand professes, supports, and pursues an egalitarian political and social system while on the other endorses an economic system which generates gaping disparities. The attempt to guarantee certain rights and to extend the principle of equality under the universality criterion inevitably imposes limitations on the market, which is designed to preserve values which are denominated in dollars. The capitalist society, which is used synonymously in this instance with the administrative state, is constantly searching for better ways of drawing the boundary lines between the domain of rights and the domain of dollars. The two are constantly in conflict because equality and economic efficiency are somewhat inconsistent. They respond to two separate institutional imperatives. In short, a possible solution seems to lie through a compromise in which 'both equality and efficiency are valued and neither takes absolute priority over the other.'[38] The compromise emanates primarily from the political process which strengthens the case for reforms in the political system if the checks and balances on the efficiency principle are to operate. It is suggested that Parliament must strengthen its legitimizing and its evaluative roles.[39]

The democratic tradition suggests that the rational comprehensive model of policy-making, which has become a dominant feature of the administrative state, should be tempered by the less structured value system of the political process.[40] The view is sometimes presented that a process of bargaining and mutual accommodation must be an inherent component of the political and administrative processes. It is further asserted that there is a pluralist dimension to the structure of scientific knowledge which facilitates decentralized decisions. From this perspective the structure of scientific knowledge is horizontal rather than hierarchical, the latter being the paradigm for the bureaucratic system.

A second source of constraint on the prevalence of management ideology comes from the political system's imperative that public policy decisions should be responsive,[41] a view which does not fit neatly in the schema which suggests that there is a consistent and logical set of relations emanating from Parliament to cabinet to department to program development, such as the Lambert commission outlined. Consultations frequently take time and they often dismantle well-established structured relations. In this regard, the planning process is different from the publication of a plan which may only be one element in the process. The administrative state may emphasize the principle of its over-all effectiveness rather than managerial efficiency. As J.E. Hodgetts has most vividly stated:

> More deeply, there is a crisis of conscience involved as we become aware of the confrontation of values in which our traditional ability to manoeuvre through compromise in a world of seemingly inexhaustible resources is sharply constricted. Thus, many of the decisions we now face on the agenda of governments are of the 'either-or' variety, where the consequences attendant on pursuing one path as against the other are irreversible. No amount of top-structure rationalization of our decision-processes can solve issues of this kind for in the end, when all the facts are in and the computers have programmed the critical path for a rational policy, there will still be the need to muster a gut response that reflects our values.[42]

The third source of restraint on blind adherence to efficiency principles has come from efforts to reform the parliamentary committee system. Recent experiments with parliamentary task forces are illustrative. Recommendations have been made by knowledge centres that they be accorded greater access to the priority-setting process in government. There has been a number of recommendations for the expansion of research and evaluative agencies both within and outside of the public sector. These recommendations have been designed to cope with criticisms that Parliament is incapable of adequately controlling the executive. It should be recognized that these recommendations would proliferate knowledge centres and so frequently run counter to the efficiency ethos,[43] especially when their financial costs are taken into account.

Thus, our analysis of the evolution and operation of the administrative state suggests that the commercial or business criteria and the cost-benefit principles must be modified under carefully examined conditions to accommodate significant needs in the political system, such as voting, the achievement of consensus through bargaining, and the national interest (the planning process). Stronger reliance on the democratic participatory tradition is an imperative. Stated differently, the administrative state requires normative guidance in order to operate effectively. I, therefore, reiterate the experienced counsel of J.E. Hodgetts who, notwithstanding exposure to the strong management ethos of two influential royal commissions (Glassco and Lambert), concluded:

For all the shortcomings and the difficulties associated with participatory democracy used as a device for formulating policy, perhaps its greatest contribution will be in fostering amongst groups of concerned citizens a clearer articulation of those fundamental values which, as I have suggested, must increasingly be invoked as the basis for the difficult policy decisions now before us. In such participatory activity resides the hope of generating within each of us that sense of being our brother's keeper, with a heritage not to consume but to conserve for future generations.[44]

1 For these three perspectives on the administrative state see the following: Emmette S. Redford, *Democracy in the Administrative State* (Toronto: Oxford University Press, 1969); Dwight Waldo, *The Administrative State: A Study of the Political Theory of American Public Administration* (New York: Ronald Press Company, 1948); and Fritz Morstein Marx, *The Administrative State: An Introduction to Bureaucracy* (Chicago: University of Chicago Press, 1957). This study presents a comparative approach to the study of bureaucracy. Marx examines the role of bureaucracy in the context of political systems under different historical and ideological conditions.

2 See, for example, H.A. Simon, *Administrative Behaviour*, sec. ed. (New York: 1957). See the discussion of his work by Peter Self, *Administrative Theories and Politics* (London: George Allen and Unwin; Toronto: University of Toronto Press, 1977), chap. I.

3 J.E. Hodgetts, 'Parliament and the Bureaucracy: Can We Keep Civil Servants Civil?' Department of Political Studies, occasional paper no. 1, University of Guelph (fall 1980), p. 1

4 Desmond Keeling, *Management in Government* (London: George Allen and Unwin, 1972), p. 32

5 (Ottawa: Queen's Printer, 1962)

6 *Final Report* (Ottawa: Supply and Services, 1979), pp. 31-60

7 (Ottawa: Supply and Services, 1979)

8 Ibid., pp. 9-10. It should be noted that the committee adopted a comprehensive view of personnel management. In this regard the personnel system must be regarded as a subsystem of the larger system. See chap. 3, 'Philosophy of Management.'

9 See Royal Commission on Financial Management and Accountability, *Final Report*, p. 35; O.P. Dwivedi, 'Accountability of Public Servants: Recent Developments in Canada,' *IJPA*, vol. XVI, no. 3 (July-Sept. 1980), pp. 757-78, and above; and T.H. McLeod, 'The Special Seminar on Financial Management and Accountability: An Appraisal,' *Canadian Public Administration*, vol. 23, no. 1 (spring 1980), pp. 105-34. For a critical analysis of the assumptions and approach of system management philosophy, see Ida Hoos, *Systems Analysis in Public Policy: A Critique* (Berkeley: University of California Press, 1972).

10 See Robert D. Lee, *et al.*, *Public Budgeting Systems*, sec. ed. (Baltimore: University Park Press, 1977), esp. chap. 2, 'Government Personnel,' pp. 261-80. It is my contention that the Lambert and D'Avignon reports implicitly utilized the approach outlined in the above study. Reference may be made also to R.D. Lee, *Public Personnel Systems* (Baltimore: University Park Press, 1979).

11 See for example, Redford, *Democracy in the Administrative State*.

12 See Hodgetts, 'Parliament and the Bureaucracy: Can We Keep Civil Servants Civil?' pp. 5-6.

13 See Bruce L. Smith, *The New Political Economy*. The author identifies five major issues with respect to public-private sector accountability: (i) sustaining institutional capacity: (ii) expenditure control; (iii) peer group accountability; (iv) administering esoteric services, for example health care; and (v) the politician and the expert. It is interesting to note that they all fall within the theme of this chapter. On the issue of the welfare state, see J.F. Sleeman, *The Welfare State: Its Aims, Benefits and Costs* (London: George Allen & Unwin, 1973).

14 On this issue, see R. Bendix, *Nation Building and Citizenship* (New York: John Wiley, 1964).

15 Cited in R.W. Phidd and O.P. Dwivedi, 'Bureaucracy, Politics and Public Policy,' paper presented to the Canadian Political Science Association, Quebec City, 1976

16 The ideals of American democracy rather than its practice are emphasized. For discussions of the contradictions see Harry Kranz, *The Participatory Bureaucracy* (Toronto: D.C. Heath, 1976), esp. chap. 2, 'Conflict between Bureaucracy and Democratic Theory.'

17 Marx, *The Administrative State*, Waldo, *The Administrative State*
18 See J.E. Hodgetts, in UNESCO, *Decisions and Decision-making in the Modern State* (Paris: UNESCO, 1967), esp. p. 31.
19 Redford, *Democracy in the Administrative State*, esp. chap. 1, 'Democratic Morality, Public Policy and The Political System'
20 See Charles Lindblom, *The Intelligence of Democracy* (New York: 1965). For a further development of this theme see Charles Lindblom, 'The Sociology of Planning: Thought and Social Interaction,' in Morris Bornstein, ed., *Economic Planning: East and West* (Cambridge: Harper and Row, 1975). For an excellent treatment of the accountability issue, see B.L. Smith, ed., *The Dilemma of Accountability in Modern Government: Independence Versus Control* (New York: Macmillan, 1971)
21 In Thomas Hockin, ed., *Apex of Power*, sec. ed. (Scarborough, Ont.: Prentice-Hall, 1977)
22 These elements were present in the Speech from the Throne.
23 See *Proceedings*, First Ministers Conference on the Constitution held in Ottawa, September 1980.
24 See, for example, O.P. Dwivedi, ed., *Protecting the Environment: Issues and Choices* (Toronto: 1974) and O.P. Dwivedi, ed., *Resources and the Environment: Policy Perspectives for Canada* (Toronto: 1980).
25 Cited by Hodgetts in 'Canada.' For more extensive treatment of the east-west issue in Canada see V.C. Fowke, *The National Policy and the Wheat Economy* (Toronto: University of Toronto Press, 1957, 1978), esp. chap. 15, '*The National Policy and the Wheat Economy*,' pp. 281-97; and his *Canadian Agricultural Policy: The Historical Pattern* (Toronto: University of Toronto Press, 1946, 1978).
26 See my 'The Agricultural Policy Formulation Process in Canada,' paper presented to the Canadian Political Science Association, June 1980.
27 See, for example, Michael Hill, *The State Administration and the Individual* (Glasgow: Collins, 1976).
28 See, for example, George J. Stigler, *The Citizen and the State: Essays on Regulation* (Chicago: University of Chicago Press, 1975), esp. chap. 4
29 See, for example, Leo Panitch, ed., *The Canadian State: Political Economy and Political Power* (Toronto: University of Toronto Press, 1977).
30 See, for example, R. Vernon, ed., *Big Business and the State: Changing Relations in Western Europe* (Cambridge, Mass.: 1974). For a treatment of the multinational corporation in the Canadian context, see P. Marchak, *In Whose Interest?* (Toronto: McClelland and Stewart, 1979).
31 (New York: Simon and Schuster, 1980). See especially Part III, 'The Global Factory: The Planning of Scarcity.' On the multinational corporation within the Canadian context see Marchak, *In Whose Interest?*

32 Marc Lalonde, *The National Energy Program*, Energy, Mines and Resources, Canada, 1980

33 Pp. 3-42

34 See Arthur M. Okun, *Equality and Efficiency: The Big Tradeoff* (Washington: Brookings Institution, 1975).

35 See, for example, Donald K. Price, *The Scientific Estate* (Cambridge: Harvard University Press, 1965). See also Smith, *The New Political Economy*, chaps. 2-12.

36 See Sir Richard Clarke, *New Trends in Government* (London: 1971).

37 See the introduction in this volume, as well as Redford, *Democracy in the Administrative State*; A.H. Hanson, *Planning and the Politicians and Other Essays* (London: Routledge & Kegan Paul, 1969).

38 Pp. 13, 88

39 Hodgetts, 'Parliament and the Bureaucracy: Can We Keep Civil Servants Civil?' pp. 5-9.

40 The position advocated here approximates that outlined by Lindblom, *The Intelligence of Democracy*.

41 For a useful discussion of these influences see Self, *Administrative Theories and Politics*, esp. his excellent chap. 1, 'The Development of Administrative Theories.'

42 'Parliament and Bureaucracy: Can We Keep Civil Servants Civil?' p. 11

43 On this issue, see J.E. Hodgetts, 'Public Power and Ivory Power,' in T. Lloyd and J. McLeod, eds., *Agenda 1970: Proposals for a Creative Politics* (Toronto: University of Toronto Press, 1968).

44 'Parliament and Bureaucracy: Can We Keep Civil Servants Civil?' p. 12

Bibliography of the Main Works by J.E. Hodgetts

This bibliography consists of all the books and articles in scholarly journals that have been written by J.E. Hodgetts. His other scholarly activities such as book reviews, letters to editors, addresses, speeches, and interviews are not included. Listings are arranged chronologically and divided into two parts: (*a*) books, and (*b*) articles and chapters in books.

BOOKS

Pioneer Public Service: An Administrative History of the United Canadas, 1841-1867 (Toronto: University of Toronto Press, 1956)

with J.A. Corry, *Democratic Government and Politics* revised 3rd edition (Toronto: University of Toronto Press, 1959)

with D.C. Corbett, eds., *Canadian Public Administration: A Book of Readings* (Toronto: Macmillan, 1960)

Administering the Atom for Peace (New York: Atherton Press, 1964)

Higher Education in a Changing Canada, edited, with an introduction, for the Royal Society of Canada (Toronto: University of Toronto Press, 1966)

with William McCloskey, Reginald Whitaker, and V. Seymour Wilson, *Biography of an Institution: The Civil Service Commission of Canada 1908-1967* (Montreal: McGill-Queen's University Press, 1972)

The Canadian Public Service: A Physiology of Government, 1867-1972 (Toronto: University of Toronto Press, 1972) with O.P. Dwivedi, *Provincial Governments as Employers: A Survey of Public Personnel Administration in Canada* (Montreal: McGill-Queen's University Press, 1974)

ARTICLES AND CHAPTERS IN BOOKS

'Problems of Canadian Federalism,' *State Government*, vol. XVIII, no. 6 (June 1945), pp. 95-100

'The San Francisco Conference: Old Worlds for New?' *University of Toronto Quarterly*, vol. XIV, no. 4 (July 1945), pp. 431-40

'Parliament and the Powers of the Cabinet,' *Queen's Quarterly*, vol. LII, no. 4 (winter 1945-6), pp. 465-77

'Administration and Politics: The Case of the Canadian Broadcasting Corporation,' *Canadian Journal of Economics and Political Science*, vol. XII, no. 4 (Nov. 1946), pp. 454-69

'Unifying the British Civil Service: Some Trends and Problems,' *Canadian Journal of Economics and Political Science*, vol. XIV, no. 1 (Feb. 1948), pp. 1-19

'Royal Commissions of Inquiry in Canada,' *Public Administration Review*, vol. IX, no. 1 (winter 1949), pp. 22-9

'Canadian Administration Faces the Fifth Decade,' *Journal of Politics*, vol. II, no. 4 (1949), pp. 715-35

'The Public Corporation in Canada,' *Public Administration*, vol. XXVIII (winter 1950), pp. 283-94

'Dives and Lazarus: Three Reports on the Teaching of Political Science,' *Canadian Journal of Economics and Political Science*, vol. XVIII, no. 1 (Feb. 1952), pp. 88-92

'The Role of Royal Commissions in Canadian Government,' in *Proceedings of the Third Annual Conference*, Institute of Public Administration of Canada (1951), pp. 351-67

'Our Early Peripatetic Government,' *Queen's Quarterly*, vol. LIX, no. 3 (autumn 1952), pp. 316-22

'Adolescent Bureaucracy: Some Features of the Canadian Civil Service before Confederation,' *Canadian Journal of Economics and Political Science*, vol. XVIII, no. 4 (Nov. 1952), pp. 419-30

'The American Election,' *Queen's Quarterly*, vol. LIX, no. 4 (winter 1952-53), pp. 512-18

'The Coming Federal Elections,' *Queen's Quarterly*, vol. LX, no. 2 (summer 1953), pp. 199-207

'Responsibility of the Government Corporation to the Governing Body,' in *Proceedings of the Fifth Annual Conference*, Institute of Public Administration of Canada (1953), pp. 389-99

'The American Debate: Four Votes for Sanity,' *Queen's Quarterly*, vol. LXI, no. 2 (summer 1954), pp. 248-54

'The Public Corporation in Canada,' in *The Public Corporation: A Comparative Symposium*, edited by W. Friedmann (Toronto: Carswell, 1954), pp. 51-92

'The Liberal and the Bureaucrat,' *Queen's Quarterly*, vol. LXII, no. 2 (summer 1955), pp. 176-83

'The Civil Service When Kingston was Capital of Canada,' *Historic Kingston*, vol. 5 (1956), pp. 13-24

'Public Servant Extraordinary,' *Canadian Forum* (April 1957), pp. 9-10

'The Civil Service and Policy Formation,' *Canadian Journal of Economics and Political Science*, vol. 23, no. 4 (Nov. 1957), pp. 467-79 (awarded the President's Medal, University of Western Ontario, for best scholarly article published in Canada in 1957)

'The Fowler Commission Report on Broadcasting in Canada,' in *Proceedings of the Ninth Annual Conference*, Institute of Public Administration of Canada (1957), pp. 301-7

'The Role of the Executive in the Modern State: Canada,' *International Social Science Bulletin*, vol. X, no. 2 (1958), pp. 198-212

'The Public Corporation in Canada,' a paper prepared for the Fourth Triennial Congress of the International Political Science Association in Rome, September 1958. Reproduced in Italian and Portuguese for scholarly journals in Italy and Brazil

'The Grand Inquest on the Canadian Public Service,' *Public Administration* (Australia), vol. XXII, no. 3 (1963), pp. 226-41

'Grasping the Nettle: Parliament's Special Committee on Defence,' *International Journal*, vol. XIX, no. 2 (spring 1964), pp. 213-18

'Should Canada be De-commissioned? A Commoner's View of Royal Commissions,' *Queen's Quarterly*, vol. LXX, no. 4 (winter 1964), pp. 475-90

'Challenge and Response: A Retrospective View of the Public Service of Canada,' *Canadian Public Administration*, vol. VII, no. 4 (Dec. 1964), pp. 409-21

'La Empresa Publica en Canada,' *Informacion Comercial Espanola* (March 1964), pp. 125-33

'Regional Interests and Policy in a Federal Structure,' *Canadian Journal of Economics and Political Science*, vol. XXXII, no. 1 (Feb. 1966), pp. 3-14

'The Role of the Executive in the Modern State: Canada,' in *Decisions and Decision-making in the Modern State*, compiled and edited by Jean Maynaud (Paris: UNESCO, 1967)

'From the Inhabited World,' Installation Address, 12 October 1967, printed in *Victoria Reports* (Dec. 1967) and University of Toronto *Graduate* (Christmas 1967)

'The Changing Nature of the Public Service: the Canadian View,' in *The Changing Public Service*, Comparative Development Series, no. 3 (Feb. 1968) (Institute of Governmental Affairs, University of California, Davis)

'Public Power and Ivory Power,' in *Agenda 1970: Proposals for a Creative Politics*, edited by Trevor Lloyd and Jack McLeod (Toronto: University of Toronto Press, 1968)

'Canadian Political Science: A Hybrid with a Future?' in *Scholarship in Canada, 1967: Achievement and Outlook*, symposium presented to Section II of the Royal Society of Canada in 1967, edited by R.H. Hubbard (Toronto: University of Toronto Press, 1968), pp. 92-104

'Social Goals from the Perspective of Political Science,' in *Social Goals: Fiftieth Anniversary Colloquium* (McGill University School of Social Work, Nov. 1968), pp. 1-9

'The Contemporary University: Ideology and Commitments,' *Proceedings*, Association of Universities and Colleges of Canada (1969), pp. 77-81

With O.P. Dwivedi, 'The Growth of Government Employment in Canada,' *Canadian Public Administration*, vol. XII, no. 2 (summer 1969), pp. 224-38

'The Public Corporation in Canada,' in *Government Enterprise: A Comparative Study*, edited by W. Friedmann and J. Garner (London: Stevens, 1970)

Introduction to J.A. Corry, *Farewell the Ivory Tower* (Montreal and London: McGill-Queen's University Press, 1970)

'Modern Institutions and the Individual Values. To Make a Work That Is All His Own,' *Queen's Quarterly*, vol. LXXX, no. 4 (winter 1973), pp. 563-6

'The Public Service: Its Past and the Challenge of Its Future,' *Canadian Public Administration*, vol. XVII, no. 1 (spring 1974), pp. 17-25

'Bureaucratic Initiatives, Citizen Involvement and the Quest for Administrative Accountability,' *Transactions of the Royal Society of Canada*, Series IV, vol. XII (1974), pp. 227-36

'Intergovernmental Relations in Canada,' *Annals of the American Academy of Political and Social Sciences*, vol. 416, 1974, pp. 170-80

with O.P. Dwivedi, 'Administration and Personnel,' in *The Provincial Political Systems: Comparative Essays*, edited by David J. Bellamy, Jon H. Pammett, and Donald C. Rowat (Toronto: Methuen, 1976)

'Where Victoria Evermore Shall Stand,' in *Victorian Cobourg: A 19th Century Profile*, ed. J. Petryshyn *et al.* (Belleville, Ontario: Mika Publishing Company, 1976), pp. 221-35

'Parliament and the Bureaucracy: Can We Keep Civil Servants Civil?' Occasional Paper #1, Department of Political Science, University of Guelph (fall 1980)

'Financial Control and Accountability,' in *Proceedings*, National Government Accounting Convention, Australian Society of Accountants (Canberra, 1980), pp. 1-12

'Government Responsiveness to the Public Interest: Has Progress Been Made?' *Canadian Public Administration*, vol. 24, no. 2 (summer 1981), pp. 216-31

Contributors

Roch Bolduc est président de la Commission de la fonction publique du Québec

D.C. Corbett is Commissioner, Public Service Board, South Australia, Adelaide

O.P. Dwivedi is Professor and Chairman, Department of Political Studies, University of Guelph, Guelph

James Iain Gow est professeur agrégé, Département de science politique, Université de Montréal, Montreal

J.W. Grove is Professor of Political Studies, Queen's University, Kingston

Kenneth Kernaghan is Professor of Politics and Administration, Brock University, St. Catharines, and editor of *Canadian Public Administration*

John W. Langford is Associate Professor, School of Public Administration, University of Victoria, Victoria

J.R. Mallory is R.B. Angus Professor of Political Science, McGill University, Montreal

T.H. McLeod, on leave from the Federal Civil Service, is now with A.R.A. Consultants, Ottawa

John Meisel is Chairman, Canadian Radio-Television and Telecommunications Commission, and editor of *International Political Science Review*

R.W. Phidd is Associate Professor, Department of Political Studies, University of Guelph, Guelph

A. Paul Pross is Professor in the School of Public Administration and the Department of Political Science, Dalhousie University, Halifax

D.C. Rowat is Professor of Political Science, Carleton University, Ottawa

Richard Schultz is Associate Professor in the Centre for the Study of Regulated Industries, McGill University, Montreal

Neil A. Swainson is Professor of Political Science, University of Victoria, Victoria

V. Seymour Wilson is Associate Professor in the School of Public Administration, Carleton University, and Secretary-Treasurer, Canadian Political Science Association